an iranian at home and abroad

a bid for freedom

CYRUS KAMRANI

an iranian at home and abroad

a bid for freedom

MEMOIRS
Cirencester

Published by Memoirs

MEMOIRS
PUBLISHING

25 Market Place, Cirencester, Gloucestershire, GL7 2NX
info@memoirsbooks.co.uk www.memoirspublishing.com

An Iranian at Home and Abroad: A Bid for Freedom

ISBN:978-1-909544-16-1

chapter one

THE HEAVY SOLID METAL DOOR closed as I stepped in. It was bolted, locked, the keys removed, and I heard the officer's footsteps receding. There was somebody already in the cell.

"Hello," I said. I got no answer. "What's your name?" I asked.

Silence again from the man squatting in one corner on his ass and the soles of his feet, his knees folded up to his chest, hands wrapped round them, staring at the floor. He was so drowned in his thoughts that he probably hadn't noticed me there yet. He looked to be in his late thirties, of medium build, most of his black, thick hair shot through with grey. His bushy black eyebrows accentuated his dark eyes. When he stood up, later, he was slightly shorter than me.

I felt exasperated. I did not want to be here and expected to be released shortly. The officer had said to me, "Till you go up to see the boss, stay in this cell.

1

There are no empty ones at the moment I could let you have." My experiences back at Winchester prison in England motivated me to ask for a cell of my own, even though it might be just for a few hours, as I expected. But things weren't going my way; they hardly ever had, recently. Now I was back in Iran where there was no right of choice for a free man, let alone for a prisoner.

It was a small cell, about two metres by four, and with him in that corner looking as if he had once owned the world and now had lost it with a realisation that deepened into despair, it felt depressingly sad - just like the rest of the country. There was only one bed in the cell with a mattress that looked a century old. In the other corner, close to where a new copy of the Koran lay on the floor, a mouse, totally unaware of us, was eating some crumbs while some beetles ran about all over the cell. The walls were crowded with graffiti which, on closer inspection, proved to be short sentences or statements, most of them with a date on top and then a line underneath. One of these, typical of many others that covered the walls, gave the date: 2 Sep., 1985, followed by the terse statement, "A. Salim to be hanged for having wrong thoughts in his head." Another one, surprisingly in English among the rest which were all in Iranian, attracted my attention. It went like this: "1 Jan., 1986 - Rahman Hakim will embrace death to attend Jesus' birthday on the other side." I didn't know whether to laugh or cry. The dates suggested the walls had been painted within the last year or so. Some of the writings were followed by a remark to this effect: "Though no evidence whatsoever has been found against me, I was nevertheless sentenced to death." All those people had been there, and then probably hanged - some innocent and a few guilty. Though personally I was in favour of the death penalty, I believed it should be put into practice only in extreme cases, where first degree murder has been proven, for instance. Somehow I doubt if half those people represented there by their notes on the walls could be included in that category of extreme crime - yet, it seems, they had paid the extreme penalty and faced the rope. Anybody who believed in ghosts whose restless spirits hang about their last place of abode would have had a job sleeping there.

The man in the corner looked up, as if he had just become aware of my presence in the cell. His stare shifted from the floor to me. Blankly, he seemed to be scrutinising me.

I sat on the bed at the opposite side of the cell and his stare followed me. Smiling, I repeated my last question: "What's your name?"

"Ahmad," he answered quietly, with a look of innocence, though underneath he seemed far from it.

I expected him, mutually, to ask me the same question, but clearly not interested in my name he asked instead, "What are you in for?"

"Suspicious behaviour," I replied, and hoped that was as far as it would go. I am not all that talkative by nature and now felt even less like talking, and I certainly was in no mood to explain my situation to him. Lucky enough, neither did he choose to prolong the conversation.

A few moments later Ahmad stood up and started pacing the cell to-and-fro. He repeated this pointless march a couple of times, looking as though he was not in control of his behaviour. Then he went back to where he sat before. He stretched his legs and leaned with his back against the wall. Once more ignoring my presence, he stared into empty space beyond his feet and soon looked miles away again.

What was playing so hard on his mind to keep him so preoccupied? I was curious, but then again, whatever it was, I thought, it was best to let him be. He sat there quietly and I didn't wish to disturb the silence. Indeed, no need for me to know, for I would be out shortly to carry on with my holiday I had started that day.

I had planned to go up to the north of the country, away from the madding crowd in the polluted city of Tehran to spend a few quiet days by the Caspian Sea. I had gone to the North-Bus Terminal around noon and got on one of the buses bound for the north. The weather looked promising, the sun was shining, and everything seemed set for a refreshing break away. The bus would pass through the small city of Noor, more of a town than a city, really, that was not far from the sea and where I had been once before, enjoying myself, and hoped to visit again.

The bus travelled for over 250km mainly through mountains and some barren areas. Later, as we approached the sea, the terrain became covered in greenery, and further on the road wound through a thick forest. Just over four hours later we reached Noor. I seemed to be the only one that alighted from the bus when it stopped in the middle of the town.

Knapsack over my shoulder, my first priority was to find a place to stay, something with a roof over it, for I didn't fancy spending the night in the outdoors though that was not out of the question. There were benches set up in the forest close to the road where people used to sleep, and I had my sleeping bag with me. Going to the only hotel in the town, I found it was a bit expensive for a place like Noor, but reasonably clean so I booked a room there. Realising there were only a couple of hours before dark, I left my knapsack in the room and went for a walk on the beach. Not a soul there and so peaceful - I could be on my own, everything so quiet, even the sea without waves. In these lovely natural surroundings without people, it was heaven on earth after the congestion and pollution of Tehran. With my back to the sea, I looked into the expanse of the inland: a couple of high mountain ranges blanketed with thick afforestation stretched into the distance as far as the eye could see. It was still early autumn and it all appeared like one piece of greenery against the clear blue sky. In reality the forest curved around the Caspian Sea for about 1500km and was almost 100km wide - all of it within Iran. There were roads that ran into this forest ending at various villages. One went through Noor, with quite a few isolated villas along it, most of them privately owned by people from other cities who spent their holidays there.

Leaving the beach, it was well into the dark when I got back to the town; not many people were around now. There by the main road, feeling hungry, I entered a tea shop and ordered a cup of tea and an omelette. The tea arrived almost immediately and the omelette a few minutes later. Having enjoyed them, plus another cup of tea, I paid the shop owner and left. These northerners, I thought, certainly knew how to make an omelette! Now what, I wondered? Everything looked dead quiet apart from a few shops still open. They, too, would soon be closing. Going back to the hotel to have an early nap seemed the only option left; I could be up by sunrise and have the whole morning to spend in the forest.

I hadn't gone more than a few metres from the tea shop when I noticed two men approaching me. Without warning one produced a gun and aimed it at my head! They weren't muggers, surely, not in the middle of the town on the main road and in front of a few people who began to gather now at a safe distance to watch. No one would dare to raise a finger or utter a sound in the new regime, even if the two men robbed me, or afterwards shot my head off, and left. They weren't members of a hit squad either - how could they be, for I hadn't started writing my manuscript yet! If they were, they would be members of the secret police belonging to SAVAMA (the information and security organization of the Islamic Republic). Later I discovered they were revolutionary guards, which became apparent when they were asked to produce their cards.

The one without a gun ordered me to face the wall, put my hands on the wall and stretch my legs back. When I did so he started searching me. Satisfied that I carried nothing illegal, he told me to turn round, mentioning something about me being a stranger in the town. He wanted to know what I was doing there. I explained my intention to spend a few quiet days by the Caspian Sea and sprouted some bullshit like I supported the regime, believed in Islam and so on - mumbo jumbo that was expected of anyone placed in a similar situation; but I didn't seem to have convinced them, and, as I half expected, they ordered me to accompany them.

I was taken to the only police station in the town, which was within walking distance. It was rather big for a small place like Noor. There they handed me over to the sergeant at the desk, explained my case and left.

The sergeant wrote down my name, adding it to a list of names in the open book on his desk; then he handed me to one of the officers who stood close by, at the same time nodding to him in a way that suggested he was conveying a familiar message. I followed the officer through some corridors, and then down a few steps, which was when we came to the cell that I have already described. It was one of a few cells. He opened the nearest cell and invited me to enter. There was, as I have said, already someone in the cell and I didn't like the idea of being locked up with a stranger. Looking about to make sure no one was watching, I quietly pressed a dollar into the sergeant's hand, telling him that I would prefer a cell of my own.

"Till you go up to see the boss, stay in this cell," the officer said, adding, "There is no empty one at the moment I could let you have." Nevertheless, he pocketed the dollar.

chapter two

AHMAD, standing up, started pacing the cell again, to-and-fro. Almost simultaneously, the cell door opened, to my relief, and the same officer who had given me the cell stuck his head in, nodding to me, saying, "The lieutenant wants to see you."

I have to admit the situation called for concern: would I hit back if my Fifth Amendment was violated? The answer should have been no. I remembered talking to a friend of mine a few months earlier on the subject of hitting back at authorities, when he took a folded sheet of paper out of his pocket and asked me to read it. Issued by the court acting on behalf of the security forces, the document briefly stated (roughly translated into English): M. T. (there may not be any risk involved if I gave his real name since he has now left the country, but I would prefer to use just his initials since his parents are still in the country and they helped him leave Iran) had assaulted a sentry, a very serious crime;

since it was his first offence, the punishment would be a term of imprisonment followed by a lashing and a heavy fine; but a second offence would cause him to face the death penalty.

I met M.T. just after his release from prison; an act of slapping back in response to a similar action he had been subjected to by a sentry had cost him three years of his life behind bars, and he was not allowed a passport for five years. All politically motivated crimes banned one from leaving the country, the duration depending on how serious the offence was considered to be, and an assault on a sentry came under the same penal code. But M.T. didn't intend to wait that long for his passport to be ready. As he put it, "I will issue one myself" - showing me the dollars in his pocket.

Soon after he was released from prison he paid some human traffickers who sneaked him out of the country into Turkey, where he made another payment to the same people - that's how the money is usually paid to these people, in instalments! They flew him from Istanbul to Stockholm in Sweden, where he asked for asylum; having had a strong case to support him - namely, the aforementioned document issued by the security forces that stated he would be condemned to death if the crime was repeated; this, together with the fact that he had spent three years in jail, was sufficient reason to grant M.T. permission to stay.

I followed the officer along some corridors, all poorly lit, until he stopped in front of a door; he knocked, opened it, stuck his head into the room and said, "He is here, sir" - upon which he moved aside and I entered.

I found myself again in the presence of the lieutenant. Seated at his desk, he was the only person in the room. He looked about 50, with fair skin, two big blue eyes and dark brown hair. He pointed at the empty chair in front of his desk and asked me politely to sit down. His clean-shaven face gave me a boost of morale and some peace of mind. It might be a little hard for a non-Iranian reader (if this book ever got published!) to grasp why a shaven face should have such a salutary effect, but I should explain that there were two kinds of uniformed security forces in Iran. One was called the police (blue uniforms) consisting of gendarmes left by the previous regime; the other was known as revolutionary guards (green uniforms), in some cases called sentries, secret police included. The latter were invented by Ayatollah Khomeini, The Messenger, as he was called by the people surrounding him, and his killer disciples through the mosque of brutality and the force of the gun. Gendarmes mostly shaved their beards off and they were lenient towards people, particularly the ones brought in by sentries, because they hated these newly formed forces; and for good reason too: they have been losing position since the spread of these killer viruses (sentries) created by the cancer called revolution. On the other hand, sentries were not allowed to shave their beards off because shaving wrinkled the face and it was essential to keep good looks in Islam. And they were not allowed to let it grow too long either, because it was said in the Koran: "Holding one's beard in his fist, starting from the chin, if sticking out from the bottom, that person should not be consulted in important matters and his advice not considered trustworthy." In fact, the Koran was quite emphatic about trimming the beard shorter than one's fist's width, mentioning the duty in five different chapters, and in one of them even pigeon-holing the person who lets his beard grow as "clearly stupid". Try to tell the Taliban that!

Anyway, the two forces, revolutionary guards and gendarmes, were also stationed at different places. The former operated from so-called sentry houses, where no gendarme was quartered; on the other hand, police stations were run by both, the gendarmes and the sentries, the head man always being a sentry.

I sat down and the questioning began. The blue-eyed lieutenant asked, "Have you got any I.D. cards?"

I showed him my birth certificate. This served as an I.D., not a card but a booklet, like a notebook, issued to all Iranians at birth. It consisted of two separate pages (four in all, counting both sides of the two pages), plus covers; one's photo appeared on the top left-hand corner of the first page, while underneath it there were particulars about the bearer such as ID number, name, surname, date of birth, place of birth, parents' names, their ID numbers and signatures. The second page was for marriages, names of the children and divorces. The last pages, 3 and 4, were used for stamping whenever voting was in progress.

Speaking of birth certificates, I am reminded of an incident that happened long ago. I remember once being with a friend, also Iranian, who was driving in Basingstoke, England, when he was stopped by the police and asked for his driving license. Not having one, he showed the policeman his birth certificate and told him that it was his Iranian driving license, saying that he was hoping soon to change it for an international license. The policeman, reluctant to accept this explanation (while not doubting the validity of the 'Iranian' license), issued him with a summons to appear before the court on the grounds that he did not have the required international license. A few months later when my friend appeared in front of the Basingstoke magistrate, he again presented his birth certificate, giving the same explanation as before. He received a fine of only five pounds for not having had his 'Iranian license' changed to an international driving license!

The lieutenant opened my birth certificate notebook (you could call it my 'Book of Life!), compared the photo with my physical features, then, as if reading to himself, began, "I.D. no:1111, Name: Cyrus, Surname: Kamrani…" At this point he paused, glancing into space, thinking, trying to weigh the information of the booklet against what he could remember. No computers were available for verification. "You won't get much out of there," I thought, following his unfocussed gaze and giving his head a glance. Failing to come up with anything, he read on: "Date of birth: 1 August, 1957, Place of birth: Abadan" (a big city in the south-west of Iran, almost totally destroyed in the war with Iraq); turning the page, he read, "and single." He closed the notebook, gave it back to me and said, "What were you doing in this town?"

None of your fucking business! I felt like telling him, but I knew better - I didn't want to end up with broken limbs and body. "I have come for the purpose of sightseeing."

"Sightseeing!" he exclaimed. "A small town in this part of the country, and at such a time?"

Security forces, not so much the police but sentries, usually found a way of twisting and linking whatever you said, even if not related, into conceptions expressed against Islam. Then it was too late trying to explain otherwise. Therefore, from the start, before it could come to that, if ever, I decided to fight them with their own weapon - Islam. Though a non-believer myself, I was ready to become one as long as needs required. "But it is mentioned as necessary in the Koran for every Muslim to discover the world around him, without specifying place or time." He looked cornered, I thought. After the revolution they passed a law that stated that denying or 'correcting' any part of the Koran carried the death penalty. He didn't know who I was and sometimes officials sent spies to police stations around the country to find out about people working in the forces who argued against this law. And the fact that I was picked up in the town made my appearance more suspicious. Then I told him the exact words from the Koran in Arabic: "*Ghol seeyàroo Fel'Arz* (tell them to travel over the earth)." This was an awkward situation because all the officials had to know at least a summary of the Koran.

Without any hesitation he asked, "What is your job?"

If I was a spy sent by officials I wouldn't have told him the truth, and he knew that. So there was no way he could be sure of the answer I gave.

"I am a tourist," I said.

He gave me a nervous smile that was somehow reassuring. After a couple more questions I told him that the countryside in the area was not unlike that of England where I had lived for years. Then our conversation took a turn for the better. He started talking to me in the relaxed way two friends might chat over coffee. Of course there was good reason for this: he had a son living in Germany studying to become a doctor and he was clearly proud of him. I congratulated him and wished his son good luck with his studies. We went on to talk about England and Germany where he had been on a couple of occasions visiting his son, unrelated, it seemed, to whatever his job required of him. Once retired he was planning, with the rest of his family, to leave the country and settle abroad, preferably in Germany, and he added in an undertone, "Anywhere would be better than this shit country."

Now realizing that he could trust the man sitting in front of him (or was the reverse nearer the truth, creating in me a false sense of security that might prompt me to confide in him?), he told me why I was picked up in the town to be brought in for questioning. He started by saying, "What I'm going to tell you, don't mention to anyone, especially the chief who will question you later; though he is alright, he is still a sentry." He went on to explain: "Tomorrow is the anniversary of the killings carried out by MKO (the main Iranian opposition group, based in Iraq, that was trying to overthrow the current regime in Iran) in their failed attempt to capture the city of Amol (one I had passed through just before I arrived in Noor) a few years ago; it resulted in the death of many revolutionary guards and a number of civilians who also lost their lives; consequently security has been tight in this province (about the size of Switzerland) for the last few days and will remain so for another few. MKO still has supporters around here. Most strangers entering the province during this interval are picked up and brought in for questioning. Those behaving suspiciously are held, though hardly anyone is kept here at this time, and then released later, when the threat of rebellion is over. To make sure this doesn't happen to you, my advice is to tell the chief, when you are questioned by him, that you are leaving the province tomorrow. That should clear all his doubts."

"Thanks for letting me know," I smiled, adding: "And I suppose the chief will also ask me the same questions you did?"

He nodded his affirmation, then asked, suddenly remembering, "Where is your stuff?"

"I only have one knapsack with me," I said. "When I got to Noor..."

"Today?" he interrupted.

I nodded. "Around late noon," I informed him and continued, "First I went to the Noor hotel, got myself a room and left my knapsack there."

"What have you got in your knapsack?" he asked.

"A towel, a couple of shirts, pants, socks, a mini tape recorder, binoculars..."

He cut me short and with a worried face said, "If the chief asks you about your bag just say you haven't got one. A mini tape recorder and a pair of binoculars could keep you here for at least two months in such unsettled times. Tell him you came today and you're leaving tomorrow so you didn't think you would be needing anything."

"Okay," I said and after some more friendly chat he stood up with the words, "Now let's go to see the top man."

We left the room for a bigger one and he went to get the chief. I felt more relaxed after talking to the lieutenant who tried to be helpful. There were good people like him in the organization, I thought, stopping some extra executions. Suddenly the door opened and the lieutenant came back following the chief who looked a bit immature for the post he had been assigned to. Being so young he seemed less intimidating, which also meant his lack of experience could mean he might pose fairly simple and straightforward questions; on the other hand, to obtain higher posts, these sentries had to prove that they could be ferocious from the start. He appeared to be in his middle twenties, and at that early age he had probably been offered a good job because a member of his family had been martyred (as anyone was called who had been killed in the war against Iraq). In fact, most top jobs were occupied either as a result of this or as a result of nepotism - in the latter instance being in close contact with someone holding a higher seat and thereby gaining an appointment or promotion regardless of education and experience; and, perhaps not surprisingly, they promoted themselves whenever the chance arose. 'The higher the monkey climbs, the more he shows his tail' is a proverb well suited to the present time and often heard in Iran. Even the ex-foreign minister, Reza Ghotbzadeh who occupied a highly responsible job, didn't have sufficient education and had clearly been appointed above his level of competency. He had been to America where he had tried to enter university but had failed all the admission exams. When Khomeini went to France for a short stay, Ghotbzadeh went to see him there and later accompanied the west-chosen leader to Iran; perhaps not surprising, therefore, he was appointed foreign minister, his only redeeming qualification being that he spoke English. However, not long after trying to assassinate Khomeini, he was found out and executed. He had got his just deserts and was shot.

Another example of these people appointed to a post beyond his level of competency is Ali Eshraghi, Khomeini's second son in law, who was taken to inspect an oil well; in front of cameras he had asked to see 'a petrol well'! The remark became the joke of the month!

In a way, to maintain a firm footing in the country, the government had acted quite cleverly: key jobs were bestowed on those who would never have dreamt of holding such positions, and in return they were expected to show their appreciation by supporting and remaining loyal to the central government. Sending someone to his death, especially one labelled as an American agent, meant a step closer to another stripe or a higher position.

The head man, tall, fair skinned and sporting an auburn beard, took his place behind the only desk in the room. I sat in front of him about two metres from the desk, the lieutenant occupying an isolated chair on his right. He started asking me the same questions; we were halfway through these when somebody knocked and stuck his head around the door and called him outside. A few minutes later he returned, almost in a hurry, turned to the blue-eyed lieutenant and said, "I have to go somewhere now, I'll question him later." He left the room and I never saw him again.

To my disappointment I was taken back to the same cell.

Ahmad was still sitting in his corner, almost in the

exact position he was in before I left the cell, and I wondered if he had even noticed my short absence. He looked miles away.

As the hours lengthened into evening, I abandoned hope of being released that day and resigned myself to staying in the cell overnight. To make myself more relaxed I tried to ignore Ahmad at his corner. But was it possible? He took to his feet, looking nervous and tense, and started pacing the cell again.

"Sorry Ahmad," I ventured, "but it's irritating when you march to and fro in front of me." In an attempt to calm him down, I asked, "Have you been here long?"

He went back to his corner and sat down. "No," he answered, "we came here today; me and my three friends in the other cells; straight from prison where we spent the last three months." Then, as though talking to himself while staring at the floor, he added, "It will all be over tomorrow."

Thinking that he meant he would be released the next day, I smiled and said, "We might leave together then."

Not removing his stare from the floor, he added, "But to different places," in the same detached voice, as though speaking to himself.

I felt uneasy, having failed to grasp the full meaning of his words but sensing something was seriously amiss. Before I could say anything he suddenly came out of his shell, perhaps because he detected my accent was different from the speech he was used to hearing in the north of the country. "You're not a northerner, are you?" he said, and asked, "So what were you doing here?"

"I'm visiting," I said. "I like the north of Iran. It's so green everywhere." It was true - the countryside in the north reminded me of England where I had spent over ten years before being kicked out when my visa ran out - something I didn't tell Ahmad or the lieutenant. "I'll be spending my day in the forest tomorrow, after I'm released," I said, then added in a deliberately casual manner, "What did you mean - to different places? I suppose you'll be with your family?"

After a long pause, which did nothing to alleviate my growing sense of unease, he answered my question in the same detached voice he had used before: "Maybe, with my dead parents, but not with my wife and two kids."

"What do you mean, with your...?" - then I stopped; I felt blood drain from my head. Staring into his eyes which met mine full on for a moment before they dropped to the floor again, I realized he had a message, a very grave one: he was going to be hanged tomorrow! That was the notion I got, anyway. With a lot of effort, coming back to myself and hoping my assumption was wrong, I finished my sentence, "....dead parents?"

"We're going to be hanged tomorrow," he stated categorically, adding, "me and my three friends in the other cells; all four of us."

I looked at him as though I had turned to stone, my eyes and mouth wide open. My body had gone numb and I didn't know what to say and just kept staring at him.

Once again out of his shell, he made eye contact

with me and continued, "Yes, tomorrow, at nine in the morning. We're told the people around have been informed and there's to be a big crowd gathering in Noor, where we are going to be hanged. I suppose you came to watch the show too?"

Still in shock, I cursed myself for not having anticipated this situation. I tried to pull my scattered thoughts together. "No," I said lamely, "I didn't know anything; and it's only by chance I'm here, in the north, to spend my holiday."

"One more day," he sighed, as if looking forward to it, "and it'll all be over."

It felt scary sitting close to a man who was not suffering from any disease or infected by any viruses, who appeared to be in fairly good health, yet had only one day left in his life. We all know our birth dates, but how would we feel and behave if we had advance notice of our death dates? Probably life would take a different course altogether. Tomorrow the man would see his last sunrise - perhaps not even that, since hanging usually takes place before dawn; but then this was different because it was public. And thinking about tomorrow, I remembered that the lieutenant questioning me earlier had mentioned something about it being the anniversary of MKO's defeat by revolutionary guards. So these people, I thought, were being hanged tomorrow just for a show of power, as evidence that the government of clerics was still in full command.

I told Ahmad about this anniversary and he seemed

well informed. "They hang them every year on that day," he said, "I saw six hanged last year, myself."

Ironically, I thought, what an improvement: from being a mere spectator, a year later, he was upgraded, playing the game himself. I felt pity for the man.

Ahmad carried on: "If it wasn't for this anniversary we would have been hanged three weeks ago. They put it off because the anniversary was close."

Like living on 'borrowed time', I thought, for the last three weeks! Such 'overtime' or extra time, as it is called in football, could be stretched into months, for it has been known that, once captured, criminals in the past had to wait for periods of over two months before they were hanged. That might seem a long time but a few years later it came home to me how ridiculously swift these criminals came to face the rope, when I heard on the BBC that there was a man who had spent the last 18 years on death row in America.

"But why," I asked, "are they hanging you?" I steeled myself for whatever story he had to tell. Contrary to what people usually imagine, mainly as a result of being wrongly informed by the media, the less civilized the society, the more brutal is the crime, or so I have come to understand. Ahmad's incident, colossal in barbarity as it was, wasn't even reported in Tehran just 250km away, whereas had it happened anywhere within a developed country it would have made headlines on both sides of the Atlantic.

Shrugging his shoulders, Ahmad looked reluctant to

talk, but then, with a sigh, said, "Armed robbery and murder."

"How was this?" I was really interested to know; it would pass my time too.

The story, as Ahmad told it, was in some parts different from the version I read in the paper the next day, but went like this: he and his three friends, the ones now in the other cells, forming a group and trusting one another, decided the easiest way to earn money was to get hold of a few pistols and raid some of the villas found sporadically in the area; not the villas belonging to the locals, who were living in the north themselves so there was a chance of being recognized, but those owned by people from other cities, especially Tehran; these owners generally spent their holiday, a few weeks every year, in their northern villas, escaping the fumes of the city and enjoying the sea on one side and the forest on the other. These people usually came driving expensive cars and carried a substantial amount of money with them. They were the ones Ahmad and his friends chose to target.

The group started by raiding the first few villas, in the night or in the early hours of the morning, kicking the doors open, pistols in hand, descending upon the occupants unawares. "They were so scared that they obeyed all our orders without hesitation," Ahmad explained.

"I imagine so!" I said. "Anybody woken up in the middle of the night with a pistol to his head won't hesitate to obey orders."

"At the first villa a gang member bundled the occupants into one of the rooms," Ahmad went on, "telling them to keep quiet or else they would be shot; the rest of us searched the villa for anything worth taking. With the nearest police station at least tens of miles away, we had plenty of time. After all, who would be checking on an almost isolated villa in the middle of the forest?" They usually finished within an hour, he said. After the first raid they stole the car too, and fled.

"Surely," I said, "on short stays people habitually hide their money and valuables where you won't find them, often in a small hole under the floor tiles, otherwise keep them in the bank..."

Ahmad raised both his hands to stop me. "Soon after the first raid we realised that," he said. "Invading the second villa, we went through the same procedure, but before leaving, a member of the group pointed his pistol at the head of a 5-year-old boy occupant..." Ahmad blamed one of the other three for doing so, but the papers named himself as the one responsible. "With the boy's parents watching, he asked them for any hidden money or jewels." Ahmad said that the mother, who had her gold stashed in a neatly dug out cavity under the floor, promptly handed her valuables over. This probably saved the kid's life, I thought, reading the paper the next day. The group took the gold and again the keys to their car and got away.

They did a couple more night raids and then, growing bolder, started raids in the daylight.

"As you warmed up," I put in.

Correcting me, he said, "No, as we turned professional. Keep in mind that there were always road blocks at nights looking for stolen cars that terrorists use."

On their sixth raid the group, thinking nothing could stop them anymore, began to call themselves "Invincible" - which was when they made the biggest mistake of their lives that eventually led to their capture. Breaking into a villa, the owner, a young man, big and strong, attacked them. In the struggle that followed a bullet went off accidentally and hit the man, going right through his heart and killing him instantly. The man's wife and their 12-year-old daughter, watching the scene, went hysterical. Screaming and running for the door, they were shot too. According to Ahmad, two of his friends were responsible for the killings while he was searching the attic. "By the time I came down from the attic it was too late to stop them," he said.

What the paper reported, the next day, was in many respects different from Ahmad's version. According to this report, the group on their last forced entry invaded the premises, robbed the occupants, removed the woman and her 12-year-old daughter from the others, tying the rest up; thereupon Ahmad and another gang member raped the two females. At this point the man succeeded in freeing himself and, while attempting to attack a gang member, was shot and killed instantly, the bullet having penetrated his heart. The two females were shot too. All four of the accused confessed to have fired at least once, killing the victims.

Comparing the two statements, one told by Ahmad and the other reported in the paper, I realised that the latter might have been extracted under torture to give credence to the government's action in hanging the culprits. Nevertheless, I believed it was probably much closer to the truth than Ahmad's version, bearing in mind he was psychologically disturbed when he told me his story during those few short hours when I was with him. Whether he should have been sent to an asylum rather than face the rope is a moot point, but it may be arguable that he knew good from bad, which would have justified the sentence that terminated his life.

The fact is that rape was viewed as a very serious crime, even more serious than murder in the eyes of the authorities at the time; therefore it is only after this incident that almost half the police force plus the revolutionary guards *and* the sentries in the province, hot on group's pursuit, were mobilized - whereas prior to this last raid, though the group had committed a murder on one occasion, only a handful of policemen had been assigned to the case.

Within less than a week, before the group got a chance to attempt another raid, they were arrested, having been picked up one by one from their different houses. How this had come about the paper didn't say. Ahmad's version was that the police had found a stolen necklace the group had sold to a jeweller as a result of which they had managed to trace the culprits. If that was the reason behind their arrest, the papers never mentioned it. But then again, at the time anything connected with criminal activities was prevented by the police from leaking to the media; even if it did, the papers weren't allowed to write anything about a particular crime till it was concluded; and, in any case, nothing about the way the police had handled it was allowed to be made known. The situation has changed dramatically within the last few years to the extent that information about most criminal activities is made available to the papers by the police and is even published, encouraging people with information to come forward.

Anyway, whatever the truth, I'd like to believe Ahmad's conclusion. He was picked up at his house and "by the time they got me to the sentry house I had lost two teeth, had a broken nose and later received four stitches to my head" without the use of an anaesthetic. The group, realizing every single one of the raids they had carried out could send them to the gallows, since firearms were involved, confessed to all the charges laid against them to avoid further torture. Thereupon a couple of unsolved murders the gang members knew nothing about were assigned to them, as a convenient way unravelling the mystery presented by some bodies found in the forest. That usually was the case with serious crimes that remained unexplained. The next condemned person(s), if there was a small chance of the crimes being connected, had to bear the responsibility. What did he, or they, have to lose? They can only hang you once.

chapter three

IT WAS APPROACHING MIDNIGHT. I had been listening to Ahmad for the last couple of hours, like one watching a great movie. Thinking about midnight, the chilling thought dawned on me that soon it would be his last day. "And you said they're going to hang you tomorrow?" I said. "I don't know what to say."

Now it seemed to be my turn to stare into empty space, lost in thought. We both remained quiet for a while.

Suddenly the cell door opened and a new officer appeared. "As it is your last day," he said, looking at both of us, "anything special you'd like to eat?"

Ahmad shook his head, but realizing the officer hadn't been told about me I used the opportunity to ask for a cup of coffee and some biscuits. The officer nodded his head up and down, slowly, a smile on his face. Trying to hide his surprise, he said, "Oh, *you* can eat?" Nodding his head towards the other cells in the row, he mentioned, "Your friends couldn't."

When the officer was gone I turned to Ahmad and

said, "He thought that I was one of you." What I didn't realise was that in less than half a day how close I would come to sharing the fate of my companion, implicit in that casual remark of mine.

About ten minutes later I was enjoying my coffee with biscuits. "Did I hear you mentioning something about a wife and children, earlier on, Ahmad?" I asked, hoping I had not heard him correctly about leaving a wife and children, feeling sorry for them if he had any.

"Yes, I have a wife and two children," he said with his head bent, staring at the floor.

Although over thirty and still a bachelor myself, it was sad imagining how Ahmad's family would be feeling now. Would they be there to see him hanged? I couldn't ask him that, I realized. "Where are they now?" I ventured.

"Staying with my wife's parents. I saw them just before you came in." Then, after a short pause, as if reading my mind, he continued, "I told them not to leave the house tomorrow. What good would it do them watching me hanged?" Now I could see tears trickling down his cheeks. "Where will I be this time tomorrow?" He was half talking to himself again, staring at the floor. There was so much concentration on the man's face; had he focussed his thoughts on a box of matches, I thought, he would have moved it, or caused it to flare up.

"Ahmad," I asked quietly, "do you believe in reincarnation?"

"I don't want to be born again, and probably hanged once more," he said.

Whatever made him declare that? I couldn't stop myself giving way to a quiet laugh.

Shaking his head from side to side, he carried on, "Where do you think I'll end up tomorrow after I'm hanged, heaven or hell?"

When the time approaches even the most heathen turn to God.

"If I follow my beliefs, at this time tomorrow you are born again."

Pointing at the Koran lying on the floor in the opposite corner in front of him, Ahmad said, "According to the Koran, when one[1] dies, the first night one is brought in front of an angel who reads out all the good and bad deeds one has done throughout one's life; one is judged by weighing the good and bad against each other, then sent to hell or heaven."

Attempting to lighten his mood, I said, "If they let you choose, ask for hell; as you know, this regime has sent all the bad women there, and even some good ones; you'll be able to enjoy all those females entering that place." After the revolution they hanged many whores round the country, mainly in Tehran, among them Pari the Tall, the most famous one; the cleric ordering her execution afterwards remarked, "She is in hell now." For the first time I saw a faint smile flicker on Ahmad's face. Then I asked him, "By the way, is this your first time inside?"

"Yes," Ahmad answered. "Prior to the raids, I had never been involved in any crime."

"You started well then," I responded.

We talked intermittently till about two in the morning, when both of us fell silent. Feeling tired, I lay down on the bed and closed my eyes, and soon fell asleep. I had a bad dream that night. A group of officers followed me through the streets of Noor, the one in front with a piece of rope in his hand; he asked me to stop so that he could put the rope round my neck and hang me. I tried to shout back, telling them that I wasn't the person they were after, but my voice had gone silent and they were closing the gap between us. Then there was an earthquake and everything crumpled down. I woke up relieved to find it was only a dream. I became aware that Ahmad was shaking me. Almost hysterical, he was saying, "Wake up, wake up, Cyrus!"

I wiped a hand over my face.

He asked me, "What time is it? They'll be coming to get me in a minute."

What time is it? Time you got hanged, I felt like saying, *waking me up like that!* Opening my eyes, I tried to sit up on the bed. "Alright, alright," I said, "let me have a look at my watch." I glanced through the widow and it was light outside. Taking my watch out of my pocket, I was surprised to see that it was seven o'clock. I had slept for five hours. I rubbed my eyes and shook the sleep out of my head; when I looked at Ahmad I was shocked by his appearance. His hair, only five hours ago black tinged with grey, now appeared nearly all white; his eyebrows, too, though not to the same extent. Even the officer who gave me coffee the night before, when he came to get him two hours later, asked what was different about him.

Ahmad was hysterical now. I wanted to knock at the door and ask for a doctor but I realized it would be pointless: in a couple of hours' time he'd be examined by the best doctor in the universe - his maker.

He got hold of my shoulders and very quietly, almost crying, said, "Help me, please. I don't want to die!"

What on earth could I do or tell a man who was going to be hanged in less than two hours, to give him some encouragement and calm him down? Then, thinking, I picked up the Koran from the opposite corner where it was lying on the floor and told him, "My brother Ahmad, let me read you some verses from this holy book. It'll help." Though a non-believer myself, I had to do something to get him, even if for my own sake, through the next two hours.

There was no need for me to be nervous but I was shaking nevertheless. Opening the book, I began to read, "In the name of the almighty God..."

It wasn't long before the cell door opened and an officer asked us to follow him. Once in the corridor, with more than ten officers just outside the cell door, they handcuffed Ahmad's hands behind his back; he didn't give them any trouble, and when they made to handcuff me I said, "No, not me. I'm not with them. I was picked up in the town..."

They didn't let me finish; three of them jumped on me and one landed a punch right in my private parts.

"You think you can get away with it like that!" one put in. "Think of something new," another said, "we have heard that before!"

Almost out of breath, hands handcuffed behind my back, I nodded my head at Ahmad and, addressing one of the officers, I said, "Ask him!"

The officer just gave Ahmad an offhand glance, and what I heard that bastard Ahmad say was to remain with me for the rest of my life:

"He is one of us," Ahmad said, looking at me but answering the officer's glance.

Even now, after all these years, even as I write these lines, those words, probably the last ones Ahmad spoke, are still with me, as clear in my ears as when I first heard them. Even today I cannot get over how cruel a man could turn in the face of death.

Looking into his eyes, I was furious. "Oh, you son of a bitch!" I swore. The thought that I'd probably see him shortly on the other side flashed through my mind. Surely, surely someone would become aware that there would be one extra, when we came together at the hanging, I kept hoping! But the place was full of officers, guards and sentries; who would notice the difference?

They took us one by one, ten officers to each person; and when on the road outside the police station, to keep the crowd away, more officers joined in. Now it was even worse, impossible to tell one from the other.

Things got underway and we started moving slowly.

Is this a dream? I asked myself for a second. But it all seemed so real and, surprisingly, happening to *me!* It was all contrary to what I had always taken for granted, thinking calamities on this scale always happened to others, never to me.

It was at this point that I recalled a chilling observation made only a few days before, by the regime's head executioner, a man called Khalkhali, the most feared and ruthless individual in the country, who said on TV: "Last week we hanged twenty people out of which we now have come to realize three were innocent. What fortunate people, for they are in heaven at this moment. As I've said before, when we inadvertently hang innocent persons together with guilty ones, justice is in effect done in that the innocent have ended up where we would all love to join them."

Consumed with frustration and anger, I felt that if by some miracle chance I got away with what was taking place, I'd get hold of a weapon and start annihilating human rights organizations! Their employees had been to Iran a few times but only to interview the killers; very rarely have they talked to a victim's family; and even then, this was done in front of government officials, meaning the family had to show satisfaction, otherwise they'd end up in heaven.

With an officer on each side of me holding my arm, I had no choice but to walk in line with them, like a lamb to the slaughter. There were thousands of people around. Surely this town had never seen so large a crowd in the entire history of its existence. Most had gathered with the promise of something exciting to see. What a show: a few men were being hanged, innocent or guilty, it didn't matter which, as long as the people were entertained. Here was something to talk about for a long while to come. Time and time again they had been told that some of those hanged had been innocent, yet they crowded to throw things at the ones condemned, insulting them and watching in pleasurable anticipation.

Thinking about it, considering the people's low level of mentality, didn't we deserve the government of the Ayatollahs? Until now every time a bomb went off in the country I wondered if some of those hurt or killed in the blast were innocent. Glancing round at that crowd, I realised that in a way they represented society as a whole; they displayed the same sick behaviour anywhere in the country, wherever one took a cross section. Would anyone with a sound mind call them innocent?

Again, bitterly I thought, if I got away with what was taking place, I would start a bombing campaign myself, then go to see the victims' families and enjoy their grief. First I would have to learn how to make bombs. It may not be all that hard: gunpowder was the main ingredient, easy enough to come by. And what about an atom bomb? One could be ignited in the middle of every town, and two in Tehran where one fifth of the population in the country lived... Would it cause casualties? My galloping mind, fuelled by fear and anger, came to an abrupt stop when I saw the gallows.

I could see the gallows about a hundred metres away and already I could feel the rope round my neck. We were closing but slowly, the crowd pushing to have a glance at us and the officers holding them back. Oddly enough, now, not only I wasn't resisting the officers on my sides to be dragged forward, but actually assisting them to get through faster; the sooner this was over the better. Somehow the officers managed the crowd and got us to the foot of the gallows; four ropes were hanging from a wooden beam, each separated by less than a couple of metres, crossed above a platform over a metre high. I felt my legs about to give up. The whole thing was like a popular performance and I wondered why they hadn't started selling tickets.

Using the wooden stairs on the left side of the platform, accompanied by an officer holding his left arm, each man ascended to the platform and almost looked as though he was being assisted up the stairs. The first man up was taken to the nearest rope and placed in position in front of it; the officer, releasing his arm, took a couple of steps back and stood behind him. My turn came next. I was brought to the foot of the stairs, surrounded by a number of officers; like the one before me, there I was handed to another officer who accompanied me, holding my left arm as we climbed up to the platform; he took me to the second rope that hung motionless and placed me in front of it. Only then was my arm released. He stood in line with his colleague behind me. Looking down, I saw a trapdoor underneath my feet. It would open in a minute. I would fall through it and nothing would be heard about me till the following week when the man in charge of Friday prayers held in the town would say, "...of the five people hanged last week one was innocent, so he is in heaven now..."; and the crowd would shout, "Hooray. Hooray!" - for a man had inadvertently ended up in the land of honey and milk.

One by one the rest were brought up and placed in front of the remaining ropes. Ahmad was the last one. Like the others, he was accompanied by an officer. As he passed in front of me I took the opportunity and kicked him up his ass. He tried to turn back but the officer holding his arm pulled him away.

Thinking about it now, maybe those four words I had heard Ahmad say and which were still buzzing in my ears weren't his last words after all.

The officer took Ahmad to the end of the platform and, finding no more free ropes there, looked up at the beam, puzzled.

What could that mean? One rope short, or a man innocent?

Next to me, on my left, stood a brave young guy of not more than 25, staring at the crowd, almost smiling.

I was hit by a tomato. A small group on one side, fists in the air, were shouting, "Down with MKO!"

Now, turning the other way, I saw that the fellow on my right, the first one up the platform, had his head down, eyes closed, murmuring prayers. Just beyond him a sergeant climbing the last stair approached the man, took the noose hanging behind him, and put it round his neck; he tied the knot at the back, left him and came to me. I nearly collapsed, my legs turning to water; almost a coward, I wondered how I had managed that far to keep standing on my legs. So this is how it is meant to end, I thought. The sergeant, taking the noose from behind me, put it round my neck.

The officer who had accompanied Ahmad to the end of the platform, now leaving him there, came up and informed the sergeant of the one rope short. The sergeant, having trouble tying the knot behind my neck, turned to the officer quite casually and said, "Well, it happens now and then, there is a rope or two short, and sometimes extra." Managing the knot, he carried on, "We'll hang four and when all are done, replace one." Then, as a second thought, he went on, "Or could it be we are hanging one innocent person? I better check this with the station."

He got his walkie-talkie from his waist belt and, contacting the station, explained the situation. I heard the man at the other end telling him to wait so he could check. A few seconds later the reply came back on the walkie-talkie. The sergeant, still standing in front of me, one hand playing with the rope round my neck just like one trying a finishing touch on a tie, was informed, "According to this list in front of me four people are being hanged..." Then suddenly, as if struck by lightning, the voice went on urgently, "Look sergeant, you're not hanging one wearing a sky-blue shirt and black trousers, and looking athletic among them?"

I recognized the voice; it belonged to the lieutenant who had questioned me the night before.

The sergeant looked at me, walkie-talkie to his mouth, and answered, "Yes; in fact, I'm standing in front of him and I've just put the rope round his neck, sir."

"Don't do anything, I'll be there in a minute!" came the order from the other end.

A few seconds later a passageway opened among the few hundred officers there to keep the crowd away; then a man, looking important with respect being shown to him, was trying hard to get through. From where I stood on the platform with the rope still round my neck, my heart leapt in hope as I recognised, as he came closer, the same blue-eyed lieutenant who had previously questioned me.

Almost out of breath, he reached the platform, a walkie-talkie in his hand; pointing it up at me, he barked an order to the sergeant: "Get that bloody rope off his neck you fool!" He appeared angry.

The sergeant, coming to me, did so. I took a deep breath. Turning me round, he removed the handcuffs from my hands, at the same time trying to show concern. "Why didn't you say so?" he asked.

"Finding it fun, I let you carry on with it," I said weakly. I could think of nothing else to say as I rubbed a hand round my neck.

As it happened, I was left, after this incident, fighting

the psychological effects of its aftermath; had they proceeded and hanged me, I wouldn't have had to live with the memory of the incident or its psychological effects for the rest of my life. Obviously, my escape from that fate meant a blow for justice; on the other hand I'm almost inclined to prefer the former course since it would save the innocent from the torments of the aftermath.

I jumped off the edge of the platform, where the lieutenant stood. With his two blue eyes staring at me, he said, "Whew, that was close!" Then nodding his head, he went on, "You can go home now."

Still surrounded by a handful of officers, the lieutenant ordered them to escort me away, for I couldn't just walk away among that crowd unprotected; they would probably want to know why I was let off such a dire punishment; they might have wondered whether I had bribed the authorities or someone in a higher position to put in a word on my behalf; if they got their hands on me I was sure all hell would have been loosed! Looking back while being escorted away, I saw my place on the platform being taken by Ahmad; the same rope went round his neck. Well-a-day, mate, I thought.

A couple of hundred metres away from the crowd I was bundled into a waiting police car. The driver, responding to my request, took me to get my knapsack from the Noor hotel, where I had left it the day before. Coming out, the police car, still waiting, gave me another lift to the bus station. "Fuck you all the same," I whispered in English, leaving the car as I closed the door behind me.

I put my jacket on and kept a low profile just in case someone recognized me. Getting hold of the local paper while waiting for the bus back to Tehran, I read the story on the front page that was entirely allocated to the group and their activities: Ahmad was called a monster who had led the other three in those killings and the rapes.

chapter four

ON THE WAY BACK to Tehran I tried not to think about all that had taken place, but barely managed to do so. What if the lieutenant hadn't noticed my absence from the cell? A shiver went down my spine. By the time I reached Tehran and alighted from the bus I was shaking and could hardly function; I had just been on a four-hour bus journey and had no notion of it. When I got home where I was living with my gentle and endearing younger sister, Sepideh, and my stupid mother, I went straight to my room without saying a word to them, locked the door from the inside and threw myself on the bed. Closing my eyes and feeling very tired, I fell asleep. A few hours later when I woke up there wasn't much I could call to mind from that near fatal miss-incident; or perhaps a stronger uncontrolled mental power was blocking my memory. I recalled escaping some disaster, but beyond that everything became elusive; all I was aware of then was that my journey north had been cut short due to some or other reason.

The next few days I spent in a kind of limbo, keeping to myself. It was a long time before, slowly and painfully, I started recalling things; probably not everything, but, on the other hand, certain scenes came back in lurid detail. For instance: as the sergeant was putting the rope round my neck, I remembered him whispering close to my ear, "It won't be long now; you'll feel no pain."

The incident left psychological scars on my mind. Was it beyond repair? Thinking I'd never be normal again frightened me. I sought treatment from a psychiatrist who advised calm. But how do I remain calm? "Think of those few thousands in your situation who went up the gallows but came down being carried away," the psychiatrist reminded me. Yes, I was lucky, I thought, trying to calm myself down. Soon afterwards I developed a twitch on the left side of my neck that reached the left corner of my mouth. This was to stay with me for a long time, though eventually went away. "You don't want to be thinking of revenge at any time," the psychiatrist cautioned me; this was wise advice, for doing otherwise a couple of times drove me to a point where I became so furious my whole being started shaking with my head in a high fever. Giving way to anger would only do more damage.

A few nights later I had a horrible nightmare. My head came off, falling through the trapdoor, while my eyes remained open, a revengeful smile on my lips; my headless body suddenly emerged from underneath the platform; people screamed and took to their legs. I woke up with sweat all over me. The nightmares persisted and I stayed awake drinking coffee to avoid them.

Keeping myself busy was a salutary way to get over that near disaster. The psychiatrist had advised this too. I cut my holiday short and went back to the factory where I'd been working for the last year. Everyone was surprised to see me returning so early; and now, worse than before, I found it impossible to get along with that stupid semi-literate bunch.

Quitting my job at the factory, I started working for my uncle the next day, selling car spare parts at his shop. He had sacked his employee, accusing him of stealing, so he was in need of someone to run the place, and who better than me to fill the vacancy?

It was a small shop and I worked on my own there. Starting at eight in the morning, I had only a few customers to attend to during the day. During most quiet periods I listened to the BBC on my shortwave radio, and wove a 0.5 x 1m carpet I had started a few days back to keep my mind busy. Then I brought my few dumbbells to the shop from home. A weight trainer almost all my life, I started exercising much harder, two to three hours a day, sweating all the way through. After a while I reached a point where I trained the whole morning, and felt relaxed afterwards - an effective remedy to overcome mental problems.

I usually stayed till six in the evening. My uncle would come round about then from where he was working for the oil refinery. I would then hand the shop over to him with the day's work and leave.

I spent most of my evenings, always alone, in the park close to where I lived. I would go back home in time for supper, listen to some more BBC and soon after hit the sack.

Days drifted by slowly. I had been working in the shop for a year and began to feel bored; there was no progress, though I didn't mind that; everything was just so monotonous. I hated my surroundings, the people, the country, the government, everything. Before I ended up in bedlam, I decided, it was time to leave the country. I'd go somewhere to prosper, and if that failed, at least I could try to live a normal life. Seeing new things and meeting different people would surely make me forget and break away from the last two miserable years of my life I had experienced since being deported from England.

A few days later I bought myself an air ticket to Istanbul and quitted my job at the shop.

Listening to the BBC, I was given to understand that Austria was granting asylum to outsiders once inside its borders. That sounded like good news; it offered an opportunity for a new beginning and a promising future. But how was I to get there? The Austrian embassy in Tehran only issued visas to those Iranians with a family member already living in Austria. I had my parents and both sisters in Iran then. My hopes of an easy and straightforward entry into Austria were therefore dashed. Paying some human traffickers to shift me over seemed another option, but I didn't have the sort of money that they would require; this left me in the end with only one last alternative I could think of - to enter Austria illegally.

Looking at the map a couple of days before my flight I planned my route, beginning with Istanbul - one of the few places on the planet where Iranians were not subjected to visa regulations to enter. It would be the first time I visited this ancient city, so much talked of through history. I would stay in Istanbul a few days enjoying myself, trying to put the past behind me with all the sightseeing opportunities the city presented. From there I would leave for Bulgaria, which required a visa from the visitor's home country preceding entry - so I called at the Bulgarian embassy in Tehran, and for a few dollars they issued me a three-day visa. It was more than enough, for I would only be passing through that land in order to enter the then Yugoslavia, a neighbouring country of Austria. Following my journey on the map, so far, I had the promise of a lot of exciting mileage ahead of me. Inquiring from the Yugoslavian embassy about a visa, surprisingly, I was informed that Iranians, as in the case of Turkey, didn't need a visa ahead of time to enter the country; instead, they were issued at the border when entering the country. Once in Yugoslavia I would sneak across the border into Austria and ask for asylum.

A three and a half hours' flight took me from Tehran to Istanbul. Upon my arrival at the airport I was given a three months' tourist visa - a red circular seal, about an inch in diameter, stamped in my passport. When I emerged from the airport everything looked colourful, probably, I thought, because, apart from black, dark blue, white and perhaps one or two other colours, the rest were banned in Iran - red especially, or anything close to it; probably for that reason the colour attracting my notice more than any others now was red, perhaps the most brilliant of all the colours.

Istanbul is a beautiful place. Securing myself a room at one of the cheapest hotels, I started touring the city. Knapsack over my shoulder, I walked for hours not feeling in the least tired, in fact enjoying every minute of the surroundings.

The next morning I left the hotel early to look for a weight training centre. I asked a policeman and found one called the Shampion Club, in the Galatazarai area of Istanbul. I had a good workout there: I wanted to keep fit for sooner rather than later, I felt, being in good form would serve me well. Leaving the club, I carried on with my walk. When I revisited the club the next day to exercise, I noticed, on entering, a big, amazingly well-proportioned muscular man sweating while working out in a corner; he looked more imposing than the best bodybuilders ever seen in magazines, and I recognized him at once: he was Ahmet Enulu, the 1980 bodybuilding world champion, from Turkey; such a nice person too, talking and laughing with everyone, and he honoured me by shaking my hand before leaving.

I stayed in Istanbul for nine days during which time I met a number of Iranians who had all come in search of a better life. It seemed more roads were open to other developed nations from this neighbouring country. In fact, most hotels in Istanbul were crowded with people from Iran. Estimates showed that three million Iranians were living in Turkey at that time, most of them youngsters escaping compulsory army service and therefore without passports. Paying human traffickers, they had been sneaked into Turkey across the border. The few I met, no doubt typical of most, were waiting for their forged passports, usually prepared by the traffickers themselves, so they could leave Turkey for countries like Canada, Australia or New Zealand, where they could live like humans. Some had paid up to 12,000 US dollars, in all, to cover the entire cost, from the application to the final destination. Prices varied and were determined on the 'quality' of the country, so to speak, with Canada topping the list.

During the course of my short stay in Istanbul, I also came across a couple of other Iranians who told me they had been to Yugoslavia but had been sent back at the border. No reason given, apart from the information that only Iranian students attending places of education in Yugoslavia were allowed entry.

That was a disappointing piece of news, but I nevertheless decided to risk the journey. Those turned back were not able to speak passable English, I told myself, therefore were probably not able to get round the authorities when greasing their hands with a few dollars. But then again, I thought, that kind of misconduct, which Iranians were only too familiar with, didn't need much language.

Meanwhile at the hotel where I was staying I met a few Yugoslavians, all from Prishtina and fluent in English, who informed me, when asked, that their police were corrupt. This was music to my ears for it meant they might be open to bribes. The Yugoslavians, like the Iranians, were well represented in the city, though most were there for a different reason from us. A few more I encountered, through other Iranians, were traffickers. One tried to sell me a Yugoslavian passport for 2,000 dollars; and to change the photo he wanted half as much again. That sounded too good to be true, yet not as good as an offer of 3,000 dollars plus the cost of an air ticket that would enable me to fly straight from Istanbul to Vienna. Why such a bargain, I asked? He told me because I spoke fluent English, I would get through by my own means, rendering unnecessary the expense incurred by those checking at the airport. But how could I trust him and know he was telling the truth? In any case, I did not have that amount of ready cash to risk.

At the time most Yugoslavians there made money buying clothes in Istanbul to take back home to sell; as I understood, the import tax on these goods was paid half underhandedly by some to the right person who would turn a blind eye to other imported goods.

Once again, knapsack over my shoulder, it was time to move on. I went to the main Bus Terminal, called

Topkapi, west of Istanbul, and got on the bus bound for Belgrade, Yugoslavia.

Passing through Bulgaria in the dark, travelling at night, we stopped only twice for refreshments. The sun was just beginning to rise when the bus left Bulgaria behind and traversed the neutral zone between the two countries; before long it entered Yugoslavia and drew to a stop. Looking through the window I saw a few uniformed men outside. One of them came up into the bus and spoke to the driver who handed him a sheet of paper - the list of passengers, I guessed correctly, since he looked up from it and called my name.

Knapsack in hand, I left my seat and went to the front. The officer asked to see my passport. I drew it out of my breast pocket and I handed it to him. He didn't even bother to open the passport, just looking at the cover which seemed to tell him all he needed to know; he pointed to where I was sitting, halfway to the back of the bus, and asked me if I had more bags. Shaking my head, I put my knapsack over one shoulder and waited for his next move.

Handing back the sheet of paper to the driver, the officer asked me to follow him out of the bus. Heart in mouth I followed, not yet abandoning all hope since I told myself that another way of overcoming this possible setback would present itself.

Clearing the last step, the driver closed the door behind us and the bus started moving away. Standing in the cool fresh breeze of early morning, the officer waved my passport in the air and, with his barely understandable English, informed me that only Iranian students were allowed into Yugoslavia and I wasn't one. How did he know I wasn't a student? Simple - students' passports were different in size and the colour of the cover.

"Look," I said, "can I talk to your boss please? The man who issues the visas?" Why waste time with him, I thought; to get through this problem I needed to see the man with the stamp.

"Wouldn't do any good," he answered.

I handed him a twenty-dollar note and he took me to a double storey building; entering, I noticed at the top of the swinging glass doors a sign that said 'IMMIGRATION'. Once inside this building we went up some stairs, then along a corridor; we reached the first door which he opened and just walked in with me following. The room looked like an office with a few tables covered with papers and stamps. Behind one table sat a fat uniformed man wearing a very thick moustache; obviously in charge, he was the one we went to. Only one other table was occupied, by a languid looking man, also in uniform.

From the way the fat man looked at my passport and the questions he asked, it was apparent that he was used to encounters with Iranians. He made sure I spoke English; I surmised that he had come across many who had lacked this ability and I was proud to tell him about my stay in England and that I went to university there. "So did I," he said sternly - which was the reason behind his good English, I realized.

He had studied in London but didn't have a high regard for that city. "Filthy," he called it, "unlike Yugoslavia" where, according to this patriotic man, everywhere one went was clean and proved to be "the best in Europe, if not now, then certainly in a few years' time." What he said about Yugoslavia at the time, being clean and all that, probably was right, according to the information I had received, mostly through the media; but what he didn't bargain for was the unpredictability of the future, especially concerning Yugoslavia. In less than two years civil war had torn that country apart, resulting in devastation and tragic loss of life - something that no doubt shattered the fat man's dreams. I was working in Japan at the time when everything went pear-shaped in that land; I was kept up-to-date by reading the *Japan Times* - and though I felt sorry for the people who suffered there, I recalled the fat man's impression of London and wondered what sort of impression he had of Yugoslavia following the massacres.

"Anyway, I cannot grant you permission to enter Yugoslavia," the fat man said.

"But your embassy in Tehran told me differently with respect to Iranians travelling to Yugoslavia. What is this then, don't you coordinate?" I asked.

"Yes, we do, but this is our policy."

"What kind of policy do you call that? It certainly needs reviewing!"

From our exchange of words it didn't appear I was likely to get any sense out of this fat man, and I thought about paying him. I dared not come out with it directly and tried talking to him, as it were, between the lines. "All you have to do," I said, "is just choose the right stamp, stick it in my passport, and if it costs me anything I'm willing to pay for it." Looking at his fat face I thought my message had gone home, but his response made me realise I should have gone straight to the point. "We don't stamp people like you," he informed me conversationally, then smiled at the officer still standing on my left - I suppose just in case he had to safeguard his part of the complicity. Back to me again, the fat man continued, "You pay 2,000 dollars, we look the other way, and you just walk in."

That was a lot of money he wanted, and my passport would still be unstamped. I could save myself that expense by sneaking across the border at nightfall! Or, from what I had heard, pay at the most 500 dollars to a Bulgarian who would get me through. It involved risks but was worth the money saved.

Offering a third of what he had asked for, I found myself following the officer out of the building. I cursed the fat man and wished his throat cut one day - indeed, I wonder if my wish has been granted by now? The officer handed my passport back and then my person to a border guard who in turn took me to the fences demarcating Yugoslavia from the neutral zone. There was another officer on the Bulgarian side serving the same purpose. He opened a small door in the fence, wide enough for one man to pass through at a time;

pointing, he said, "You see the man there behind that fence? He is a Bulgarian border guard. Go to him."

Reluctantly I covered the 100m neutral zone and came to the Bulgarian fence and passed through the same kind of door I had just exited. The border guard there, seeing me approaching, had it already open. And so, disheartened, I re-entered the country which less than an hour before I had left. The guard asked me to wait close by.

In no time an immigration officer materialized and asked for my passport. I handed it over and he disappeared. About ten minutes later the same immigration officer appeared again, gave my passport back and said, "You've got 48 hours to leave the country of Bulgaria."

Sent back from the west with Romania in the north and Greece to the south, and with both countries subjected to strict visa regulations preceding entry and only obtainable from the home country, it looked as if I had no choice but to go east - back to Turkey.

chapter five

I STARTED WALKING along the road pretending to hitchhike, but at the same time looking for a suitable place to hide till nightfall when I might sneak out of Bulgaria and enter Yugoslavia, though it was still early morning and a long time before I had the benefit of the cover of darkness. After walking for about a couple of miles I came to an isolated restaurant, perhaps better described as a tea shop. There were a few benches outside and I placed myself on one of them. The only man serving there came to me and said something in a language I didn't understand.

With the help of body language and at the same time talking English I made him understand that I would be there for only five minutes and so nothing was needed. He went off and a few seconds later came back with a bottle of beer, gave it to me and said, "Be my guest."

"Do you speak English?" I asked, surprised.

Word for word his reply was, "Not very much" - then pointing at a lady sitting on another bench about a few metres away, he informed me, "But she does." He asked her to join us and she did so, sitting down on the other side of my bench. She looked in her late thirties and overall of normal appearance. I offered her a drink and paid in dollars. She did speak some English, and better still, lived close to the border. That could come in handy, I thought; she might be able to help me with my problem, or at least give me a few good pointers on how to cross over. With that in mind, I didn't waste much time and told this woman about the refusal by the Yugoslavian officials to let me in and how much I needed to enter that country. Then, not knowing if I could trust her and throwing caution to the wind, I asked if she knew of anyone who would take me there. "I'd pay too, 500 US dollars," I said.

That was a lot of money to these people and I saw her eyes widen. She stood up at once, ready to look for someone to do the job. "Wait, I'll be back," she said, "even if I can't find anyone," and then disappeared.

When she was gone as well as the man, I turned back and looked in the direction of Yugoslavia. On my left, just a few hundred metres beyond the road, it was mountainous; and to my right stretched a virtually flat plain covered by a thin forest, where one could walk freely at dark and not be seen; but there was always the danger of border guards going their rounds, some with dogs, that could sniff one out in such an unrestricted area. Nevertheless I decided it would be safer and easier to leave on the right-hand side. But then again, I would wait and see what the guide said, if indeed she brought one back; there may well be a route or a strategy I was unaware of.

Time went by slowly but I was willing to wait. I lunched at the restaurant and paid the owner in dollars again; there was no need to change money into Bulgarian currency called Leva since I didn't intend to stay anyway.

Around noon, after a short walk, I sat down once again on one of the outside benches. The man came out every now and then, smiling, reassuring me with a gesture of his hand, that she would keep her promise.

And she did.

It was well into the afternoon when she came back accompanied by a man that I at once took a hearty dislike to. However, that was tough luck, I thought, for he would probably be my guide, like it or not, and in a couple of hours' time I would be over the border. The man, who called himself Vich, looked to be in his late twenties, of average build, taller than me, blond, with a round face and a slightly big nose in the middle of it - a nose I was to disfigure later that evening.

Vich knew the way; he had conducted people across the border to Yugoslavia many times and usually asked for his money in advance. When I told him he would only receive his pay on Yugoslavian soil "on the other side of the fence", he asked to see if I had the amount I offered. I showed him five one-hundred dollar notes that I had separated from the rest of my money to avoid him being confused and tempted to ask for more, then put the notes back in my pocket. Tapping the outside of my pocket, I said, "Yours, on the other side." All this was translated to Vich by the woman.

We started as soon as night fell, but with it being a clear sky with a full moon, things could be seen as clearly a few yards away as they would be in daylight - a bad omen, I thought. Leaving the road, as I had hoped, from the right side into the forest, I followed Vich in a direction that seemed to me to be parallel to the border line, though I couldn't be sure. After keeping on that course for about an hour, I noticed some single lights ahead, to the right and about two hundred yards away that appeared to be moving. They were flashing on and off behind the trees; it was hard to tell how many, but they were definitely approaching. Border guards, was my first guess.

I now hoped that Vich, who had surely also noticed the lights, would try to avoid them by changing direction to the left and take a more direct route to where I presumed the border was. Instead he continued walking directly towards the lights. Stopping him as though he hadn't seen the lights, though I knew otherwise, I pointed at the approaching danger and said, "Lights!"

"Okay," he answered - the only English word, apart from Money that he probably knew. But they didn't look okay to me and I could smell trouble. Those lights weren't border guards, I thought. I had a gut feeling that if he was trying to reach them, it wasn't part of the plan I had in mind.

As he was about to carry on, I pointed a finger of my right hand at myself and said, "Me, me", then a finger of my left hand towards the west and said, "Yugoslavia" - meaning he would be on his own if he carried on towards lights, and he clearly understood that. Taking a stand in front of me, less than a couple of yards between us, he looked aggressive - but I was on guard. He murmured a few words in his language, then put a hand in his pocket and withdrew something that flashed in the moonlight. It was a knife. I tried to keep control of myself and not to show panic. He shook the knife threateningly at me and said, "Money!"

It was too late to run now; with the knapsack over my shoulder, he would be sure to outrun me, I thought. It crossed my mind to fight him, but with that knife in his hand he looked formidable; and anyway, with those lights approaching, which probably belonged to his friends, because this was clearly a pre-set trap, I was left with only one option. Taking the money out from my pocket and deliberately separating the notes from each other, I threw them on the ground in front of him; as I expected, the notes scattered as they fell.

As he sat down to pick them up, I took a step back. There was a stone behind me, and I bent down and picked it up; it was quite a handful and felt heavy. Vich looked up but before he could react I hurled the stone at him and it smashed his nose. He gave a loud painful shout; he had been sitting on the soles of his feet and landed on his ass. I Jumped forward and kicked the knife out of his hand. I was prepared, now, to give him a fair fight if he wanted one. He held his nose, groaning. I picked the notes up, finding only four. He could keep one, I thought - he'd need it to get his nose fixed. One of the notes was wet from his blood. He was holding his nose in pain while on his knees, and when he tried to stand up I kicked him up his backside. Giving another loud shout, clutching himself where it hurt, he doubled over with pain. Now I looked at the lights: they were close enough for me to make out three advancing figures among the trees. Their movements were erratic and they were approaching fast; clearly they had heard the shouts.

Turning to face the road, I started to run like hell! To avoid the restaurant and especially the moving lights which pursued me halfway back, I kept to the right. In record time I reached the main road; out of breath, I started walking along it, undecided what to do. A few hundred yards away I came to a very sharp bend in the road and at once recognized the place - with the rubbish stand on one side and a small parking space on the other. I had passed this bend walking along the road in the morning - almost halfway between the border and the restaurant. Forgetting all about Yugoslavia, I determined to go back to Istanbul. I had had enough! I would start afresh, I thought, and think of new ways to leave.

To get a lift now, by simply standing on the roadside, was out of question. No one would stop in the dark in the middle of nowhere, even though it was not all that late yet. Furthermore, on such a clear moonlit night, there was a chance that Vich and his friends, who were probably still on the lookout for me, might spot my outline or even, in some car lights, recognise me and pounce on me.

Hiding behind one of the trees close to the roadside, I would get a lift, I thought, but in a different way.

Earlier in the day, while outside the restaurant waiting for that bitch to bring her bastard guide, I had seen many trucks passing by, each one hauling a large transport trailer. If one came along now it would suit my purpose; the bend would force the truck to slow down sufficiently for me to put my plan into action.

It wasn't long after a couple of private cars passed that I saw approaching what I had been waiting for. As I expected, the truck hauling its large transport trailer had to slow down to almost walking pace in order to negotiate the sharp bend. All I had to do to catch up with it was to run fast behind it. I grabbed a bar and hung on, at the same time pulling myself up onto the roof where I lay down.

The combination picked up speed and a minute later when it passed by the restaurant, I looked down from my hiding place and recognised the woman, the owner, surrounded by a few men; and if I am not mistaken, one of them sported a white bandage over his nose! No doubt they were talking about the way the plan they had colluded with Vich had gone awry. How many bodies, I wondered while lying on that trailer's roof, were buried in that forest - the remains of those who had followed Vich in the vain hope of reaching Yugoslavia?

The wind from the slipstream felt refreshing. I looked up and noticed the sky full of stars; it looked to me like a navigator's chart that was an omen of bad luck. I made up my mind there and then never again to try crossing borders in the way that I had attempted.

About an hour later the truck slowed down, turned a couple of times and stopped; then the driver got out, closed the door behind him, and walked away. I sat up on the trailer top and looked around. I was in a big parking area with about a dozen other truck trailers of the same kind, all parked so close together that I could jump from one to the other if I wanted to. The rest of the area was half packed with private cars.

After climbing down quietly, I walked out of the car park and came across a large, well-lit coffee and sandwich bar, almost half occupied. Adjacent to that was a sizable off license shop. I bought myself a can of drink and some chocolates; my dollars were accepted, evidently the kind of currency more in favour than their own.

Leaving the complex behind, I carried on along the road and was soon walking in total darkness. A few cars drove by, slowing down, the occupants looking amazed, heads turned, watching me. Keeping to the road and at the same time looking for a suitable place in the woods to crash out, I became aware of dim lights ahead. Getting closer, I saw that they belonged to a small isolated park with vacant benches, close to nowhere. To me, exhausted and dead beat from the trial I had been through, it looked like a 4-star hotel! I chose a bench that was out of view, behind some bushes. I settled down on the hard wood, knapsack under my head, and fell fast asleep.

chapter six

IT WAS WELL INTO DAYBREAK when I woke up. After a quick wash at the toilets in the park, I went to the roadside and it didn't take long before I was offered a lift by the same kind of truck trailer I had travelled on earlier, this time in the proper way. The driver was heading for Istanbul, where I wanted to end up. But as we approached Sofia I thought it would be a pity to have come all this way and not make a stopover to pay such an interesting city a visit, even though my available time was restricted to only half a day. Therefore, just before turning into the ring road going round Sofia, I asked the driver to stop and got out - to his surprise, since I had told him I would accompany him to Istanbul. I closed the door behind me and waved him goodbye.

The truck on its way, I started walking along the road towards the sign that said Sofia. By this time it was around noon. I had missed breakfast and began to feel hungry. But in order to get a better deal for my money to buy anything, first I would have to change some of my dollars to Bulgarian Levas, preferably on the black market, since it paid many times more than the banks did, or so I had been told. I knew that close to a hotel called Hemus, near the city centre, this agreeable currency exchange rate could be found, where dealers approached foreign looking people and asked if they wanted the ready - though, as it happened, I didn't have to go as far as that.

Coming to a bus stop a few minutes later, I got on one of the local buses. I wondered if public transport was free in Bulgaria, since no one seemed to pay and neither did I. After a few turns, talking to the driver, I found out this wasn't my bus. He dropped me at the right place to catch an electric train, which they called *terramva*, bound for the city centre; again, no fare was required.

Crowded inside, I stood close to a young man who kept staring at me. Watching him out of the corner of my eye, I felt uneasy, and wondered if it had anything to do with the previous night's incident involving Vich? Though, how could that be? Suddenly I turned round and stared right back into his eyes, ready for any action he might have had in mind. Instead, he brought his head closer and quietly said to me, "Dollar change?" I wanted to shout at him: "You scared the hell out of me, bastard!" I must have stood out like a saw thumb as a foreigner, which is why he approached me.

We got off the *terramva* and walked to some deserted corner; obviously illegal, this sort of transaction occurred everywhere, the same rules applying in Bulgaria as in neighbouring countries. Cautiously, I handed him a 100-dollar note and he gave me 400 Levas in return.

The clandestine transaction complete, I went to the nearest restaurant and had a hearty meal, plus a salad and a drink. Thanks to the advantageous exchange rate I paid a bill that was equal to only one dollar, whereas, the day before, at the restaurant near the border, a simple meal had cost me close to five dollars - which was almost the official rate charged by the banks.

Things turned out cheap; I was enjoying a drink here and there, said things to girls passing by and started feeling a bit happier, though a long way off normal yet. After all, life wasn't meant to be a monotonous affair of facing miseries, and, my spirits rising, I determined to make the most of my circumstances.

During the afternoon I went to the Bus Terminal and found out that there was a bus leaving Sofia for Istanbul every two hours, right up to ten at night. I would depart by the last one, I decided, to be at the border early the next morning and in time for my visa; that way I could continue touring the city as long as possible. But, come to think of it, since I was enjoying myself, did it matter if I overstayed my visa by a day? Impulsively, I decided I would let the last bus leave without me!

Time passed quickly and soon it was night. I came across a large park in the middle of the city; a narrow pavement encircled the park and there were benches placed at equal intervals along it, and to my surprise, none were occupied; in fact, there were only a couple of youngsters to be seen, roller skating. Soon they were gone too. I stretched out on one of the benches, knapsack as a pillow, feeling worn out, and it didn't take long before I drifted off. It was my second consecutive night spent under the stars! I was fast asleep when, in the early hours of the morning, a torch flashed into my eyes and woke me up. I shook the sleep out of my head and saw three policemen standing in front of the bench. The one with the torch spoke first. Realizing I was a foreigner, he asked in very good English to see my passport.

I sat up, got it out of my breast pocket and handed it over to him.

He skimmed through the passport, then went to the right page and said, "You have till tomorrow to leave the country, you know that?"

Or rather today, I corrected him in my mind, as it was past midnight and therefore tomorrow was already with us. I answered, "Yes, sir."

Handing back my passport, he appeared satisfied but said, "You are not allowed to sleep in the park" - and he added, "People pay a heavy fine breaking this law."

But I slept in the park last night and nothing happened, I wanted to say, but didn't; instead I lied, "I got to the city a bit late and didn't know where to go, so came here, not realising I was breaking the law."

Good enough so far, but then he ordered me to leave

the park. "There's a hotel just round the corner," he said, pointing his finger in a certain direction, adding, "Go there tonight." Then he warned me, "If I come back and see you here," his finger now pointing at the ground, meaning the park, "you'll be arrested!" Having made sure I understood, they walked away.

As there were only a few hours left till morning I didn't want to waste money on a hotel - but where else could I go? I had noticed the police station while I was walking around on the previous afternoon and I wondered whether I might be able to stay there for those few hours.

When I got there, only a short walk away, I saw a policeman, machine gun over his shoulder, standing guard in front of the entrance door. He didn't know a word of English and, thank heavens I did not have much to do with him. It was as though he had been programmed about what to do when faced with a person confronting him, like myself. When I addressed him he stuck up the palm of his hand, indicating that I should wait. He then went inside, came back a minute later and held up his palm again, indicating that I should wait a little longer. Not knowing what to expect, I heard a phone ringing, the sound coming from inside the police station, just beyond the door. Using his hand to point at the door and nodding his head towards me, the policeman gave me to understand that I should go in and answer it. I did so. I picked up the receiver and a woman's voice came over the line: "What is the problem?" she asked with the brisk tone typical of people of the communist block trying to speak English.

"I was sleeping in the park when..."

She cut me short: "You are not allowed to sleep in the park! People pay a heavy fine breaking that law" - repeating almost word for word what the policeman at the park had told me. Then she said, "Wait a second," and started talking in Bulgarian to another person on the same line; clearly it was a triple connection. A male's voice replied and she gave me the translation: "My boss says you go to a hotel!"

"I haven't got that kind of cash to part with," I lied. "Besides," I added, "I'm leaving the country early in the morning so there is no point spending money on a hotel for only a few hours..."

She cut me short again: "What else can you do, walk around the streets?"

"Would you let me sleep in the police station for a few hours? I will leave at first light."

She conveyed my reply to her boss and after receiving his reply, she addressed herself to me and said, "Go to the airport and sleep there."

"Where's the airport?" I asked.

"Get a taxi, the driver will take you."

"That'll be too costly," I countered, all the time trying to sound American; if she knew my real nationality I would spend the night in the police station, and not for the sake of temporary accommodation.

Back to her boss, then a few seconds later to me, she

said, "Okay, Just wait in front of the station - a police car will come in a minute to take you there."

I put the phone down, went outside and waited. Almost to the minute a police car arrived, two policemen occupying the front seats, the driver and the other in the passenger seat next to him. I was told to get in the back. Being early in the morning with no traffic about, the driver went fast and hardly took notice of any red lights. It didn't take long to reach the airport. I thanked them, got out of the car and walked inside.

It was the Bulgarian International Airport in Sofia, the capital, and presumably one of the biggest in the country, though ridiculously smaller than the domestic airports I had seen in some big cities in Iran. There were only about a couple of dozen passengers there, each horizontally occupying an old worn-out bench full length, in deep slumber. Finding an empty one I did the same.

Dawn had just broken when I left the airport. After walking for some distance, I caught a bus that was heading for the city centre; though still early, it was crowded. *Terramvas* were moving at full capacity, too. This was communism and everyone had to work, I guessed.

After enjoying a sumptuous breakfast around midmorning I found another park, a different one from the night before. There were a few people around and some kids playing. I sat on one of the empty benches, looked at communism for a while, then took my diary out of my knapsack and started writing:

17 Sept., 1988. Sofia, in a park:

> Left Istanbul 3 days ago. Passing through Bulgaria, I wasn't allowed to enter Yugoslavia, where I was hoping to start the second leg of my journey in a different direction altogether. Then I tried to get there illegally... meeting a woman at the restaurant ... later she got me a guide by the name of Vich. I followed him trying to cross the border but he turned out to be a thief. Remembering Vich with his knife drawn, standing in front of me in a forest, even now, far away in this park 2 days later, sends shivers down my spine. I got a lift in an unusual way, hanging on to a bar at the back of a trailer... and spent the night in an isolated park. Another lift to Sofia in the morning; walking around enjoying myself, I decided to overstay my visa and ended up spending the night at the airport...

Then a few lines on politics:

> ....clearly these people feel positively towards their government... I hate a bastard communist regime myself...

As I was writing a young girl of about eighteen, perhaps

even younger, came and sat next to me. I gave her a glance and she said, "Hello."

"Hello," I said, taken aback.

She didn't waste much time and went straight to the point: "You want madam?"

While in Istanbul I had heard that in some communist countries, especially Romania and Bulgaria, girls as young as thirteen went round whoring freely; so her offer didn't surprise me. I put the diary back in my knapsack, faced her and asked, "How much is it going to cost me to want a madam?"

With her average English she said, "Twenty dollars one time."

Meaning, I assumed, that much for a fuck.

She got off the bench and stood up facing me; nice figure and almost pretty, I thought.

"I give you one hundred Levas," I offered, which was more than twenty dollars.

Accepting the offer, she wanted to know if I had a place I could take her to.

"No. Do you?" I asked, though I knew the answer; most took their clients to their own places.

"Yes. But you have to pay for that as well. Only twenty Levas."

"Let's go," I said.

"By taxi it would take 15 minutes, walking almost twice as long," she informed me, waiting for an answer.

"Let's call a taxi. I have to come back and catch my bus to leave the country." I had decided on the 4 o'clock bus so that I would be at the border just before midnight when the immigration officer would be impatiently waiting to change shifts and would be unlikely to bother with someone who has overstayed his visa by half a day; sometimes, I heard, you could get away with two days overdue, and later came to experience that that was indeed the case. "But where are we going?" I asked.

"To my aunt's place," she said.

About 15 minutes later the taxi stopped in front of a block of flats. I paid the driver and we got out. It was a ten-storey building with rows of flats, a handful on each floor.

We went up the stairs. I had to admit I was a bit nervous; if anything happened to me here no one would know. But desire prevails over caution in carnal cases, and I was badly in need of a woman.

In the taxi she told me her name was Lynn, just 18 and that she came from Sofia; she lived with her parents but was on good terms with her aunt.

We reached the fourth floor and stood in front of flat no. 43. She knocked and a few seconds later a woman's voice from inside said something, out of my hearing. Lynn answered back and the door opened. A middle-aged, medium-sized woman, wearing glasses appeared at the doorway and asked us in.

Following Lynn and entering the flat, and closing the door behind me, I found myself standing in a narrow corridor less than 5 metres long. There was a door to the immediate left, two on the right and one ahead of us, into which her aunt had just disappeared. "Leave your knapsack here," Lynn said. Pointing to the door on the left, she explained, "Toilet and bathroom, if you need it." The first door on the right was open, revealing the kitchen, but the second one was closed. The door ahead had been left wide open and, looking inside, I saw Lynn's aunt comfortably ensconced in an armchair watching TV. It was apparently the sitting room.

I was half-expecting the closed door to open with guys rushing out to beat me up, take my money and dispose of me as they chose. Nothing like that happened and Lynn opened the door. "We will use this bedroom," she said. I gave a glance inside while she talked to her aunt. It was a tidy room. Shortly she turned back to me and asked, "Twenty for her plus my hundred."

I paid her the money and she gave it all to her aunt, and we entered the bedroom. Once inside I locked the door; hearing the click she said, "Don't you trust us?"

"Just a precaution," I smiled. I didn't want to sound suspicious, though that was the case.

The curtains were drawn but some light managed to seep through from the outside. As we were taking our clothes off I could see her breasts were fully developed. We got into bed and in a moment I was making love after a period of celibacy of almost three years. It was beautiful but didn't last long.

When over, she got out of the bed and started dressing.

I got out of bed too, but before I put my clothes on,

pointing at the bed, asked her, "Do you want to go back in and stay a bit longer? I'll pay you well for it."

She shook her head. "No, sorry, I am in a hurry - I have to get my brother from school; then meet a friend and after that attend my computer classes."

"What about when you're finished?" I asked.

"I probably won't until late."

"Doesn't matter, I could meet you then," I said and mentioned my wish to spend a longer time with her the next time.

"I thought you said something about catching your bus and leaving the country today," she reminded me.

"That can wait for a while." I would stay for another month if it meant being with her. The experience of that brief time with her was exquisite.

She said, "I'll be back here at ten; and how long do you want me for?"

"Let's say till morning?" I ventured, putting my clothes on.

"That long!" She seemed to be thinking in terms of money. "I have to ask my aunt to see if it'll be okay to stay overnight."

After unlocking the door she went to her aunt who still appeared to be engrossed in her TV programme. I stood by the bedroom doorway and watched the two women talking; the words *dollar* and *Leva* cropped up a couple of times. At the end of the discussion, Lynn turned to me, smiled and said, "It'll be okay."

As for money, I would have nodded acceptance even if she had demanded twice as much.

We went to the door and she opened it. I picked up my knapsack and as I stepped outside, I gave her a quick kiss on her sweet lips and said, "See you tonight." I left with a sense of elation, eagerly looking forward to our meeting later that night.

It was 2 o'clock now and I had to be back at ten, which meant I had eight hours to waste, or rather to enjoy more novelties. Forget about leaving the country for a while, I told myself - a couple of days' delay, if spent embracing the ultimate pleasure, as I had done with Lynn and was expecting to repeat, would more than compensate for any risk that might arise from the delay. An exquisite experience like that should be praised or even legalized as valid grounds for extending a visa! Furthermore, I hadn't had a woman for nearly three years - eleven months spent in jail without one back in England, then the two years after being deported back to Iran. Not that I couldn't have had any, since there were more loose women in Iran than anywhere else in the world; it was just that I didn't want to get involved with anyone in such a troubled country. But in the end it all proved worth waiting for and I was well rewarded. It brought to mind the preaching of those clerics in Iran with their message that God has his ways of rewarding patience; I should listen to them more often, I reminded myself.

I started walking towards the city centre, the place I enjoyed hanging around in most. It was a nice area; the whole area cobblestoned, and there were the other intangibles, the atmosphere, the friendliness, the pretty girls, all cheering and boosting my morale. Life seemed to have taken a sudden turn for the better.

There was a leisure centre close by too which I had noticed wandering around yesterday. Though not feeling up to it, I dragged myself in and spent an hour there weight training. I had a shower afterwards and felt a different person.

Coming out of the leisure centre, I got myself something to eat, had a few drinks and started, again, saying things to girls passing by. I was feeling better; another step closer to normality.

Later in the afternoon I went to the same park where I met Lynn and skimmed through the 4-page local paper in English; nothing but a pack of lies about communism being better than the 'imperialism' of western countries. Then, feeling tired - reading often had that effect on me - I drifted off while still in a sitting position! I woke to find myself flat on the bench with the knapsack having somehow insinuated itself under my head. Luckily there were no policemen around. Though the weather had turned dark, it was still early and I stayed stretched out on the bench for another ten minutes. Soon afterwards I left the park.

Time dragged on but eventually the appointed hour approached and I started to make my way towards Lynn's place, thinking I wouldn't be spending the night under the stars again; on the contrary, I would be having fun and at the thought my heart missed a beat! I found the building, climbed the stairs to the fourth floor, stood in front of flat no. 43, and knocked. A few seconds later the door opened and Lynn stood there.

"Hello," I said, almost not recognizing her.

She had make up on and looked quite pretty; for a second I thought I was meeting someone like her but a lot more attractive. "Better not waste much time," I told myself. She had a long red close-fitting dress on showing her nice figure in full; and her beautiful long straight brown hair hung loosely around her shoulders. With a lovely smile she answered "Hello" and opened the door wider, moving with it, inviting me in. The dress enhancing the curve of her back made her look all the more desirable.

We entered the living room where her aunt was as usual watching TV. I sat on an armchair while Lynn went to the kitchen and came back with a cup of tea. She gave it to me and drew up a chair close to me. I was aware of her captivating perfume. Leaning on the arm of the chair, she said, "Tomorrow morning you have to leave early, at six…" I kept staring at her loveliness as she continued, "…because my aunt will be meeting someone around that time and wants you out before she leaves."

"So we better start then," I said breathlessly. I couldn't wait to get even closer to her.

"When you've finished your tea," she smiled.

I drank it fast, gave her the money, and we went to the bedroom. Again I locked the door from the inside, but now I could hardly see her. Reading my mind, she asked me not to put the light on. Indeed, I was about to do so.

We took our clothes off and got into bed. Not having had a woman for so long apart from that earlier far too brief encounter, my appetite for her was intense - and now a young girl of 18, never mind pretty, proved far too sensational!

It was one of the best nights I would ever remember.

We rolled over one another and held each other tight. I couldn't stop kissing her, the pleasure of just being with her almost overshadowing the fuck. Like all blissful times, this one especially, the night sped away and morning came far too soon. Then there was a knock on the door and the old aunt muttered a few words behind it. Lynn, translating, conveyed the message to me: "It's 6 o'clock and you have to go."

It's hard to put my feelings into words, and it's an understatement to say that I was reluctant to part with her.

We got out of the bed and put our clothes on. I left the bedroom and went to the bathroom, had a quick wash at the sink, brushed my hair, and when I came out she was standing by the door, still looking devastatingly pretty.

Clearly it was time to say goodbye; she gave me my knapsack and opened the door. As I was leaving, I just had to come out with the way I felt or I would never know the answer she might have given me. "Listen," I said, looking into her soft brown eyes, "I'll get a place and you can move in with me; I wouldn't mind looking after you." I felt uneasy about expressing the next words, but I went on, "You don't have to sell your body anymore to earn a living."

Smiling, she shook her head. "I'm going to save a lot of money earned this way so I can pay to leave communism and go to America," she said. Then she said goodbye. The door gently closed and I stood there for a moment, feeling hurt and lost.

I shouldn't have allowed myself to be carried away by my feelings, but there was no denying that they were beyond my control. Walking down towards the city centre I tried not to think of her, but the image of her kept floating back in my mind; she was right in front of my eyes, distracting my vision.

"Well, that's another chapter closed," I thought to myself. There was no more for me in this country, and it seemed time to quit - though I didn't want to leave. People looked so friendly, especially the girls with their smiles; something their counterparts in Iran, since the revolution, hadn't displayed very much.

I reached the Bus Terminal not long after noon and waited till 4 o'clock (for the reason I pointed out earlier), then got on the bus bound for Istanbul. At the border just before midnight the immigration officer looked impatient with the people standing in the queue before him. When it was my turn at the counter, I handed him my passport. He paged through it, found the right page, and said something about my having overstayed my visa by two days. I pretended to be ignorant of this; he hesitated for a second, then stamped my passport and saying no more, gave it back to me.

Entering Turkey, I was granted another three

months' visa, the same red circular seal being placed in my passport. It appeared at the bottom of the page where my Bulgarian visa, the size of a postage stamp and no longer valid, was stuck.

chapter seven

ARRIVING IN ISTANBUL early in the morning, I left Topkapi and went back to the same hotel where I had stayed before leaving. Minus some good memories, it felt like I was almost back to square one. The receptionist told me to wait since rooms would only be available at 10 o'clock, when a few guests were expected to leave. If they stayed beyond that time they would be obliged to pay for an extra day.

I placed myself on one of the chairs in the small lobby, next to an Iranian who was also waiting for a room. He appeared about my age, much taller, bigger and somehow looked good natured. Now, who would have guessed that in less than a couple of days, this same guy whose name I did not even know at the time and with only a few words exchanged between us, would accompany me as we tried together to sneak out of Turkey into Greece! Though an intrepid spirit, he got cold feet halfway through the venture, stopping me in the middle of the night, reluctant to continue; feeling scared, though not admitting it, he wanted to turn back rather than face the unknown hurdles that lay ahead.

Ali had left Iran with the same aim as others: seeking asylum in some developed country. Australia was his priority, a country where he could own a piece of land, breed lambs and earn a good living by selling the wool and the meat; describing his dream as if he had spent years in Australia, he hardly knew where it was placed on the map. How I came to start on such a trek with a person in that state of mind is a question yet to be answered. He seemed to be living in a world of his own and would have carried on elucidating his dream if I hadn't changed the subject.

I told him about my aborted attempt to enter Yugoslavia. He had met a similar fate, going through the same trip. Lying low inside the cabin of a truck that had given him a lift was his second attempt to enter Yugoslavia. The first being in the normal way, travelling by bus, from which he was simply pulled off and made to face east again when the immigration officer had discovered him. A lift back by another truck trailer, almost non-stop through Bulgaria, missing a lot of fun, returned him to Istanbul. In fact, sitting on my left, he, too, had just closed a chapter in his life.

Talking to Ali, for some reason, perhaps because I found the man honest or in the same boat as I was, I trusted him and confided in him about my next move. I told him how, waiting at the Bus Terminal in Sofia for my transport to leave the country, looking at a map of Turkey, I had come up with a new plan.

He seemed interested.

I saw some guests leaving and at the same time the receptionist called us both and informed us of some vacant rooms. We both stood up and I said, "It was nice meeting you, Ali. I better go and get some rest." As I left I said, "I'll see you down here tonight and talk to you more about it then." We were handed some room keys, went up the stairs but to different floors.

At 8 o'clock that night I came down and saw Ali sitting in the lobby area watching TV. He was more than happy to see me. Drawing up a chair, I didn't waste much time: I got the map out of my pocket, unfolded it and let him hold one side. Tracing the route with my finger on the map, I told him of my plan: "...first we go to this place here... under the cover of darkness we sneak out of Turkey... somewhere there... and enter Greece..." Folding the map I added, "Nothing to it - we will manage!"

Then our conversation took a turn for social exchanges. Ali told me that he was married with one kid. After being granted asylum by Greece, or any other country, he would ask to enter Australia; and once there, would send for his wife and kid to join him. He gave me his phone number in Iran just in case we didn't make it and went back, so I could get in touch with him again.

Quite casually, I asked him, "What did you used to do in Iran?"

From his pocket he pulled out a photo and an I.D. card and gave them both to me. The former showed him in full uniform with a loaded holster at his waist; somewhat swiftly I turned to the card; there was a smaller photo of him at the top left corner, showing only his face wearing a cap. It said: *Border Guard.*

Astonished, I looked at him. He was laughing.

"So," I said, "watching people trying to sneak in or out of the country, you now find yourself on the opposite side of the fence? Right, we'll start tomorrow - early in the morning!"

I left Ali in the lobby and went out. It was a bit late to go training then, so instead I decided on a walk around the area. Coming back to the hotel, the lobby almost deserted, my companion gone too, I went up to my room. We had a long journey ahead of us the following day so I took to my bed.

Early the next morning I saw Ali in the reception area and after paying our bills, we got a taxi and headed for Topkapi. It was beginning to become a familiar place. We had our minds set on a place called Edernè, though any border town close to Greece would have done. But, then again, looking at the map, we didn't have many options; another place, a village called Ipsala, accessible by the southern road, seemed the only other alternative.

Getting on the right bus, it was past noon when we arrived in Ederne. At a teashop at the Terminal there, we had something to eat and when we left, a short dark man, who was in the teashop too, followed us out. He caught up with us and asked in poor English if we wanted a taxi, his two light blue eyes, almost transparent, staring at us in such a meaningful way that I realised he had more questions to ask or information to impart.

Ali's English was close to non-existent - he only knew a few Turkish words, so I did the talking. I studied the man for a second. It was written all over his face that he knew why we were there, and that the taxi meant a lift to the other side of the border. Straight to the point, I dared to ask, "Can you take us to Greece…?"

He cut me short: "Ssh…" - then, with a movement of his hand he asked us to follow him. We went round the back of the Terminal where it was quiet and he asked, "Are you from Iran?"

"Yes, we are from Iran," I said.

By means of body language and his hardly understandable English, the dark man told us that he had taken many people, almost all Iranians, across the border to Greece. Once caught sneaking four of them across the border, he said, he had spent two years in prison - which, I assumed, would mean a high levy on his service in view of the risks involved. "But anyway," he said, "I'm willing to help you for a small amount of money."

"And how much would that small amount be in American dollars?" I asked, expecting somewhere around a thousand for each of us.

He surprised me when he replied, "Five hundred dollar two of you."

"And how are you going to get us there?" Now I suspected there might be some trick involved.

"Wait here," he said, "I'll be back in a minute."

While he was gone I explained our situation to Ali. In view of the circumstances we took the quick decision that, no matter what transpired, the dark man would receive his money only when we found ourselves in Greece.

A few minutes later he came back accompanied by an individual, a tall, fair skinned man with brown hair who he introduced as another trafficker. Pointing at him, the short fellow said, "If you pay him now" - meaning the amount he had asked for - "he'll take you somewhere close to the border tonight." All we would need to do then, he explained, was to simply walk a few hundred metres and we would be on the other side.

Did he think we were born yesterday? Slightly on edge, with my finger close to tapping his shoulder, I said, "We want to be in Greece, not near the border." Then a bit louder, to make sure he realized our position, I carried on, "And we won't pay now but when you have got us in Greece, right on the soil inside!"

It was like a declaration to end all negotiations.

The incident made us realise that there would be more people crossing our path whose assistance to further our purpose could be bought.

We moved out of the area and got on a local bus that was heading for a destination that was close to the border. In the bus I met a university student who knew of a few people who had been on the same trip. "But," he said, "not from here. The best place to do the crossing is around a village called Ipsala." That was the alternative we had come up with on the map. I would try that later if all else failed, I thought.

Half an hour later, getting off the bus at the right place in terms of the route we were following on the map, we asked some locals for directions. They told us there was a passport office about ten minutes' walk from where we stood. We were of course fully aware that if we went to the passport office we would be turned back since Ali and I were both well aware of the visa restrictions Iranian nationals faced, restrictions imposed by the neighbouring country. Nevertheless, it would be a good strategy to test the situation and present ourselves at the passport office, since it would give us a good opportunity to evaluate the surroundings to further our purpose; the area was patrolled by soldiers who once stopped us to know what we were doing there.

The passport control office, rather more like a shack, big enough for only one man to sit inside talking to travellers through an open window, was placed next to some sort of movable barrier blocking the way to a long and narrow bridge linking Turkey to Greece. The immigration officer asked to see our passports; we had them ready. I looked beyond the check box and saw a Greek soldier on the other side of the bridge; his counterpart, machine gun over his shoulder, stood guard on this side. The official behind the glass looked at our passports and, as we had expected, refused us exit; he added, "Iranians are not permitted to cross because they are returned by Greece."

We got our passports back and as we were leaving I gave the other side one more envying glimpse; so close, but then again, so far to reach!

Never mind, as I had planned, we'd issue the visas ourselves, so to speak, either tonight or at the latest tomorrow night. And this time I took heart that there were two of us, not yet realising that my sense of security was flawed, for I had been misled by Ali's strong appearance which made me think I could rely on him.

On the way back I surveyed the surroundings, more observant now, and realized that it would be hard to do the crossing anywhere near the vicinity. A wide river separated the two countries, banked by high walls; also, the bridge overlooked a wide area.

We returned to the town, had a drink and went to a hotel. That night I studied a map of the area, a new one we had bought in the town, which showed more detail; and I saw Ipsala village was situated almost at the border.

In the morning, as we were checking out, I was bold enough to ask the receptionist about the best place to jump the boundaries to Greece! If he called the police I would deny ever asking him anything. Quite urbanely, however, he referred us to the village of Ipsala, which was in keeping with the advice we had received before.

Therefore, all set, as we had decided the night before, we determined to try our luck there - the option we should have chosen in the first place. For some reason, it seemed, we had at first picked the wrong one of only two alternatives and now had the right alternative confirmed.

At the Bus Terminal they told us there was no direct transport from Edernè to Ipsala, and in order to get there we had to change our bus somewhere on the way for a minibus.

Looking through the window during this journey I enjoyed the scenery, for Turkey had its own natural beauties. We went through a few villages, very rural, before it was time to change our bus. In the minibus we sat right at the back where there was room for five people. I sat by the window, Ali next to me on my left, and a young man of light brown hair, white skin, thin brown beard, apparently in his early twenties, next to Ali.

Getting off the minibus at Ipsala I tapped the young man on the shoulder and when he turned towards me, I said, "We are looking for a hotel" - though I could see one in front of us - "do you know of a good one?" Somehow I wanted to evaluate this young man before I turned to my main subject. We were in a border village now and I had to be cautious. I had also told Ali to keep a low profile, though luckily I imagined we blended in well with the locals - apart from when we spoke which caused a couple of heads to turn towards us.

The young man signalled with his hands; his English was limited to only a few words, but by now I had mastered the body language of the country, being conversant with relaying and understanding messages, though assisted also by the Turkish I had picked up during my previous stay. We followed him round the corner and entered a large hotel with two hundred rooms; apparently all were empty apart from one occupied by a middle-aged whore. I asked for a room and we were given one on the third floor right opposite hers, a narrow corridor separating the two doors. She was standing in the doorway leaning to one side.

The bellboy left and, together with the young man who was still with us, we entered our room. He introduced himself as "Osman" and, taking us by surprise, said, "Are you going to Greece?"

"Yes. Can you get us there?" I asked.

The same old story and probably true: he had taken many people across, quite a few Iranians, during the last few years. Then grassed to the police by a friend, he had been sentenced to five years in prison, but after serving only two years was paroled and released. It would nevertheless be an easy crossing, he continued to tell us; cross a few fields, a narrow stream and then "we will be in Greece. Nothing to it!"

"How long will the whole crossing take?" I asked.

From where he proposed to start, at the most two hours.

"You said we have to cross a stream?" I asked. He had just referred to it as the final frontier. I waited for an answer to make sure I had heard him right. Nodding his head, I carried on, "How deep and wide is this stream?" I had seen it on the map specified as a 'river' called *Maritza*.

He put his right hand to his chest and said, "Up to here." Though short myself, 5'7", he was shorter than me by four inches. Asked how wide it was, he said about the length of the room - about six metres. I wanted to know if it was a turbulent stream, and to convey my next question I made some wild wave movements with my hand and at the same time gave out some rough river noises.

Shaking his head from side to side, Osman said "No", then to convey a smooth-flowing calm stream he moved his hand slowly in a straight horizontal line, at the same time making a barely audible sound with his mouth.

It all sounded good, if true.

That being the case, the prospect of wading across this final stage no longer troubled my mind. The hurdle would be surmounted without much difficulty, I thought. Perhaps it was just as well that, as I found out later, the river was much deeper and at least ten times wider than what he gave us to believe, presenting a barrier that almost caused me to give up.

"How much do you want for this crossing?" I asked, not foreseeing his answer, since he looked shrewd and I was beginning to wonder if he could be trusted.

"One thousand US dollars for both of you," he replied.

It sounded a fair deal, but whether he agreed to it or not depended on my next statement: "We will pay you by the stream."

Reluctant though he seemed, surprisingly he accepted the arrangement.

We would start that same night. That settled, we went for a drink.

Coming down from the room, we spoke to one of the receptionists, Alper, a youngster of about twenty, dark, slim, midway between my height and Osman's. He had spent twelve years in Germany and could also speak English well. My mind was put at rest when he told us that Ipsala was a mining village and people from all over Turkey came to work there. I realized, then, that we wouldn't just get picked up, going out, if seen by the police, provided we didn't speak; the place was full of strange faces, which also explained the reason for the presence of hotels with so many rooms in such a small village. Alper told me that had I come in the evening a room would not have been available. At the weekend though, luckily a couple of days away yet, it would be a different story and the village would be deserted.

Alper could be trusted, I decided; therefore, in the evening, just before leaving, I would call the guy up and ask him those few questions Osman avoided answering. I would also ask for his opinion of the whole undertaking and see what he advised; after all, he looked to be a clever boy and the kind who knew his way around.

We went for a drink and, coming back, at the hotel entrance, Osman reminded us again that "we would start tonight", then left to join us later. Going to our room I saw the middle-aged whore still standing by her door, winking at me, and I asked her in. Ali seemed inclined to have a go at her, but when I told him what Alper had said about the rooms all being occupied by miners at nights, and how they never used condoms in Turkey, he changed his mind. Having decided on no sex, I thought, we could still spend a while having some laughs with her; after all, we had a fair amount of time on our hands. Using my standard language of communication I pretended, with some help from Ali, to be interested in what she was offering, I asked her, "*San, kach para* (you, how much)?"

We didn't understand the amount she wanted from her speech so I handed her a pen and paper and she wrote down, "20,000 liras."

She had valued herself far too high! In view of the place abounding with foreigners, I had expected a price in excess of the amount usually paid by Turks, but not a four-fold jump! I answered, "*Chok pahaleh* (too expensive)."

"*Chok pahaleh, yok* (not too expensive)," she said.

Then I tried to explain to her that at the brothel in Istanbul called Karkhaneh, where whores were placed behind windows like items in a shop from which one chose, you could have a whore as young as 16 for 10,000 liras - so how come, when she was old and almost useless, she was asking twice as much?

Looking disgruntled, she got out of the room and we never saw her at the doorway for those few hours remaining.

Around eight o'clock Osman came back. He was a bit drunk and I noticed he had an open knife in his pocket. *I don't have to face another Vich I hope*, I told myself; but, if the situation demanded, this time I would make sure we were both armed equally. By now I had come to realize that, though on the big side and tall, Ali didn't seem the kind of person who could be relied on when times were hard; and from the trouble I sensed brewing from Osman, I anticipated a situation that I would have to handle on my own.

I went to my knapsack pretending to get some tissues to wipe my nose, took out my flick knife and, without them noticing, put it in my pocket. Ali, reclining in the only armchair in the room, appeared deep in thought. I went and sat on the bed and a moment later Osman came and placed himself next to me on my right. Watching him out of the corner of my eye, I pretended to be in deep thought, like Ali, at the same time with my left hand in my pocket holding my knife, head down and staring into empty space. It didn't take long before I felt him touching my pocket. With one quick movement, grabbing his hair, I pulled him back, at the same time taking the knife out, flicking it, holding it to his throat. My action, so swift, surprised even myself and created such a frightening atmosphere that Ali jumped from his chair and got behind it. As I was sitting on Osman's chest, with my knife still to his throat, I said to him, "I thought we had a deal! No payment till you get us to Greece. Understood?"

Whether he did or not, he nodded his head signifying compliance; he probably gathered that was the answer expected of him. He kept staring at me and looked quite sober now.

Our plan seemed shattered, at least for the time being, and I felt like pushing the knife right through his throat - but that wasn't in me.

I put my free hand in his pocket, got his knife out, still open, and closed it; then, getting off his chest, I went to Ali who was still standing behind the chair looking confused. I told him about Osman trying to pick my pocket.

Ali thought that it would be best if we abandoned the whole plan and went back to Istanbul. He had heard of some Burmese bandits taking people to Australia for as little as three hundred dollars. But I had come a long way and wasn't going to give up now; going back halfway across the world to find out the Burmese bandits were probably worse than Osman felt stupid.

I went to the phone and picked it up. Alper answered and I asked him up. A minute later he was in our room. I told him what we were up to; indeed, he had guessed as much the moment he first saw us. Not giving up on making a fresh restart the same night, I asked him, "Can Ali and I make this crossing ourselves without help from Osman?"

Nodding his head, he invited me to the window. Looking through it into the darkness outside, my eyes followed the direction in which he was pointing. I could see some lights a couple of miles away. He said they belonged to a border village in Greece. But he informed me, "Trying to sneak out from Ipsala is dangerous; army units have recently been placed on the border side of the village." Our best bet, he explained, would be "to go outside, get a taxi - there are some just round the corner - and ask the driver to take you towards a village called Merich. After going for about twenty minutes you will pass under this very tall bridge which is halfway through construction. Go for another ten minutes and stop the taxi - anywhere there will be a good place to start."

"Come on Ali, let's not waste much time; it's easy, we could do it ourselves without this bastard's help," I said, pointing at Osman.

Ali was scared. "We don't know the way and it's dark out there."

Osman, realizing what we were about to decide, cut in, "Just give me 500 dollars and I'll take you both there."

"But no tricks. Okay?" I retorted.

We went downstairs without our bags; Alper would take them to the reception later and if he ever got an address, would post them to us; otherwise he could keep mine. Going outside, there were not many people about; walking round the corner, all four of us, we came to some parked taxis. Alper spoke to one of the drivers, a fat man with a big belly, and told us to go with him.

Before we got into the taxi I asked Alper offhandedly, "So we can trust this driver you spoke to?"

"Yes, a very good man; he is my father," Alper answered.

Osman sat in the front, Ali and I in the back, and we started on our journey hoping to reach Greece.

As Alper had told us, about twenty minutes later, driving on an isolated narrow road, we passed under a tall bridge. After another few minutes Osman asked the driver to stop; paying him, we got out. It was dark, in the middle of nowhere, and we could hardly see one another. Overcame by a sense of loss, we would have probably gone back by the same taxi if Osman wasn't there to guide us. He took the lead, me behind him and Ali following in the rear. We hadn't been going for ten minutes when Osman stopped, tapped the ground with his foot and pointed down towards it and said, "Greece. We are in Greece now."

I took my knife out, flicked it, pointing the tip downwards, at the same time tapping the ground with my foot in imitation of him: "No Greece," I said. "Another two hours, as you told us, then maybe Greece!" So we carried on along these narrow muddy paths between what seemed to me to be rice fields. Ali brought up the rear, every now and then shouting quietly, "Wait for me!"

It was easy-going for a couple of hours. Then I saw four solitary bright lights, about a hundred yards away moving in a direction that would intercept ours if we maintained our course for another fifty yards. The lights they were carrying were so bright they almost illuminated the area for about ten yards around them.

"Border guards," Osman said, turning back.

Indeed they were. Now coming a bit closer, I could make out the uniforms, caps and the rifles over their shoulders.

We stopped, stayed low and watched; we would let them pass and when far enough, continue on our way. But suddenly the four of them disappeared into a small hut we managed to make out in the light of their torches.

Thinking they would be in the hut for a while before showing up again, we decided to carry on. Another fifty yards and we came to a water ditch, just over a couple of metres across, that stretched in both directions before us. The border guards, it seemed, had been walking along this ditch. Suddenly overcome by a sense of loss, I felt disoriented, wondering where exactly we were. Was this the Border then, I asked myself?

Osman thought so. Pointing to the other side of the ditch, still calling it a stream, he said, "Greece", and that was as far as he would go. It was clear that he intended to go no further.

We had been going for over two hours and the presence of the border guards seemed to verify Osman's claim. But could such an insignificant narrow ditch stand as a boundary between two countries so close to war with one another?

Alper had also told me, I recalled, that when we passed the river we would be in Greece. What I was looking at was clearly a ditch, not a river. But maybe because Alper didn't know the word *ditch*, I thought, he had used the word *river* instead.

I said, "Okay Osman, here is your 250 dollars." Like the time following Vich, I had the money separated from the rest for the same reason - to prevent him from suddenly developing a desire for more. Though the situation was different here, I was the one with the knife.

What was left of my money, plus my passport and diary notebook, I had wrapped in a small plastic bag, all safely in my pocket, so that when crossing the river these items wouldn't get wet.

With the light of his watch, Osman looked at the three notes one by one, making sure two were 100s and one 50. He held them tight in his hand.

I turned to Ali and said, "What are you waiting for? Give him your half of the money and hurry up."

Ali looked scared. He put both his hands up as if a gun had been pointed at him and said, "No, I'm not coming with you, and *don't insist*." Nodding his head towards where we thought Greece was, he grumbled, "It looks all dark there and I don't know what's lurking for us in that nowhere. I'm going back with him," and he pointed at Osman. Again he started mumbling something about Burmese bandits who took people to Australia charging just over a couple of hundred dollars.

Coming all this way and now going back was stupid, I told him. But he had made up his mind and wouldn't change it. My feelings towards him until then were reasonably positive and now I felt let down. But then the realisation that from that moment he would no longer be a burden was like a heavy weight lifting from my shoulders.

I shook hands with both of them before they turned back. A few seconds later they disappeared into the darkness.

chapter eight

I WAS ALL ALONE NOW, looking forward to the future. All my hopes were upbeat. I didn't feel scared and, in fact, I was smiling inside. I climbed down the half metre slope that led to the ditch, then went down to the water. I was in the middle of the ditch when, turning to look back, I saw the border guards approaching. It seemed too late now to get out of the ditch. If I climbed up the opposite slope, they would see me. My body fully immersed and hiding my head in the long weeds that were shooting out of the water, I watched them as they got within ten yards. Two were walking on top of the slope I had just left and the other two I couldn't see, just their torches moving in the air as they lit an area half a metre lower down on the flat ground. Would they see me if they looked? Too busy talking and laughing, the two on the top, heads turned the other way towards the two lower down, passed within a couple of yards from me and didn't notice me.

When they were far enough, I got out of the ditch, crept up the short climb, threw myself on the other side and lay down on the slope. All wet, my heart nearly bursting out of my mouth, I took a deep breath.

Shortly after getting myself back together, I started walking again; no more fields around, just dried mud under my feet. Was I in Greece then or still in Turkey? The latter more likely, I thought, for the dark gave me no clues. Going for about half an hour further I came to a forest, sparsely wooded with thick tall trees, but with dense shoulder-high thorn bushes covering the forest floor. Wouldn't such a barrier mark out the border more convincingly, I asked myself, than that stupid narrow ditch, which in the daylight could probably be jumped over? I was still uncertain which country's soil I was standing on, but hopefully it was Greece. But would a forest like that conceal water beyond it, like a river, since there was no proper river on my side? Would I still have to cross a river? I had to pass through the thickets to make sure. But every time I tried to get through the bushes, their thorns pierced my jacket and stopped me. I walked for about a hundred yards along the edge of the forest either way, looking for a clear cut or opening to avoid this thorn infested domain, but I couldn't find any. All hopes of crossing gone, for the time being, and nearly exhausted, I decided to sleep until dawn and try again then, when there would be more light to see by.

Taking my jacket and trousers off, still wet from the

ditch water, I hung them on the bushes; keeping my shirt and pants on, I lay down on the ground. Everything was so quiet, no wind, and I listened to the sound of silence I had heard so much about. If not in Greece yet, I'd soon be there; so far there was no trouble to speak of and the rest would go smoothly. The future seemed bright. Once in Greece I'd ask for asylum; it might take a while to sort my papers out, but the longer the better for I'd be able to see more of the country; they said Greece was beautiful, after all. I might even get myself a job in the meantime and start earning some real money. And finally, when granted asylum, they usually asked which country one wanted to go to. Me, New Zealand! I've always wanted to go and live there. To start with, it was green, something I liked, and small, unlike Canada and Australia. Yes, I'll ask them to send me to New Zealand, and once there, I'd start a new life. It all sounded wonderful with a bright future ahead of me.

I was lost in thought when suddenly a shooting star brought me back to the present. Looking at the stars, their arrangement seemed different, I noticed, from that night following Vich. I had tried to sneak out of Bulgaria less than a week ago and the memory was still fresh in my mind. Looking up at the spangle of stars again, I thought my horoscope, whatever that meant, hopefully promised success.

The light was beginning to tinge the night when I woke up. The watch in my pocket showed five o'clock. My clothes had dried overnight and I put them on. The forest stretched on either side as far as I could see. I looked behind me, at the barren field I had crossed the night before. I had come all that way, yet the problem still remained: I had to overcome the thickets. It didn't take long before I found a way and I praised my horoscope! About ten yards from where I had slept the night before there was a small tunnel cut neatly through the bushes. I had passed it close by last night in my search and hadn't noticed it in the dark. Surely someone must have made this passageway for the same reason I meant to use now - to sneak across the border. The bush corridor was narrow with overhanging branches so I had to bend down as I walked. It took me about ten minutes to pass through; at the end of this bush corridor the ground became soggy with mud and puddles. When I stood up and looked in front of me, I nearly took a step back in shock

Yes, it *was* there, and it stared me right in the eye. "You have come all this way but I'm going to use all my strength to stop you," I heard this great river telling me. The worst was the horrifying confirmation that I was still in Turkey.

My legs felt like collapsing under me. I sat down in despair and looked at the river, drowned in my thoughts. So Ali was right last night when he said, "I don't know what's lurking for us there in that nowhere." Come and have a look for yourself, Ali - the greatest challenge of the entire journey is waiting here!

You son of a bitch, Osman! I remembered him

putting a hand to his chest, the lying bastard, when asked how deep the river was. His height multiplied three or four times would surely not fathom its depth, and yet he said it would only reach his chest! In fact when I tried to cross it the next day, after walking for only five yards into the river, the water came up to my nose; and I guessed it probably measured more than fifty yards across.

I almost gave up; and, in fact, had I known what awaited me in Greece, I would have remained low till nightfall and then gone back. Anyway, I hadn't come all that way to be stopped by this river. It seemed I had no option but to swim it, though I didn't feel up to the task and was reluctant to get my clothes wet again. However, the trees and bushes bordering the river up to the bank made it hard to avoid standing in the water. Looking to the left I could see for about a hundred yards ahead, beyond which the trees and the bend of the river obscured the view; to the right, about ten yards away, there was a huge tree with its thick branches arching over the river more or less cutting off the view beyond. Under all that and close to the trunk, something looked out of place. Bending down to look under the foliage in order to see what it was, I almost rubbed my eyes in disbelief. Was I hallucinating? There was a small boat tied to one of the overarching branches.

Hardly believing my luck, I waded through the water, got to the boat and untied the rope. There was a long stick lying inside the boat. I climbed in, picked it up, then, pushing the boat by forcing the stick to the bottom of the river, I got to the other side. The bank there was much higher than the bank I had started out from and I had to pull myself up by hanging to whatever branch came to hand. I let the boat go with the current and it slipped away under my feet.

On the top bank, passing a few trees, I came across a dirt road a couple of yards wide; on the other side of the road corn fields stretched as far as the eye could see. I walked through a field and, emerging the other end, I came across a railway line. Looking to the right I saw a railway station, and beyond that, a small town. It seemed the whole atmosphere had changed from one side of the river to the other. The rails had no barriers, so I just walked over them, then turned right towards the station. It was close to seven in the morning now. A man in uniform stood on the platform, apparently the only one there. I went up to him and said, "Good morning sir. When does the next train leave for Athens?"

The uniformed man, fully aware of where I had just come from, looked at my mud dried shoes and trousers. In very good English, he answered, "First you go to Alexandropolis and from there to Athens. And the next train to Alexandropolis is at 10:56." He paused for a second, then asked, "You want to call at the UN office there?"

"Yes, to ask for asylum," I said.

"You don't have to go all the way to Athens for that," he said, "just walk into the village and ask someone to call the police for you. They'll come and take you to

Athens." Over a period of years working at the station he had seen numerous people crossing the border as I had done. "Once in Athens you'll be given a job and then, when granted asylum, they'll send you to the country of your choice." Later in the village I heard the same story repeated by a young student and then another one, confirmed again by those who gathered around me. In fact this was the procedure, they believed, their government exercised towards those entering Greece illegally, or at least by way of the river by which I had crossed. I was to find out differently.

"Is there a coffee shop nearby in this town?" I asked the railwayman. I needed a drink, a hot one especially.

He corrected me, saying it was not a town but a village called "Sufli".

As I was making my way towards the coffee shop the railwayman had just shown me, the people, mainly students, stood on both pavements watching me. A new face in the village, I supposed, and what else could it mean but an illegal entrant?

At the coffee shop a young man sitting next to an elderly lady at a table in the open air in the forecourt asked me to join them. A small sized cup of coffee arrived and had just touched the table when I gratefully grabbed it. Before long a few students plus some village people started crowding on one side, staring at me as if I were some strange creature. One of them, a young man of about sixteen, asked me if I had crossed by the way of the river; when I replied in the affirmative he repeated what the railwayman had told me in regard to seeking asylum in the village, and I heard some of those standing by saying, "Yes."

Victorious at last, I told myself! Though tired and muddy, I felt like a conquering hero. I had arrived in civilization and as some of these people pointed out, a bright future beaconed. They'd send me to Athens, that magnificent city I had heard so much about. The Acropolis! Yes, I'd go to see that great historical monument. I remembered something about the Acropolis: over 2500 years ago Xerxes, the great king of Persia burnt it down. But now, 25 centuries later, I had come for a different reason.

An army jeep arrived and an officer with a few stars on his shoulder stepped out and made his way through those standing around me. Seeing me, he said at once, "Would you like to come with us please?"

We got into the jeep. I sat in the back next to another soldier, the officer occupying the passenger seat in the front. The vehicle pulled away and half an hour later we arrived at some barracks. I was taken to a big solitary room in one corner of the building and left alone. It wasn't long before an officer followed by a soldier holding a tray came in. The tray was laden with chips, corned beef, eggs and a can of coke. Placing it in front of me, the officer said, "If you need anything else please let us know." He left, but the soldier remained.

So far so good; they were treating me well. I was hungry so finished the whole lot.

A short while later another young soldier, a bit taller than me, slim, brown hair, light green eyes, entered and walked up to me and said, "Hello, I'm Mike," extending his hand.

"Pleased to meet you Mike. I'm Cyrus," I said, shaking his hand.

Mike was born in America to Greek parents and in order to stay in Greece as a male citizen, had to serve twenty-one months in the army, compulsory for everyone. His brother had done the same and was now living in Greece permanently.

Soon another officer entered the room, nodded to Mike, and in response the American turned to me and said, "Now you'll be moved to another barrack, but as your identity still needs to be verified there are certain necessary precautions we have to take."

I was blindfolded, led out of the room and into a car; pulling away it sounded like the same jeep that had given me a lift earlier. A short drive later the vehicle stopped and Mike helped me out of it. After walking for a few metres, a door opened and we moved inside. The change of atmosphere was evident and I sensed with my ears that we were in a room. I recalled a talk I had heard on the BBC how some people born blind could even tell the dimensions of the place they entered. I felt the touch of a chair behind my knees and I was asked to sit down. The blindfold removed, I found myself at a desk with a middle-aged uniformed man, pen and paper in front of him, on the opposite side. He didn't look friendly. Mike sat on his left, acting as an interpreter, though the man didn't seem to be in need of one.

A soldier with a rifle over his shoulder stood by the door.

The man asked to see my passport.

Extracting the plastic bag from my pocket, I got my passport and handed it to him.

"Your name is: Cyrus, surname: Kamrani, date of birth: 1 August, 1957, nationality: Iranian, place of birth: Iran." Writing all this down, he asked me how I had got to Greece, mainly interested in establishing the final hour of my journey.

"...I crossed the river... and that was it," I explained, receiving my passport back.

"Did you see any military build-up anywhere in Turkey?" Mike translated to me.

I shook my head and said, "No."

"Or any of their soldiers near the border, soldiers you tried to avoid?"

I gave the same negative answer.

"And now you are here asking for asylum, am I right?"

"Yes, sir," I responded.

Then he asked the question I'd been waiting for: "If granted asylum, where would you want to be sent to?"

"New Zealand." I almost thought myself there already.

No further questions, the man stood up and said, "Well, that's about it," and walked out of the room.

Mike, the soldier with the rifle over his shoulder and I left through a different door for another room with more people there. A few minutes later, once again, an officer followed by a soldier carrying a tray full of food entered and the tray was pushed into my hands. I didn't have much appetite now and placed the tray untouched on the table apart from the coffee that I couldn't resist.

There was a bed in the room. Mike noticed I was tired and invited me to use it. I did and soon fell asleep.

A few hours later Mike woke me up. "Do you know what time it is?"

I sat on the edge of the bed. He gave me a cup of coffee and after I finished it he said, "Now we'll be taking you to another place."

Blindfolded again, I was led outside. After a short walk I heard keys rattling and a metal door squeaked open, and we moved inside. Half a dozen metres away another door closed and Mike said, "Now you can take that blindfold off."

Doing so, I found myself locked in a cell with three solid walls, the fourth wall consisting of iron bars that went right up to the ceiling; within the bars was a normal sized door which presumably I had just passed through. On the other side of this iron barred wall, accompanied by three other soldiers, Mike asked me to give him the blindfold. I handed it over and they left through a corridor that stretched to the left of the cell; a few seconds later I heard a solid metal door being shut closed, keys rattling.

chapter nine

MY CELL measured about 3x4m, had a bed in one corner and a dirty mattress with some blankets on top. I was still tired. Spreading one of the blankets on the bed, I lay down on it. Why had they imprisoned me? Was this part of the procedure before they sent one to Athens? Or did it mean back to Turkey? It was dark in the cell, though a mini-size barred hole in one of the walls, close to the ceiling, let in some light from the outside. Many thoughts tumbled through my mind before I fell asleep. When I woke up it was totally dark and I could hardly see anything. The watch in my pocket showed ten o'clock: it was late yet still no news. About an hour later I heard the keys again: a metal door opening, lights switched on, footsteps approaching in the corridor. Mike accompanied by the same three soldiers stood in front of the cell. One opened the barred door and asked me out, then led me along the corridor into the open air. Once there, I was surrounded by about a dozen soldiers, Mike on the right and the man who had interviewed me earlier, behind two soldiers, on the left.

"Sorry Cyrus," Mike said, "but the army has decided that you should go back."

I had half expected such mistreatment, though I thought there was more than a slim chance of success; nevertheless, I showed my utmost surprise. He carried on, "Yes, and we usually send them back the same way they have come."

"But this is wrong!" I protested. "I overcame a lot of hurdles to get here thinking you'd be helpful. Please accept my asylum and soon you'll be rid of me; and I'm willing to support myself till then."

Mike shook his head. "I'm afraid the decision has been made; you are going back."

"Where to?" I asked.

"Turkey."

It sounded barbaric. Surely what they were meant to do was incompatible with UN laws in connection with asylum seekers. Then I remembered the young student in the village that morning, and those around him, as well as the railwayman earlier. With a sarcastic smile I said, "And the people in the village think you send us to Athens and then to the desired country." Shaking my head from side to side, I continued, "And is that why you proceed at night so that no one will notice what actually happens…?"

Mike cut me short. "No, due to precautionary

measures. We don't want to draw attention from the Turkish side. Though every time we send one back we are well prepared for any surprises."

"And every time you send one back," I said, pointing with my left thumb towards the man who had interviewed me in the afternoon and now kept low standing behind two soldiers, almost protected by them, "it's because this son of a bitch has decided. Yes?" I turned and faced him; the two soldiers closed in on me and, looking into the eyes of the man, I called him a bastard.

"That's enough!" Mike said. "Do you want us to use violence on you?" Receiving no reply from me, he continued, "Now we are going to take you to the river you crossed this morning, then take you back by a boat to the other side and leave you there. Don't try to come back because that part of the river where you will be dropped is very deep and full of snakes. Just cross the forest and get yourself to a nearby town, away from the border, before light, because if the Turkish soldiers catch you anywhere close to the border area, no matter what, they'll probably give you a hard time. You were not meant to leave without permission."

It didn't sound too bad after all, I thought; once on the other side I only had to repeat the last part of my journey: crossing the river. And this time, probably, without a boat. Though demoralized, I didn't feel as frustrated as they might have thought. I'd been well fed and rested. And next time after crossing I would get myself to Athens and call at the UN office there; they followed the rule book, I hoped.

Mike continued: "Now we have to tie your hands behind your back and cover your mouth."

One of the soldiers standing in front of me, with a piece of rope in his hand, moved in on me, unaware that I had a surprise for him. When he was close enough to me I took him off guard. Yanking the rope out of his hands, I gave him a hard punch on the side of his face. He went down and I jumped on him. But before I could put the rope round his neck, threatening the others to keep back, I was overpowered. They held me down, forced my hands back and pulled the rope out of my grasp and tightened my wrists with it. Then they covered my mouth with a strip of wide sticking tape and stood me up.

Two soldiers, veritable giants, each holding one of my arms, took me to a colossal army jeep, the kind I had only seen in Second World War movies, about a dozen soldiers all armed sitting at the back on each side; another two soldiers were waiting at the opening and I was picked up as if weightless and handed to them. I was manhandled into a sitting position with one huge soldier on each side, holding my arms tight. A few seconds later we started moving and another army jeep of the same size followed behind. Out of the barrack, we reached the main road and I noticed traffic there.

That's where I should have stretched myself this morning, I thought, and hitchhiked to Athens. Never mind, I'd be doing that tomorrow night: cross the river in the morning, stay in one of the cornfields, then, as soon as it was dark, I'd be on the move. After following the main road for a short few minutes we turned up a narrow muddy one and entered the wooded area. Another short drive and both vehicles stopped. I was handed down from the back of the jeep and placed on the ground. In the darkness I saw a few dogs moving around while this veritable army of soldiers noiselessly led me through some trees. Reaching the edge, looking down, there it was: the quiet, deep and powerful river! Descending some steps cut into the slope of the bank, we reached a boat with six armed soldiers, all wearing life jackets, who had been waiting there. I was placed in the middle and two soldiers at both ends, in a skilful way, started paddling. We got to the other side and a soldier sitting behind me took me out, holding my arm. He was carrying a knife and used it to cut the rope, freeing my hands, and went back to the craft. Paddling away, they disappeared from sight.

First like one gone mad, I tried to get through the bushes, but it seemed impossible; thorns entering my jacket just like the night before stopped me dead. There were only a couple of metres, where they had left me, where I could move freely, an area obviously cleared in advance. Beyond that bushes and the river hemmed me in. Like a chained tiger, pacing from one side of the clearing to the other, I wanted to break out of that restricted place, but all my attempts proved useless. Soon I came to myself and realized that I was acting irrationally. I sat down. There wasn't much I could do in the dark. For the time being resigned to my fate, I picked up a few pebbles and started throwing them, one by one, into the river. Having used up all the pebbles, I felt acutely depressed. I lay on my back, considering whether I should really let myself risk another attempt to enter Greece.

Deciding that I would, since otherwise it would be back to square one again, I dozed off to wake at daybreak. I remained there, stretched out on my back, till full light. Even then, I realised that if I wanted to cross this river, I had no choice but to swim it.

I took all my clothes off, everything including my shoes, and made them into a single bundle which I held above my head as I entered the water. I anticipated that, from what I had heard, it wasn't deep. I hadn't gone far before the water came up to my neck and started taking me with it. Lying on my back, holding the bundle in the air and using my legs to keep myself afloat, I was close to panic, thinking that I might drown any minute. I managed to paddle back towards the bank but landed downstream a good many metres from where I had started. I climbed out of the water finding myself in a relatively clear area of up to ten metres between the river and the bushes and the trees that stretched in either direction parallel to the river. I let myself dry - it was a hot sunny day - and put my clothes back on and started walking along this open strip, hoping to find something, anything, that would enable me to cross the river. Everything was quiet with not a breath of wind. I hadn't gone far before I spotted a boat under a thick bush. Whoever had left it there had made a lousy attempt to hide the small river craft there.

I tried to pull the boat towards the river and managed a couple of metres when a shout stopped me. I looked back and saw four soldiers, their guns pointing at me. They were standing halfway between the clearing and the river. One of them put his rifle down, came to me and said something in Turkish which I didn't understand. He turned me round roughly and handcuffed my hands behind my back.

That was when I said goodbye to all dreams of ever setting foot in Greece.

chapter ten

I WAS PUSHED ALONG unceremoniously by the soldiers. Crossing the forest where they had cut through the bushes, we came to the same old mud dried field I had passed only two nights earlier. It didn't look much different in the daylight from what I had imagined in the dark, almost barren with some weeds sprouting here and there. Crossing it again we reached the ditch. It all seemed like they were showing me the route I had taken earlier but unable to see because of the dark. Walking along the ditch for about a mile, we crossed it using some planks already laid across it. Going for another mile, we came to a narrow dirt road that ran through some fields. I could see some locals working there now. As I had guessed a couple of nights earlier when passing them, most of them were rice fields. After walking for over an hour on this dirt road I could see where they were headed for. Just ahead of us was a very high round hill surmounted by a watchtower with an antenna stretched high into the air.

We climbed the rise and entered the building. It was quite small inside. A young officer, after asking what my nationality was, got behind the transmitter and sent a message in Turkish. I could make out the word *Iranian*. That over with, he turned to me, removed my handcuffs and said, "Commando come" - probably the only English words he knew. I wondered why he told me that. I'd just have to wait and see. Then, surprisingly, I was offered a cup of tea. Five minutes later the commando duly arrived. Looking smart, in his early thirties, he came straight up to me, put a friendly hand on my shoulder and with his broken English said, "Why you go to Greece?" Not waiting for an answer, he carried on, "You money?" I got whatever cash I had out from my pocket and handed it to him. He counted 2520 US dollars, gave a whistle, took the 20 dollar note at the end, put it in his pocket, and handed the rest back to me. "Your taxi money to Merich," he said.

The commando led me out of the watchtower and we climbed down the hill. There was an old Peugeot car waiting at the bottom with three people already inside. The commando occupied the empty seat in the front next to the driver and told me to join the other two in the back. I did so and the car pulled away. On my left there was a white skinned, light brown curly haired guy who looked to be in his mid-twenties, and on his left a uniformed man with a machine gun on his lap. The curly haired man next to me looked like an official, but later when I shared a cell with him, through his non-existent English, I found out he was a Czech running away from communism. He had left Czechoslovakia (then a communist country), flying over to Bulgaria from which he had sneaked into Turkey, then attempting to enter Greece in the same way I had tried. Whatever his story beforehand, in the end he had been met by a similar fate as me: hands tied behind him, something stuck over his mouth and sent back.

Twenty minutes later we were handed over to Merich police station - a sizeable double storey building on one side with a large yard in the front, surrounded by tall brick walls, where Curly and I were left in a corner next to a few trees and a rectangular patch of lawn. We made ourselves comfortable on separate benches. The station was well guarded: two soldiers marching in front of the gate and three more on the roof of the building, all five armed with machine guns. I gave Curly another glance, still unaware of who he was. Suddenly turning round, our stares met and he smiled. I decided it was safer to ignore it.

About half an hour later a soldier came out of the building, gave a shout and asked me to follow him inside. Curly, looking the other way, didn't even bother to turn around. Just beyond the entrance to the building there was a door on the right through which I was pushed. An army sergeant about 30 years of age, very good looking with dark straight short hair, tall and well proportioned, said something in Turkish from behind his desk. His words were beyond my scope of the language and I shrugged my shoulders to convey my inability to comprehend him, then asked him if he spoke English. He shook his head 'no' and said, "Terjomeh" - the same word we have in Iranian, meaning 'interpreter'. Picking up the phone, he motioned me to sit on one of the chairs away from his desk. After a few words into the receiver, he replaced it on its cradle and said to me, "Oun degigeh" (ten minutes).

The translator came on time. Just looking at her lifted my spirits! I kept staring at this tall, slender blonde with two big blue eyes under dark eyebrows; with her willowy body in tight blue jeans she looked like a dancer. Nature hadn't made a mistake in perfecting this specimen of female humanity. She was smiling, the most disarming smile I had ever seen. This girl was the veritable rose without a thorn - no wonder the sergeant hadn't wasted much time calling her, I thought. Drawing up a chair she sat by his desk, one leg crossing the other. I could see her full on and couldn't help mentally undressing her, hastily putting her clothes back on when the sergeant gave me a quick observant look.

Though slow, she was capable of maintaining a good conversation in English and knew all the words. I was there to be questioned, a procedure in normal circumstances I disliked, but now, thanks to her, how I wished it would never end!

Mesmerized by her two big tits standing proud under that light red jumper that thinly covered her top, I wondered what it would be like to have some fresh milk from them. They were paying twenty pence a bottle for milk in England, and I would be willing to pay twenty pounds a drop here.

The sergeant started by asking me (through the rose without a thorn) the first primary universal questions and while looking at my passport, wrote my answers down. Then he wanted to know about the degree of my education.

"I went to college in England, passing 3 A-Levels, then to university doing Mechanical Engineering," I said. Since education meant a lot to these people, I didn't mention that I had dropped out during the second year, never finishing the course.

Personal information done with, he charged me: "You have been caught in the prohibited area trying to leave the country illegally, which is why you are here." After I received the translation, he asked, "Have you got anything to say?"

"No, nothing to say, sir," I replied.

Now that they realized I had lived in England, been to university there and spoke English, their behaviour became friendlier towards me.

I asked if the charge I was facing was serious and what the consequences were.

After conferring with the sergeant, the translator began by answering the second part of my question, which conclusively answered the first part, too. "From here you'll be taken to another prison, kept there for a few days, then brought back to Merich again to appear before a court; this should be a warning to you not to repeat violating the border regulations; after that you will be released." That, apparently, was what usually happened to those caught around the river.

Surprised, I asked, "Am I not going to be deported out of the country and back to Iran?"

No, deporting apparently wasn't part of the procedure in this case. Once the present procedure was over, I'd be let free in the middle of the next town called Ozon Kopru.

In the end this is what happened, but not before the lapse of two long torturous weeks.

For the next hour they asked irrelevant questions, mainly centred on England, which the translator would love to visit, in particular to see Buckingham Palace. She was 22 and still single, and I dared to quote the English phrase, "a rose without a thorn", saying that it suited her perfectly. She smiled again. The sergeant turned out to be a nice person too, laughing along though he didn't understand half of what we were talking about.

The time came to say goodbye and she stretched the back of her hand towards my mouth. I responded by taking the hand and kissing it. "This has been the greatest moment in my life, madam," I said, returning her hand. The sergeant and I accompanied her to the yard outside. There she turned back, waved and walked elegantly away.

The sergeant jerked his head towards where Curly was sitting, indicating that I should join him. He watched her leaving through the gate, then went back inside the building. Shortly afterwards a soldier entered carrying two rice plates. One was given to me, the other to Curly - which evidently proved him to be a prisoner too. After the meal another soldier led us out of the yard to the back of the building, where we were taken down some stairs into a cellar; there were a few cells there and we were placed in one of them. It was a tiny cell, about 2x3m, a single bed and one chair in it, with a small barred window at ground level outside.

Curly sat on the bed and I occupied the chair. Then for the first time I heard him speak - and what a surprise that was! He talked non-stop, and in the way one usually spoke to a countryman of the same tongue. He went on for a couple of minutes, though I understood not a word of what he was saying. Eventually I decided to stop him. "Hey, hey, stop, stop!" I said, holding up my palm. He stopped instantly, like a speeding car coming to a sudden halt. "Do you speak English?" I asked him.

Whether he understood me, I cannot say, but in effect he took no notice and in a moment resumed his blabbing in the same way. Stopping him again and while pointing at myself, I said, "Me, me," then using more body language than words, I said, "no understand you!"

It didn't work.

In fact two weeks later when we were released together in the town of Ozon Kopru and were picked up by the police soon afterwards and taken to the police station, he kept on talking in the same animated way till the policeman hit him on the head and told him to shut up. Only then did he stop!

Coming back to the present: Curly carried on for another minute, then, realizing I wasn't listening, my back turned towards him, he tapped me on the shoulder and said something that sounded like, "Why don't you listen?" Taking my time, just using words without any physical movement, I answered, "Because I don't understand you." Speaking again, he seemed to say, "I know you don't, but you can still listen!" I muttered, "You're fucking crazy." This was going too far. He tried to carry on and I put both my palms up in the air once more and stopped him; then, with a lot of patience, pointing at myself, I said as plainly as possible, "Me, me, country, Iran, Iran." Then pointing the same finger at him, I said, "You, you, country - where?"

No, he wouldn't give in; but before he could start again, I cut him short: "You, you, Russia, Bulgaria, Romania?" He spoke a few more words, then while pointing at himself, said, "Czechoslovakia."

Christopher Columbus discovered America, Galileo the telescope, and I, this man's country of birth! Once out of that dungeon I would register this discovery in my own name. "Ah, ah, you Czechoslovakia. How interesting!" Then, and I'm sure only then, when I made him understand that I was from Iran by repeating the name a few times, he realized that I didn't speak his language. Talking to him a bit longer with the aid of a pen and paper he was carrying, I found out about his flight from Czechoslovakia to Bulgaria and so on which I mentioned earlier.

A couple of hours later the same soldier came and took us back to the yard. We sat on separate benches, Curly and I, close to one another, but with hardly any words exchanged. Around late afternoon a group of soldiers arrived, apparently from military exercises. It amused us watching them cleaning their guns in one corner of the yard. Before long they disappeared into the building; presumably there was a dormitory inside. Tired of being inactive for so long, I took a short walk alongside one wall of the yard, to-and-fro - until nightfall when we were led back to the same cell. Before leaving, the soldier said, "Sleep, sleep," banging the door shut, bolting it from the outside. Did that mean we weren't going to get anything to eat that night? In fact, while captive in Turkey, no supper came my way at nightfall. It looked as if prisoners in some third world countries were not allowed dinner. Has this law been issued by the human rights organizations so that the prisoners wouldn't be sleeping on full stomachs? Doctors suggest it causes tummy upset - a good pretext for not feeding one, no doubt. Curly offered me the bed, but I refused; and it was too small a bed to accommodate both of us. I put two blankets on the floor and, lying on them, went to sleep.

Woken up at seven in the morning, we were let out of the cell and led into the yard. Then two soldiers each carrying about a metre long chain appeared and fastened these to each of us; we were like two dogs being taken for a walk, only instead of being secured by the neck we had the chains round our right wrists and padlocked, the two soldiers holding each end. One more soldier joined the throng and all five of us left the police station. By now I had come to realize the police station was run by the army and more or less like a small barrack. We started walking towards the Merich Bus Terminal, as I found out twenty minutes later. Two people being led on chains, going right through the village, seemed an exciting spectacle to these villagers who had probably not much to amuse themselves with. They started coming out from everywhere, doors, windows, roofs, joining us, walking behind us, their numbers increasing by the minute. Added to this was the commotion they made! By the time we reached the Terminal it looked as if the whole village was out following us to enjoy the spectacle.

At this point one of the soldiers, the higher in rank, said that Curly and I had to buy the bus tickets for us all. But, where to? When I asked, no one answered. I didn't have any local currency on me. When I pointed this out to the soldier, he responded by pulling on my chain and escorting me to the bank next to the Terminal where he told me to change some of my dollars into Turkish liras. I took a hundred dollar note out from my pocket, gave it to the man behind the exchange counter and told him that I only wanted twenty dollars changed. No problem doing that, but the remainder he could only give back in Dutch marks for they didn't have any dollars in the bank. "No thanks," I told him and got my note back. We left the place for the only other bank in the village which was across the road. The soldier, the bastard, kept pulling hard on my chain! We entered the bank and were informed that here they had no exchange section to deal in foreign currencies. But before leaving the place, an employee from behind his counter grumbled a few words to my uniformed guard. At this, I noticed, his face went red. Then turning to me, with his broken English, the employee carried on, "I told him that he has been paid for the trip by the government, so why is he trying to rob you as well?"

The soldier looked angry. We left the bank, the soldier almost jerking on my chain. We hadn't gone a few metres before he turned and punched me on the shoulder. I took a great risk and punched him back! He stumbled back and the chain fell out of his hand. Now, looking really mad, he took the rifle from his shoulder, cocked it and pointed it at me; he shouted a few words in Turkish that I didn't understand, but obviously meaning to shoot me. In the blink of an eye the villagers, tens of them, surrounded us in a circle, apart from where a bullet might pass if fired in my direction! Everyone was dead quiet, my heart racing double its normal speed. What great excitement that must have been for those villagers; it would be something to talk about for the next few months, here and in the surrounding villages! Less than a year later, living near the forest close to one of the villages in the north of Iran, by the Caspian Sea, I found it amazing to see how fast in those communities news got round by word of mouth. Every time an item of news was passed on, from one mouth to the other, it was rehearsed with added incentives till, in the end, even a small item of news will have grown and provided sufficient material for a full-length movie. This is true for most third world countries, and Turkey is no exception.

I put my hands up and said, "You don't shoot an unarmed man!" Regardless of whether he understood me or not, what if he pulled the trigger? Who would mind or care? Certainly the villagers wouldn't dare come forward afterwards and give evidence to the effect that the prisoner had his hands up when he was shot - which would call for a murder trial. Even in Istanbul with all those educated people living there, the army and the police were well in control - for every 100 metres covered, no less than four to five policemen were encountered, and the people were evidently cautious of them. And that in Istanbul, a big city, never mind Merich, a small village and therefore with people who were more 'obedient' or intimidated by the police. Even my own supposed protector, the Iranian government, would probably not raise a finger in protest; no, not in defence of one who had deserted his country seeking asylum somewhere else. They would emphatically label such a person as a traitor who would therefore be deemed worthy of the bullet he had received. Indeed, officials at the Iranian embassy in Turkey wouldn't concern themselves with a fellow citizen of that type. Neither would human rights organizations, which often turn their backs and say, "....an internal affair so the organization is not allowed to interfere..." This was the answer I received from the United Nations office at Geneva, Centre for Human Rights, when I wrote to them after being deported from England on grounds of having entered into a marriage of convenience. Though it was only my wife's words against mine, I spent eleven months in prison, then sent back to Iran. I quote from the letter I have in front of me while writing these notes: "I regret having to inform you that the Secretariat of the United Nations is not in a position to be of any assistance to you in the matter raised in your communication, because your case comes within the domestic jurisdiction of the state concerned."

Everyone was waiting for something to happen, and it did, but not in the way they were expecting. Somebody in the crowd shouted, "Allah Akbar!" ("God is great!") It was taken up by a few more, and consequently the soldier, under the influence of his religious beliefs, put his rifle back over his shoulder. I brought my hands down and he came to me and took the chain. We went back to the first bank with the exchange section and I changed a hundred-dollar note into Turkish liras. As we were leaving the bank the manager came forward, wished me good luck and shook my hand. By doing so he meant to show his revulsion, I realised, towards my watch and the military as a whole.

You could say that this kind of hatred was apparent everywhere. People had strong religious feelings and wanted an Islamic state, but the military and the police were stopping them by every means available. Even most of these soldiers themselves were Islamic fanatics. I remember the night before we were being released I was sitting in the yard of the Merich police station, Curly as usual on a different bench, when this same soldier appeared and placed himself next to me. Before saying anything he looked around to make sure no one was close enough to hear him. Then he asked me if I was a Muslim. In reply, though an atheist, I gave him a positive answer - for I didn't want more trouble with this sick bastard. He wanted to know to what extent I was a devotee and he told me to read him a part of the Muslim prayers called Tàshàhod. I had been taught how to pray at school, the ritual repeated every day of the year, and remembering the part, I read it to him: "I give evidence that God is one and has no associates... and I give evidence that Mohammed is His messenger, praise be to Mohammed and His descendants." I finished reading the verse to him in the standard language (Arabic); he nodded satisfaction and asked me if I prayed. I said no and he kicked me! I kicked him back; at the same time the sergeant came through the gate and he left.

Now out of the bank, in possession of enough Turkish liras, I paid my half share of the bus fare, an equal amount having been paid by Curly, and we got on the bus. I still didn't know where we were heading, but over two hours later we arrived at a place I recognized: the Edernè Bus Terminal. Getting off the bus, the same head soldier told us that we had to use a taxi to reach our next destination which was Edernè Police Station, Curly and I paying again. Glancing quickly around the Terminal, a familiar face caught my eye - the same short dark man who had offered to take Ali and me to a place near the Turkish-Greek border four days earlier was standing by the same teashop entrance watching. He gave me a sarcastic smile, satisfaction written all over his face. I smiled back meaning: "Your offer of dropping us somewhere near the border would have probably resulted in worse, and we were wise not to accept. At least this way I set foot in Greece."

We went towards the taxis and there I also saw the tall guy, the short man's friend, who had offered to drive Ali and me in his cab close to the border. We exchanged a quick glance. A pull on my chain brought me back to the present and we got into a different taxi, and about ten minutes later were delivered to Edernè Police Station. A sergeant there writing our names down told us to wait in the yard. It didn't take long before we were approached by three plain clothes MIT (secret police in Turkey) officers. We were bundled into a van, then blindfolded, and kept low on the back seat while the vehicle moved off. Manhandled like this by people in suits and wearing ties who looked like the mafia, I felt as though I were being kidnapped to some unknown destination, later to be released on ransom. The movement was rough, for the vehicle was probably driving over some earthen road to a place acknowledged only by a few, and presumably in the security wing of the country. About half an hour later the van stopped and we were led out of it, still blindfolded, and entered a building. My hand was placed on some railing and I climbed down a lot of stairs. It took a good while to reach the bottom and I seemed to be in a very quiet place. We walked through what I sensed was a well-lit corridor, then entered a half dim room at which point our blindfolds were removed. We were searched while we had our hands on the wall. My diary notebook and the watch I was carrying in my pocket were taken away, but my money was left untouched. Finally our shoes were examined. They left me in the cell but took Curly with them. The door closed and was bolted on the outside.

chapter eleven

IT WAS A VERY BIG CELL, 4 x 6 metres, three sides nothing but walls, the fourth, on the left, a solid metal door with a square at head height, 10 x 10 inches, with metal bars. On the right at the same level was a large hole in the wall covered by heavy metal gauze, through which a floodlight sent a faint yellow colour into the cell, leaving the rest of the cell in darkness. A single bed with some torn up dirty blankets was to be seen at the left-end corner. One thick pipe a few inches in diameter went across the longer length of the cell close to the 3-metre high ceiling. It seemed unwise that they left the prisoner with his belt and shoelaces; in an unsettled moment, in such a demoralized state, the chance of hanging himself by the way of this pipe might well present itself. Thinking of hanging, I recalled the day Ahmad and those three met their ends, and came close to wishing I had shared their fate. My dilemma, my quest for escape, would have been ten times over by now. Looking through the bars of the door I could see a well-lit corridor, just over a metre wide, walls on both sides and the ceiling the same height as the cell I was in. To the left, a few metres away, the corridor turned right; looking the other way, it stretched beyond the cell, my view limited, again, to only a few metres.

Turning my attention back to the cell, I started walking to-and-fro. After doing so for about ten minutes I took my jacket and shirt off and started exercising - press ups, sit ups, squats and elbows; no weights, yet I found it harder without them. Sweat all over me, about an hour later I stopped, my spirits high again. I walked towards the bed, picked up half a blanket, spread it on the floor and sat on it with my back against the wall. It was probably about twelve noon now. In this subterranean prison I thought of the many stairs we climbed down, well below ground level, and with no lights from outside to get through. Soon I'd have no awareness of the time, of day and night.

We've had nothing to eat since yesterday afternoon and surprisingly I wasn't feeling hungry. No books or reading materials in the cell either; and later when I asked for some, my request was denied. So how did they expect the prisoner to amuse himself? Staring at the floor into empty space, shortly afterwards, letting my mind wander freely, was the only recourse to entertainment.

I thought about my father back in Iran who was wanted by the police there, and if caught would be stoned to death for running away with somebody's wife. He, in his late fifties, had been living with a woman called Mahin, in her late thirties, a little on the fat side but not bad looking, for the last two years in an unknown location. It's just possible she was someone I knew. When I entered the country (after being deported from England), father came round and took me to his place. Mahin was officially married to a man by the name of Hassan, who was still pursuing her and hot on her heels. To get her back, when her affair began, he went to the police and reported the incident. They came round to our house and searched it; finding my father absent, they questioned us - me, my mother and sister - about his whereabouts. Mum and my sister, Sepideh, didn't know and I kept quiet. Then the police told Hassan that if he wanted his wife found he had to give them a photo of her so they could put it in the papers as someone who was wanted in order that she might be located. However, they also told him that once she turned up she'd be stoned to death. Perhaps because of his two daughters he did not pursue this option - for how could he explain to them that he had sent their mother to such a savage end? But it was a different story when it came to our mother. She, consumed with jealousy, took one of father's photos to the police asking them to put it in the papers. Fortunately she went to the second person in charge of the station, a policeman and not a sentry, who took her to a corner and privately told her that if the photo was printed in the papers my father might be found and, if so, certainly stoned to death. Would she ever forgive herself for bringing about such a dreadful fate to her own husband and the father of her three children? The policeman very kindly endeavoured to change her mind. She came back home, told us the story and also that she was going to decide whether to take action or not. Two years later she was still uncertain what to do.

My father, out of work, began to deal in drugs with his girlfriend and together they were making a lot of money. They went to the south of the country where they bought opium and brought it back to the capital where they sold it many times higher than the purchase price. The further south the cheaper the narcotics were; but the danger increased proportionately since coming back meant the prospect of encountering more checkpoints controlled by sentries. These anti-drug guards searched most cars; nevertheless many carrying narcotics - mainly opium and heroin, the commonest with the highest profit in the market - managed to sneak through. Risky? Those caught faced a grave punishment: anyone found in possession of more than five kilos of opium or hashish was hanged; with heroin and its derivatives, the so-called hard drugs, only thirty grams and the same penalty applied. Anything less was dealt with by imprisonment and flogging. However, if caught a number of times, once the total sum of the banned substances discovered on each occasion reached the fatal figure just mentioned, regardless of the punishment that might have been meted out in the previous convictions, the accused found guilty faced death. In all cases, the vehicle carrying narcotics that were deliberately hidden in secret places, such as inside doors, petrol tank, or tyres, would be confiscated, regardless of the amount; but if the narcotics were found just lying about, like on the back seat, in the boot, or on the dashboard, the vehicle, after a thorough search, was usually returned to the owner.

Every year twenty thousand people find their way to the gallows of which fifty per cent are drug related convicts. However, this figure represents the ones who hadn't been able to bribe the authorities and therefore escape the rope; and nearly half are Afghans - with no proper government to stand up for them, some have met their death just through word of mouth alone.

Then for some reason within the next few years we were to witness a rise in the number of people supposedly in possession of the banned substances subsequently to meet the ultimate sentence; but we found out it was due to the increase in pressure from international organizations on Iran for executing too many political prisoners; henceforth the government decided to hang them under the name of drug dealers. In one of these hangings, which usually took place in famous squares in any city, but this one in Tehran, a friend present among the crowd later told me that the guy who was about to be picked up by a crane, threw a piece of rope round his neck and bravely announced,

"I'm a prisoner of conscience and not a drug dealer" - and then was hit by an egg! Can you imagine a mob of that mentality - trying to save the people, he lost his life for them! "Some among the throng even looked entertained," my friend said regretfully, "watching and at the same time eating chips and breaking nuts!"

My father usually bought his opium from a city called Kerman, the main centre for this kind of drug in Iran, if not the world. "You can have a lorry loaded with a ton of opium in less than an hour," he once said to me. The last time I was at his house he was unloading 4.5 kilos of opium from the bottom of his Renault. He had welded a small sheet of metal there, quite unnoticeable, where he usually placed his purchases. I certainly didn't have the courage to play with my life like that, whatever the rewards; then again, it seems that what drove most people to embark on this dangerous business were the very harsh times they were facing earning a living. My father was certainly a brave man, something that had been proved to me many times.

I was lost in thought when the cell door opened and a man in his mid-thirties entered. He was good looking, about my height, thick dark hair and moustache, one hand holding something wrapped in newspaper and the other a plastic cup of water. He was followed by about seven or eight younger men of between 18 and 22. They all appeared to be friendly, just there to make fun of the prisoner and have a few laughs; perhaps to cheer him up too. One of the youngsters sat next to me, put his hand on my shoulder, smiled, and said a few words in Turkish I didn't understand, but obviously funny since the rest laughed. They stayed for a couple of minutes, taking the piss out of me, the prisoner; the man who first entered gave me the newspaper wrapping and the cup of water before they all left. Going to the door and looking through the bars to the right, I could see they had gathered together about a few metres away. My view was limited, for I could only see a couple of them standing in the corridor. I heard a door opening and realised there was another cell next to mine. My first guess was that it was Curly's. They entered his cell, just as they had entered mine, one talking and the rest laughing; more talking was followed by more laughter. They stayed there as long as they had stayed in my cell. Then I heard them leaving the cell and they gathered in the corridor again, closing and bolting shut the cell door. They moved away, beyond my field of vision now, but I heard another door being opened. I realised then that I was clearly wrong thinking that Curly occupied the cell next to mine, for I now recognised his voice and his manner of speaking which was unmistakeable: he began talking as soon as the men entered his cell. He kept on grumbling in his language, and when I heard them laughing, Curly turned up the volume, almost shouting. Then I heard heavy movements like someone being chased, followed by a lot of laughter. They must have stayed in Curly's cell the longest, but eventually came out, door shut, bolted it and moved off.

Apparently there were no more cells beyond Curly's.

When everything was silent again, I waited for a while, then shouted quietly through the bars of my door: "Czechoslovak man? Czechoslovak man?"

The answer was a few words in Czech.

"Okay, Czechoslovak man?" I asked.

"Okay," he answered.

And there our conversation ended. So, after all, Curly was only about a few metres away.

I turned my attention to what they had given me. I unwrapped the paper to reveal four slices of bread and some cheese about half the size of a small matchbox. I wondered why they bothered to wrap it up. The meagre meal was hardly enough to replace the energy I had lost through my physical exercises: with this kind of grub one would find it hard, even with activities eliminated, to get through half a day. Surely they'd feed us properly later, I hoped, or at the most tomorrow morning? With the help of some water from the cup I managed to get the provisions down. After walking to-and-fro for a few minutes, I stopped all forms of exercise.

I was lying down on the floor, about to drift into sleep, when I heard a few knocks on the door. A young man called, "Toilet?" I didn't really need the toilet but just to get a glance of my surroundings, I answered, "Yes." I went to the door and my hopes of seeing anything further than my limited vision were dashed right away. Another young man was also there; I hadn't left the cell before the blindfold went over my eyes.

Going out, I was turned right, walked a few metres along the corridor and stopped. One of them opened a door on the left, almost opposite Curly's cell, I imagined, pushed me in and at the same time took the blindfold away, closing the door behind me. Apart from the toilet, there was a sink with one cold water tap over it, and a barred window covered with opaque glass so nothing could be seen through it. I had a small pee and ran the water and wet my face and hair to wake me up. Then, before coming out, as I had been told, I knocked and the door opened. Blindfolded again, I was led back to my cell. My escorts were two good natured youngsters, by the look of it, so pointing at my wrist while one was closing the door, I risked asking, "Time?" He showed me his watch: 10:10.

The place was extremely quiet. I dozed off again, later to be woken up by a loud shout, wherever it came from. It took me a minute to shake off the sleep and realise what was happening: the UN's Fifth Amendment was being violated, for someone was being tortured! By the sound of it, there were two people involved; one who kept sobbing, at the same time talking and every few seconds giving way to a loud scream as if subjected to pain; and the other, I could make out, the torturer, who shouted at him and presumably applied the pain. I went to the door. The sound was coming from just beyond the right bend to the left of my cell. Later I found out there was a room, if you came out of my cell and turned to the right, that they called 'Torture Chamber'. Both were Turks, for listening I could make out a few words in their conversation; among them, *sikim* (the word meaning 'penis', but widely used as 'fucking' in Turkish) and also *Islam*. The torturer used both words, the former more often, but the one being tortured only the latter word. My instant guess: a political prisoner, most probably an Islamic fundamentalist, was under torture.

In fact, two weeks later when we were released in the town of Ozon Kopru and got arrested by the police there again, we were told, when taken to the station (after telling them our story and that we had just been released), that we had been kept in the political section of this prison.

But back to the present: I was listening to the agony of someone under torture, which went on for another ten to fifteen minutes. The prisoner, who sounded like a man not more than thirty, suddenly gave the loudest shout and then went all silent; evidently he had passed out. After another couple of minutes I went back to my blankets and lay down as before, staring at the ceiling, my mind a blank, unable to think.

During my detention there I was woken from sleep on two further occasions by the sound of someone being tortured. Each time the pattern was much the same, with someone sobbing.

The same youngster as before, at eight in the morning, knocked at my cell door and asked "Toilet?" I didn't want another look around so I shook my head 'no' and just pointed at his watch to know the time.

A couple of hours later two of the youngsters showed up. I was blindfolded and taken out of the cell; turned right, passed the first cell, then at Curly's, we stopped. A bell was rung and I heard a door right in front of me opening and I was pushed through; the door closed behind me. (The same young men later took me back, so it seems that in the meantime he waited outside the cell or room I was now in.)

A man's voice from about a couple of metres ahead, in good English said, "There is a chair on your right, sit down."

I did so.

He carried on: "I can see that you have been educated in England." Obviously he was looking at my record filled in Merich police station, through that Beauty Queen translator. "Where exactly there?"

Judging by his accent, he had lived in England, and his question suggested he was also familiar with that country. "I went to college in Basingstoke and to university in Guilford," I replied. He was familiar with both places.

From what I had heard, in Iran also, where they kept political prisoners, the men questioning them had spent long periods living in England and America.

"Guilford, a nice place," he said, then as if that subject were over, he went on, "I've got your passport and diary notebook here. First, looking through the former I couldn't find your visa for entering Turkey. Was it done illegally?"

Though I had my passport wrapped in plastic, going through that ditch where I left Osman and Ali, some small drops of water got through and spoiled part of the writings in my passport. The red circular mark, my Turkish entry visa, had lost some of its colouring, and unless one knew where to look for the mark, it was easily missed.

"No, sir," I replied, "I was issued three months visa, legally, at the border upon my arrival from Bulgaria…"

Cutting me short, he asked, "Where is it then?"

"At the bottom of the page where my Bulgarian postage stamp-like visa is stuck." It was the only one of its kind in my passport.

I heard him going through the pages and then stopping. After a short pause, he said, "Correct." He had found it. "So you entered this country on 19th of September," he continued, the tone of his voice suggesting a smile, "and were leaving us so soon?"

"I didn't stay long last time either."

"Yes," he replied, "only a couple of days; then, passing through Bulgaria, you went to Yugoslavia, but weren't allowed in. It is in your diary: the last entry. Let me read it to you and refresh your memory: '17 Sep., 1988. Sofia, in a park… Leaving Istanbul 3 days ago…'."

He read from the diary and I thought about Lynn: how she let me down; if only she had accepted my offer of living together, I wouldn't have been here today. And also even much further back, my wife Sue in England: if only she had been satisfied with one man, then none of this would be happening.

He drew my attention to the part which read: "'... trying to sneak out of Bulgaria to Yugoslavia, I followed Vich...'.'" After a momentary halt there, he said, "Do you always leave countries you enter, illegally?" Not waiting for an answer, he skipped the next few paragraphs, almost right to the last part where I had penned some remarks about communism; he seemed very interested in that and carried on reading, "'...anyway, I hate a bastard communist regime myself...'.'" He stopped and everything went quiet. I felt him staring at me; he couldn't be in favour of communism, I thought, for Turkey was too pro-American.

"So you don't like communism," he said, as if making a statement.

I kept listening - uncertain; with the blindfold over my eyes, his feelings were hard to guess.

Reading my mind, he carried on, "Nothing to feel uneasy about, I'm against communism myself." Giving a short laugh, he spoke to someone else in the room of whose presence I was unaware until then. His attention coming back to me, he said, "You seem disciplined and, since you are educated, we have decided not to send you to the Torture Chamber."

I didn't quite realize what he meant by sending one to the torture chamber until a few minutes later when Curly was questioned in this very place and then directed there.

He carried on, "Now you'll be returned to your cell, then I'll come and set you free in a minute."

That 'minute' took almost two weeks. Back in my cell I started pacing to-and-fro, impatient to be released soon. Then I heard another cell door being opened followed by Curly's voice. He was taken to the same room I had just left - as I surmised by the sound of the bell ringing. I could still hear him behind closed door. They didn't keep the Czech there long - probably tired of him talking in his language. Instead of Curly being taken back to his cell, two young fellows escorted him, blindfolded, each holding one of his elbows, I saw them pass in front of my cell. They turned right and stopped, and I heard a knock on a door, which meant there was a room there. All three went in and closed the door behind them. As soon as they were inside, I heard Curly being slapped; he shouted, and they hit him again, then he almost screamed. Another man shouted back, and I recognized the voice: it belonged to the same vile bastard who had practiced his devilish art before, torturing the prisoner I had heard the night before.

I didn't know whether to laugh or cry. I heard chairs and tables being thrown about, followed by some heavy running that almost shook the building. This went on for another couple of minutes; then as swiftly as it had all started, everything stopped dead. I heard Curly no more. Had he been knocked out? So that was what they meant by 'torture chamber', I thought.

Then the door opened and I saw them coming out. Passing in front of my cell, the two youngsters dragged Curly on his heels, supporting him under his armpits; his head was bent backwards, his face covered in blood. He was taken back to his cell, the door closed and bolted.

I nearly felt sick; sitting down, I tried not to think about it. Idi Amin ordered a worse treatment for his opponents and it passed. This would pass too. But then, it was repeated again.

Trying to concentrate on any other diverting subject, I remembered we hadn't had breakfast either. Torture followed by no food - the first two basic rights of a prisoner clearly violated. I cursed the Human Rights Organizations for the hundredth time. In fact, the same feeding routine went right up to the day we were released. They fed us once a day: at about six every evening the same man followed by a number of youngsters, entered the cell; having had a good laugh, making fun of the prisoner, though not in a very humiliating way; one talked to the prisoner - not so that he could understand what was said but to provoke confusion or puzzlement, which was the cause of more laughter. A couple of days later, finding it comic myself, I started laughing along; then looked forward to six o'clock. They left the prisoner with four slices of bread and a small piece of cheese, funny enough, always wrapped in a newspaper, plus a cup of water. On Fridays (and I was there for two Fridays) a few olives were added.

Some time later Curly came round: I heard him talking in his cell. What kind of a state he was in remained to be seen. Shouting quietly through the bars of the door again, he sounded in no immediate need of a doctor. It seemed ridiculous to think otherwise - the prisoner's right to fair treatment. He would be examined by a doctor only when his heart stopped beating - and then only to make sure he wouldn't be leaving his cell faking his death.

A few days later I was becoming quite weak when a guard came to my cell door, cautiously looked in either direction, and spoke quietly to me, "Hey mister, you want juice?"

"Yes, of course," I answered.

"Twenty Liras," he said.

I gave him the money and a few seconds later he came back with a bottle of pure cherry juice. It sure gave me some energy! I felt stronger at once - almost as soon as the liquid went down my throat. He was waiting outside the door to take the empty bottle. Giving it to him with a 100 liras note, I said, "Get me two more bottles please and two for that man in the cell at the end." I knew the Czech would never understand him if asked so felt it was up to me to take the initiative. "And keep the change," I added. Those bottles of juice were worth more than their weight in gold here, I thought - my kind Samaritan was a fool to offer them so cheap.

Coming back with four bottles, he gave me two, and walking away he handed the other two to the right person - I knew that because Curly's voice was unmistakeable.

He was back again to fetch the empty bottles. I asked

for more, but he said, "No, too dangerous." I wondered what made him suddenly so cautious. However, paying twice as much, I managed to get one more bottle from him, and the same for Curly, the day afterwards. But apparently it was the end of our party. "Too dangerous," the guard kept repeating.

With no reading materials and no exercises, time dragged on slowly. Then one day they came round to my cell. I was blindfolded, led through some corridors, up a lot of stairs, and out of the building. Deprived of sunshine for so long, it was good to feel it upon me again, though only for a few seconds. The Czech was brought out too. We were taken to a waiting car, made to lie down on the back seat, then driven off; like the last time travelling in a car, the movement was rough. Thirty minutes later we came to a halt and they pulled us out of the car.

Blindfolds away, I found myself back at Edernè Police Station. Curly stood next to me. I was seeing him now after so many days; from the time he had been half dragged, half carried past my cell. I saw now that he had a big cut over his right eyebrow and had lost some weight. So had I. We got drawn to each other and we shook hands. A couple of soldiers soon put us in chains. From one sort of handicap to another, I thought.

All four of us got into a waiting taxi which moved away. Minutes later we arrived at the Edernè Bus Terminal. It looked as if we were travelling backwards along the route we had taken more than two weeks earlier. We got on one of the busses there and for a few hours had the benefit of a reasonably pleasant journey sitting by the window. I didn't take my eyes off the view until the bus arrived at the Merich Terminal. Again, we were pulled by our chains, walking through the village; people stood by watching us, finding the spectacle of men being led by chains amusing. In this way we were brought to the Merich Police Station where our chains were removed. One of the soldiers jerked his head towards the benches, indicating that we should sit there. We sat on two different benches, Curly and I, close to each other, but kept quiet. Soon the same sick head soldier joined me; we exchanged a couple of kicks; when he left the good looking sergeant who had questioned me through that beauty queen appeared. I wondered where she was - would I get to meet her again? The sergeant came to me, shook my hand, gave me a friendly smile and left the building.

About late afternoon a soldier brought us two plates of rice. I finished mine in record time, Curly even in less time! I could have done with another helping. At nightfall they took us back to the same cell we were incarcerated in more than two weeks earlier, at the back of the building, down in the cellar. It seemed, fortunately, that a life of solitude in that underground prison had left Curly with a diminished inclination to talk; or perhaps this was due to the beatings he had received in the torture chamber. He lay on the bed and we exchanged a few of words while I spread a folded blanket on the floor and stretched myself over it.

In the morning we were led out of our cell and taken back into the yard. The rice dish I had consumed the day before had given me energy, and I managed to do some press ups in the fresh air. Around mid-morning - no breakfast forthcoming - our guards came round, as expected, to escort us to appear in court. Curly and I, oddly divested of our usual excursion chains, were loaded into an army jeep at the gate. Half an hour later we entered the court building: the time 10:00, date 7 Oct., 1988, as I noticed, on the clock inside.

Going by what the sergeant had told me in his earlier questioning, we would be released today. However, in a country like Turkey, by now I'd come to realize, anything concerning a prisoner, plus delays, could happen. I felt more despair than hope.

We were told to sit on a bench placed in the corridor outside a room that bore the number '5', a soldier standing guard over us. I was impatient to know what would happen to me. And apparently, it seemed, the same thing was true of Curly, though he was in a worse situation than I was, since he had entered Turkey illegally in the first place, and was not able to speak English. Since I could speak English, I was the one always asked forward.

A person in Bulgaria caught trying to leave without permission would face six months imprisonment. I had spoken to people who had served that sentence; and not in a better place than the dungeon we had just left. As the time went by I grew more anxious; they say waiting is the worst part.

Suddenly, almost out of nowhere, the same good looking sergeant appeared. Tall and walking strong, he entered room '5', the one we were expecting to be called into, closing the door behind him. For some reason, his presence made me feel easier. It didn't take long before the same door opened and a man from inside, sitting just beyond the door - the sergeant on another chair next to him - pointed and asked me to come closer from across the corridor. It was a small room, a desk with a chair behind it in one corner; but where these two were sitting, on chairs, they looked more like spectators than officials. They called it 'Court number 5' - different from the ones I had seen in England. I stood by the door talking to them.

The man in his early forties, quite fair skinned and speaking good English, first told me that leaving Turkey illegally was a serious offence and anyone breaking that law faced imprisonment. Haven't I been through more than two weeks of it already, I thought, or maybe that didn't count in Turkey? I had spent three terms on remand in England, amounting to six weeks, nine days and eleven months, all for the same charge of having entered into a marriage of convenience, but it is the two weeks in detention spent here, in Turkey, that I always remembered most vividly. My interrogator then wanted to know why I had chosen Greece. Still standing just inside the room by the door, I told him the reason but he cut me short; he then told me to return to the bench, closing the door behind me.

"Surely that didn't conclude my court case?" I asked myself. Shortly afterwards the sergeant came out of the room and, jerking his head, told us to follow him.

Leaving the building, we were taken back to the army jeep. The sergeant joined us, taking a seat in the front next to the driver; the doors were closed and the jeep sped away. About half an hour later we entered a town. The jeep stopped right in the middle of the town and we were told to get out. We did so, as did the sergeant who came to me and said, "Don't go near the river again." He spoke like one who had remembered a phone number which, once dialled, was forgotten: he uttered the sentence word for word in English, as though he had memorised it for the occasion. I had a good idea who had 'programmed' his instructions. Having delivered this message, he turned back, got into the jeep and left. It was the end of the ordeal, and that went for the Czech national too - something I never understood since he couldn't possibly have entered Turkey legally. Though I hadn't seen his passport, he nevertheless gave me to understand that he had entered Greece legally - but maybe I had got the wrong message.

We were in Ozon Kopru. Curly had been there before: he knew his way around and asked me to follow him. We entered a shop and the owner recognized him; not much was said, but he changed some of Curly's Greek Drachmas into Turkish liras. Curly had changed all his money to Drachmas thinking he would never be back: unlucky none of us got far enough.

Leaving the shop, I wanted to get something to eat. At one of the restaurants in the town I soon made up for the time we were denied the pleasure. Out of the place, going round, finding it interesting, we decided to stay and leave the day after. Preceding the need for sight-seeing, however, was the need to wash. We rented a room at one of the hotels and I was getting ready to wash, taking off my shirt to go for a shower, when the door opened and two policemen walked in. The one who appeared to be of a higher rank asked to see our passports. I showed him mine and pointed out my Turkish entry visa, since I knew he wouldn't find it. He took the passport, turned the pages and said, "Greece!" - noticing the water dispersed writings, evidently a well-known sign of crossing the river - possibly based on years of experience in regard to foreigners round there. Now I had to explain all that to him, I thought. Then Curly handed over his passport and the policeman went through it, once more, and again, in search of something not there. The Czech was simply illegally in the country. Confronting a questioning stare, Curly just shook his head and said several words in Czech.

We were taken to Ozon Kopru Police Station. After being searched thoroughly, emptying our pockets, one of the policemen glanced at my dollars and Curly's drachmas on the table. He pointed at his watch, completed four circles round the face of it with his finger, trying to make us understand that they meant to keep Curly and I there for 48 hours to find out the reason behind our stay in so insignificant a town. I tried to explain why we were there but they wouldn't listen. Now Curly took over; in his language he started and went on. The policeman twice told him to shut up but the Czech man kept talking. I kind of realized that he was nervous and not fully in control of his actions. The policeman, running out of patience and finding no other option, hit Curly hard on the head. It worked! The Czech man went very silent. I'd probably try that myself later if found necessary.

We were locked up but not for long. Hours later they took us out and said we could go. Just before leaving one of the policemen, who had apparently made inquiries about us from other sources, said, "Sana (you)… Merich police… after… Edernè zindan (prison)… shèbè siyasy (political section)…"

That cleared my doubts, for that was when I realised those prisoners being tortured were politically motivated.

We went back to the hotel, had a shower, as it was still early yet for bed, and left for a walk round the place. It was dark and dead quiet everywhere. We had a few drinks in one of the bars. It was late when we left the place. No more policemen appeared and we spent a peaceful night at the hotel.

Early the next morning I said goodbye to Curly, wishing him all the best. I left for Ipsala to get my knapsack from the hotel where I had left it over two weeks earlier. Funny enough, I had to change busses at

Merich Bus Terminal; waiting to do so, some of the people there recognized me. Around noon I reached Ipsala. After alighting from the minibus and walking round the block, I entered the hotel. Alper behind the reception desk was busy reading and didn't notice me walking in. I went quietly to his desk and said, "Hello."

He looked up, surprised to see me. "I thought you went to Greece," he said.

"I got there but they sent me back." That went as far as I felt like explaining. Then I inquired about my friend Ali and also Osman. "What news of them?"

That same night we had left for Greece, Alper remembered, "both came back to the hotel around four in the morning; Ali got his bag, then they disappeared together." He had seen Osman in the village a few times since, but not Ali.

I received my knapsack which was intact, said goodbye to Alper and left the hotel. Once outside, I felt like going back in again, rent a room and wait till dark, then once more try for Greece. This time I'll get myself to Athens and submit to the authorities there. But there was no guarantee that they wouldn't do what their army did to me at the border. And the thought of being caught by the Turks again was daunting - I would be spending quite a while down that dungeon, next time, followed no doubt by a lot of imprisonment facing the same court, which would not be so lenient the second time round.

Walking away from the hotel, coming to where the taxis were parked, I heard a man from inside a half-crowded minibus shouting, "Istanbul!" I got on. Soon all the seats were occupied and the minibus set off. On the way, feeling downcast, my eyes wet with tears, I called it another loss, the close of another chapter in my life.

chapter twelve

IT WAS DARK when we got to Istanbul. After walking through the city for a couple of hours, I went back to the same hotel where I had stayed on both previous occasions. It now felt like a place of refuge to which I returned after every defeat. Inside my room I cursed those authorities in Iran who had missed the opportunity of hanging me that day along with Ahmad and his three friends.

In the morning I left early going around looking for a job. I still had 2,400 US dollars on me, but it didn't seem like the sort of money, now that I had to pay for my food and lodging, that would last for long. Calling at a few hotels I found most were fully staffed, or they wanted someone familiar with the local language as well. The same applied to restaurants. Regarding factories and most other places, I didn't even bother to check, for I was given to understand they always asked to see one's work permit. Around noon, coming out of the biggest and best hotel in Istanbul, Etap Marmara, by the famous square, Taksim, I was making my mind up as to which way to go, when a hand came over my shoulder; turning, I was surprised to see Curly! He had come to Istanbul too, but to do what? Since he was almost in the same situation as me, I was interested to know if he had any good plans. Why not join a Czech man on the next trek, I thought? It might turn out successful. Though the idea was mine, it occurred to me that the last time I joined forces with anyone - Ali, to be precise - I at least had the benefit of a companion who shared that initial initiative, or spark, if you like, to get us on the way. Using my standard of communication to convey this idea, he responded in his language; when I asked him if he was planning to enter Greece once more, he said, "Ne, ne" - which I presumed meant "no, no!" As for the rest, I didn't understand a word of what he said. It simply wouldn't work, I concluded: the one speaking the same language left half way, let alone with no language... Shaking hands, we parted, never to see each other again.

As I'm writing these notes, thinking of Curly, Czechoslovakia is no longer communist, so he might even be back in his country, living a happy life. Would he ever remember me, someone who shared the same cell with him at one time?

Giving up my plans, I went back home to Iran two days later. I felt it was almost the only option open to me for the time being. When I got to the flat my elder sister, Soheila, and her two sons were there too. She hugged me and cried. There was something wrong, I sensed, for she didn't usually show so much emotion on seeing me. Soon I found out the facts: her husband, Sohrab, had been arrested for being a Bahaii (a religion associated with Israel, declared illegal by the authorities in Iran). We had always anticipated some sort of happening along these lines and had advised him to leave the country, but he had stayed. Where had he been taken to? She didn't know. "Five nights ago we were sleeping when the front door got kicked open," my sister explained quietly while tears rolled down her cheeks. "Four sentries, guns in hand, rushed into our bedroom! They got Sohrab out of the bed and took him away." And since then, all the women of the household, plus the two young boys, were in despair. They had been waiting for me to come home and advise them what to do. They were worried for me too, away for so long with no news, and they wanted to know where I had been. With all this trouble, what good would it do, I thought, apart from adding to their misery, if I told them the truth? "I was in the north. Liking it, I extended my stay," I lied. Thinking of what really took place, I sighed in my heart. In fact, if this book is ever published, and my sister gets the chance to read it, only then will she know where I had actually been during those weeks that coincided with Sohrab's arrest.

My sister, Soheila, now quite naturally wanted to know her husband's whereabouts. But there were problems; people belonging to the Bahaii sect, once recognized, were arrested, then treated as opponents to the regime. At the mere thought of this a shiver ran down my spine, for anyone inquiring after this type of prisoner often ended up in a worse predicament. So all we could do was just wait.

Soheila and her two sons, it seemed, were likely to stay in my flat for a long while to come. A few days later, though scared to go back, she returned to her lodgings. This still left six of us in my two-bedroom flat, which included Soheila's two sons and my younger sister, Sepideh, as well as my repulsive whore of a mother who had always tried to separate Soheila from her husband so that she could have him for herself; not surprisingly, she was the only one who did not look displeased by the turn of events. This old woman who I felt ashamed to call mother, for two reasons, didn't like my younger sister, possibly simply because she was young, and in fact she displayed the same hateful attitude towards all girls under the age of wrinkles; the second reason for my feelings of shame towards her was that, as far back as I can remember, she had always tried to molest me.

Things began to smooth out a bit, if not for everyone else in the flat, at least for me, as time moved forward. A few days later I started back working at my uncle's shop again, doing the same thing - selling spare parts for cars. On my own, there were only a few customers to attend to and I followed my previous routine: tuned into the BBC while exercising in the mornings; spent the afternoons weaving a new and bigger carpet - till it was time to quit for the day. I finished around six in the evening and from the shop headed straight for the park. Apart from the keepers, only a handful of people were there, which was the reason I frequently visited the place. I stayed as long as I could see my way back so only left when the light began to fade. When I got home, I had something to eat, listened to more BBC, then crashed out.

One evening lying on my bed reading *Time Magazine* - I always kept the door of my room closed - I heard a loud scream from Soheila who had been watching TV in the sitting room. I jumped out of bed and reached her in no time, wondering what had happened. She was speechless. Sepideh, by her side trying to comfort her, explained, "It was announced on TV just now that 40 Bahaiis were hanged this morning!"

A minute later I put my clothes on and left the house. What a night it was! Just recalling it makes the hair stand up on my body. Going towards the newsstand, I was half numb with fear. I had to get hold of the evening newspaper. Those hanged were always named in the papers - either today's or at the most tomorrow's. But I would go insane if I had to wait for another day, so I bought the paper; my hands shaking, I could hardly turn the pages. I found a topic relating to the Bahaiis - it seemed the one I was looking for. First there was the headline: '40 Bahaiis found guilty of having connections with the regimes in Israel and

America were hanged this morning.' Beneath this were a few lines of lies about their activities, followed by their names in columns. I could hear my heart beating; it would come out of my mouth in another minute, I thought. My eyes in full control of my brain, I tried to force them down along the rows of names. They were reluctant to look and I tried once more and managed a quick glance before, involuntarily, both my eyes moved away again. I cursed myself for being a coward, my hands now shaking so badly I couldn't keep steady. Stopping a passer-by, I handed him the paper. I asked the man if he saw the name Sohrab Norouzi in any of the rows. I felt sick, as he read. Taking his time, he went through the columns; then, turning to me, he shook his head and handed back the paper. I took a deep breath, thinking that he might have missed the name in one of the columns; now less nervous, I ventured to look at the columns of names myself. To my relief I saw no Sohrab Norouzi there.

Now I realized my brother-in-law's place had been taken by another. The family of someone else will have looked for their relative's name tonight and noted his name among the rows. A number of people will be mourning for the next few days, I thought; but secretly, since the families of those executed were banned from expressing public sorrow. And the rest of the people had learned to remain indifferent to this type of news. As long as those in their immediate circle were not involved, who cared what happened to those implicated?

I got home and found they were all waiting to hear from me. I tossed Soheila the paper and at the same time said, "His name's not in there." She visibly relaxed, relieved not just for herself but for her two kids.

Not surprisingly, the day after, listening to the BBC - the main news at 13:00 hours GMT, the one I never missed - the fate of Bahaiis in Iran was commented on. The news went like this: '...UN has condemned Iran's action for executing Bahaiis without a proper trial... 40 Bahaiis were executed...'

And when this condemnation didn't work, a few days later the UN issued a warning, flagrant statements threatening Iran with sanctions for her human rights violations.

Whatever the reason, due to these warnings, or perhaps even by sheer chance, three months later Sohrab was freed. He phoned us minutes after his release, and gave us the news; he couldn't wait to get home to tell us his good news in person. Soheila and her two kids opened the door on him, a couple of hours later, when he knocked. He had been inside for more than six months, with no news, and we were overjoyed to see him back. He had been incarcerated in Evin prison - the very name sent shivers down people's spines in the country - where politically motivated prisoners were kept. "In underground cells and blindfolded everywhere we were taken to," he told us. My memory was still fresh as to how Turkey treated her political prisoners - in the same way! I wondered, was there a higher authority that dictated the pattern of how political prisoners were to be treated?

Sohrab hadn't changed much, certainly not in the talking department! Famous for being a chatterbox and often an exaggerator, now we were to be told virtually every minute about his 6-month long imprisonment! He began like a runaway train, nothing able to stop him. Sharing a cell no bigger than 3x3m with three other prisoners, he had learnt riddles and jokes.

Excusing myself half an hour later, I left them and went to my room. It was ten when I got to bed, and when I got up around two in the morning to use the toilet, Sohrab was still talking to the rest of the family.

Now we had to get him out of the country. We were living under the sword of Damocles, uncertain whether at any moment some people might come round for him. Bahaiis were not allowed passports which meant he had to be smuggled out. Not so serious a problem, since hundreds were leaving the country illegally daily. Traffickers engaged in this venture had a booming business. People were paying with all their belongings to reach a developed country. And for those who could barely afford it, priority was given to their male youngsters who needed to be smuggled out to avoid joining the army - for joining the army would mean going to war, followed by martyrdom which, against all promises, the clergy bestowed on these so-called heroes. "If your son gets martyred he will enter heaven," Khomeini was saying from his stronghold built under and well inside the mountain, Jamaran, in the north of Tehran, and the people just didn't believe him anymore. They answered, if martyrdom was good for their sons, it was surely good for *his* son and grandson too, "not hiding in that luxurious cover where nothing can penetrate." This is what the people were heard whispering to one another, and sometimes wrote on walls in the streets. As for Rafsangani (the president at the time), the ministers and, on the whole, all those holding key jobs in the country, their sons were exempt from joining the army, notwithstanding the promise of heaven that Khomeini was saying martyrdom would bring. One cleric even went to the length of describing the place where the martyrs would end: "...thousands of fountains all with different colours of water... trees with foliage the same colour as the sky..."; he went on to describe the heavenly girls: "... on her forehead she has 'In The Name Of God', on her right cheek 'God is Great', and the same on her left cheek..." The dirty bastards, always thinking of women! The next day some of the customers at the shop were saying this, in spite of what my uncle had written on a piece of prominently displayed cardboard hung on the wall: *Do Not Discuss Politics Here*.

Preaching wasn't working anymore. Khomeini's words began to fall on deaf ears, so they resorted to force. Youngsters were rounded up by sentries, were loaded into minibuses seen almost at every corner, and taken to barracks, given only a few days of training, then sent to the war zones. No wonder Iraq with her population of only twelve million was holding out against us with our seventy million, and at times even gaining ground.

As a result the death toll was staggering. Once I heard on the BBC: '...the number of people killed in this war has reached more than that of west Europe during the whole of World War II.'

Most programs on TV and radio were devoted to war and Khomeini's speeches. Once the tyrant addressed the people from his throne, making it clear to those who were showing some unrest towards the continuation of war, that he was the ultimate decider not only on that issue, but on all matters; this was relayed over TV and, the next day, printed in the newspapers. He announced: "If the whole population of the country said 'Yes' and I ruled it out, it will always be my word that goes - and vice versa." So the wheels of the war kept rolling upon one man's decision.

The only way to escape that decision was to flee the country. Turkey was certainly considered the prime choice of destination, but not the only one. Pakistan and Dubai were well crowded with Iranians entering illegally; new routes were found nearly every day, people anxious to try any means of escape. Families would start their arduous journeys, among them often pregnant women who, we were told, now and then gave birth in one of the villages on the way.

Back to Sohrab: like most, he also decided on Turkey to begin with, and knew someone who was in the business of smuggling people out of the country and sending them there. If I remember correctly, through one of his cell mates while in Evin prison, he had come to hear of this person. To expedite his plan to leave the country - he had had enough - a few days later he invited the man over to our place, mainly to discuss the price and, as most human traffickers asked for their money in advance, to access the reliability of the man and whether he could be trusted. Unfortunately, like most illegal activities where there was easy money to be obtained, and on that scale, some swindlers had joined honest criminals in this trade and distinguishing one from the other was not easy. People paid but never left. In most cases an honest trafficker was known through close friends who have had someone smuggled out by him.

The man, called Mohammad, duly arrived. He was of medium stature, quite ugly, one eyebrow lower than the other. His appearance well suited the job he was into. He asked for 12,000 US dollars to send Sohrab, first to Istanbul and from there to Canada, Australia or New Zealand. The price he asked for these three Western destinations, the highest in the market at the time, was the same. The European countries, Sweden, Norway, Spain, the Netherlands, England, Belgium, Germany, Denmark, Italy and Austria, would be 6,000 dollars each. Munching through two apples, he informed Sohrab, "Nearly all of Europe at present accepts people seeking asylum." Apart from the communist states, I thought, remembering the Czech man, where even some of their own citizens fled. Mohammad went on to say that once papers were obtained from any of the countries mentioned Sohrab could leave to enter America and stay there - "where you can get yourself a good job and earn a decent amount of money," he explained. Until then, we thought, it would be a long time, and might even prove to be an unobtainable dream.

And how would Mohammad like his money to be paid? "All in advance," he answered, when asked.

Sohrab wanted to end up in Australia, but 12,000 dollars amounted to a lot of money to entrust to Mohammad, someone he had never seen before.

"How much would you charge just getting him to Istanbul?" I asked, giving voice to something on my mind.

"3,000 dollars," he said, swallowing two more apples.

In spite of his dubious appearance, Mohammad didn't seem dishonest. And finding my idea of using Turkey as a stepping stone, when I suggested it, Sohrab decided in favour of going to Istanbul and taking it from there. Being a Bahaii he would have the benefit of support groups in Turkey, funded by Israel and America, who would arrange their papers in a very short period of time, sending them anywhere they asked for - something that soon proved to be true. Then, in regard to money, we had to see if we could cut some kind of deal with Mohammad.

Sohrab said to him, "I'll give you 1,500 dollars now, and when you got me to Istanbul, you can have the remaining half." He pointed at Soheila. "You'll come here and ask my wife for it."

It was not the usual type of transaction ratified by human traffickers, but times being as hard as they were, clutching at straws was not to be dismissed. Mohammad, who also found our family honest, accepted what Sohrab proposed. He received 1,500 dollars on the spot, and they thought it expedient to leave the next day. First they would go to the city of Salmas, north-west of Iran, and from there to a border village; then at nightfall and on horseback, they would sneak out into Turkey.

Early the next morning Sohrab left, but before leaving, for the twentieth time, said to his wife that once settled in a so-called 'good' country, he'd send for her and the kids.

Now came the worst part - waiting. The moment he walked out of the door Soheila took up a position by the phone; two days later she was still sleeping close to it. Every phone call was answered at the first ring. We were all waiting for news from Sohrab. Before anything, on getting home from work in the evenings, often cancelling the park from my schedule, I asked, "Did he call?" There was no news from Mohammad either.

On the 5th day Sohrab phoned - from Istanbul and in good health! He had an easy journey and we all felt over the moon. So that was the first leg of his journey, insignificant as it seemed, nevertheless successfully completed. Though I've spoken to him many times on the phone since he left early that morning almost 20 years ago to the day (at the time of writing these notes), and I have yet to see him in the flesh, the details of his journey, to Istanbul and beyond, are still unknown to me. A couple of months after he left he called again, this time from Spain. The authorities there had granted him asylum, based on his religion, and it wasn't long after he received his papers that he decided to leave for America.

Mohammad duly came round and collected his remaining 1,500 dollars. One good turn deserves another and he was introduced to a neighbour who wanted a son removed from the country.

chapter thirteen

I WENT TO SEE MY FATHER. I hadn't seen him for nearly four months. He had changed his address, but asking his friends, telling them who I was, I managed to find him. As always he was healthy in body but looked older than his 57 years. He was still dealing in drugs and had got rid of his old car. "In this business there are two changes that are absolutely essential and which should be made frequently," he stated. "One is your address, but better still, your car. These changes make it hard for the sentries to catch up with you."

He inquired about the family and I told him they were okay. Since he was on sour terms with his son-in-law, Sohrab, I never mentioned him; and I didn't inform the old man that he had left the country. Sooner rather than later he'd find out for himself.

"How is business going?" I asked.

He was building a summer house in the north of the country by the Caspian Sea, soon to be finished. Then in a couple of days' time he would be going to the south (the city of Kerman), for a consignment of opium, 14 kilos, which he had arranged to bring back.

His girlfriend, Mahin, was there too. When she gave me a cup of tea I told her, "Your husband's been around again asking about your whereabouts."

Mahin, who looked a bit worried, gave my father a glance. "You won't tell him where we live, will you?" she said.

I shook my head to assure her. For two people under the sentence of death by stoning, if caught, they were both acting bravely. I wondered how far one would go for the love of a partner. Once I heard on the BBC about a King in England who gave his throne up for the love of a woman. Was this the furthest one had ever gone? How many get the chance of a kingdom? Or know that if they carried on what awaited them?

"Your husband is not giving up, is he?" I said.

"Has your mother?" she asked. Not expecting an answer, she smiled sarcastically.

"I don't talk to her much," I said. Then I asked for a cup of coffee instead of tea, drank it and left.

For the next few months, life went on smoothly for everyone at the flat with little new developments. Still working in my uncle's shop and coming home one day from the park, Soheila was especially pleased. "Sohrab's in America!" she announced. He had phoned from there giving them the news. He was soon to receive the State's green card after which he would be able to send for his wife and kids to join him. That was certainly good news, but as in the life of the unfortunates, happiness often happens at the cost of sadness: a few days later I received a letter from my father saying he was in prison. He had been caught with 9 kilos of opium, so was now, I assumed, under the shadow of death. Five kilos of the substance was enough to send one to the gallows, and he had been caught with nearly twice as much. I felt weak and had to sit down. The opium, wrapped in a plastic bag, had been found in his Peugeot's petrol tank. He had played ignorant but to no avail.

The captured person is usually taken to a prison nearest to where he or she had been caught, and my father's letter was sent from the city of Yazd, next to Kerman, on the way to Tehran - almost 600km away. He had asked me to go and pay him a visit.

A few days later I took a bus bound for the south from Tehran's South Bus Terminal. After almost 12 hours of journeying along one of the most hazardous roads in the country, which claimed tens of lives every year, I arrived at Yazd Terminal at 6 the next morning. I was told that the prison was situated on the other side of the city, about 5km away. The visiting time was 9 o'clock in the morning, according to my father's letter, so that left me almost three hours. I decided to walk the distance. Yazd is a small city but full of historical sights. Through dynasties, as a great trading place, different clans had met and some settled there. The city, to a large extent, amazingly enough, also harboured another religion, apart from Islam and a few other minor ones, all Zoroastrians. Wherever these were in the country, they all claimed to come from Yazd. Later, after visiting my father, I decided I would visit one monument - and probably stay overnight.

I sat down on one of the benches just outside the main gate of that medieval looking prison since I still had more than an hour to wait before being allowed in. I noticed the tall thick walls that surrounded the prison, made of red bricks with barbed wire on the top. At each corner there was a watchtower, in each a soldier with a machine gun trained on the prisoners in the yard.

I hadn't answered my father's letter, so he didn't know I would be visiting him today; neither had he any confirmation that I had received his letter, for that matter. Talking to him later, he asked me whether I had received his letter or found out about his imprisonment through his girlfriend.

It was well after 9 o'clock that the main gate of the prison opened. Nothing happened on time in the country apart from prayers. An officer appeared and invited the visitors inside. The prisoners were in their cells. After being thoroughly searched, we followed a sentry, crossed the yard and entered the visiting room: a wide corridor divided into half along the length; from the waist upwards was a glass panel, partitioned every half metre where one talked to the prisoner through a small hole in the glass. To my surprise it was a clean room, newly carpeted and walls recently painted. Giving the name of the inmate one wanted to see, each visitor took up his position at a different partition. It was a Wednesday: men's day to visit. Five minutes later the prisoners came and I spotted my father who looked the oldest among them: almost white hair, his beard grown a couple of inches, not a strand of black to be seen in it. For a moment it felt as though I was watching the movie 'Papillon'; my father reminded me of the way the actor Steve McQueen looked, coming out of the prison called 'The Man Eater' halfway through the movie.

He was surprised to see me, though the identity of his visitor was not unexpected - who else, apart from his son, would have travelled 600km just to pay another relation a visit?

"How do you find your new life?" I asked, bearing in mind it was his first time inside.

For someone shortly to be under the sentence of death, he looked indifferent. My father was either the bravest man I had ever seen, or his apparent indifference was because those all around him were in the same situation.

"I can take it," he answered, unaware I had served behind bars myself, several times.

We went through the usual trivia... how was everyone at home?... he had someone to finish his summer house in the north... Then he explained his case, "Do you remember that 14 kilos I told you about, the last time you were round my house?" It was not a question but a statement. He carried on, "I was caught with that." In his letter, however, he had mentioned 9 kilos. Reading my mind, he said, "You always find a few kilos missing" - pointing at the other inmates occupying the partitions on his right and left. And what about the 'not guilty' bit, again, mentioned in his letter? He had told the authorities that the day before his arrest he had taken his car to a garage, which he actually had done, and someone there must have placed the opium where found. Trying to shift the blame to others - the usual manoeuvre played in this game. Nevertheless, the sentries had been to the garage, which was almost half the size of a football stadium; they had questioned a few of the 100 workers there, but no arrests had been made, as my father had expected.

"How did you put it in that petrol tank and how on earth did they find out?" I asked.

He had dismantled the petrol tank from the car, cut the top part out, placed the opium inside, well wrapped around with plastic, welded the part back then put the tank back in place. He couldn't have done a good job of it since the merchandise was discovered, I pointed out. "Some of the sentries at these check points are expert mechanics," he explained. Still, a number of people carrying narcotics managed to slip through, I thought.

Whether for good or bad, in the eyes of Islam dogs were just as dirty as pigs - something certainly not for me to judge; but it explains why dogs were not used when searching cars, otherwise more people would have found their way to the gallows. Was nature playing the right cards, awarding dogs with a heightened sense of smell? Some people tried to keep a dog at home, a habit picked up as usual by watching foreign movies, seeing people taking the animal out for a walk. In Iran they passed a law prohibiting anyone from going out on the streets with this kind of pet. But then again people always found ways to beat the system. A friend of mine, a truck trailer driver who took goods abroad, said all vehicles were searched using dogs at the border between Poland and Hungary; more so, evidently, in Germany, where these animals were highly trained to find narcotics. So, I asked him, how he managed to get two kilos of opium through the last time he left. "I got a wet piece of cloth," he explained, "and smeared it well with opium, then rubbed it round the trailer. In Hungary, searching the vehicle, the dogs sniffing became confused, barking and jumping everywhere, up and down the trailer and back. The handler, apparently puzzled and wondering what had gone wrong, withdrew them, then personally just checked inside the cabin and under - far from where I had the opium hidden; and he asked me to carry on." The same thing happened in Germany.

But back to my father. One of the sentries inspecting his car had noticed that the tank had been placed there recently - which could happen, I thought, but this gave him a good reason to check it. Draining all the petrol out of the tank, then refilling it, he noticed that the amount of petrol used to fill the tank was scarcely half the amount usually required for the type of car being searched. The petrol began to overflow far too soon. The petrol tank was therefore dismantled, cut through, and the rest, as they say, is history.

My father had been in prison for over two months now and was expecting to appear before a court in three to four months' time. Already presumed guilty - the word *acquittal* just didn't exist in the vocabulary of the justice system in the country - he faced a mandatory death sentence, horrifying though it might sound, even though it was his first time inside. Such punishment was inevitably conclusive, if the course of justice was not interfered with. There was nothing much one could do to avert it since the reputation and living of the people in high places depended on this cast-iron judicial system.

Those responsible for running the narcotic section of the judiciary system, for a suitable amount of favour, often tampered with the evidence and changed the figures, the old man informed me; and while in prison he had learned how and who should be approached. "It is not wise to favour anyone at the moment in an attempt to influence the final judgment," he said and explained that the best move was to bribe the judge himself - the judge appointed to his case; and he wouldn't know who that might be until the day of his trial.

Someone from the other side of the corridor shouted, "Time's up!"

We had been talking for almost two hours, not realizing how quickly the time had passed. "I have to go now. Make sure you write again, and let me know about the date of your trial," I said, and in view of the travelling inconveniencies another visit would incur, added, "I don't think I'll pay you another visit until that day, again."

The same sentry led the visitors back across the yard and then outside.

Walking away, leaving the prison behind, I felt sorry for my father: an educated skilled man who used to have a good job with a well-paid salary in the previous regime, he now found himself in prison facing death. In fact, thousands of people like him were at that moment behind bars, had already been put to death; or were yet to be caught, involved in some kind of illegal activity, all just trying to make ends meet. Those keeping out of trouble were living on what they had earned in the previous regime; but inflation running at 200 per cent, how long would their money last? War was ravaging the country, but worse still, corruption among the top people was rife, even to an extent never known in the history of this country. Only one man, Ayatollah Talèghani, had done his job conscientiously, having earned his money in a responsible and honest way. He feared no one, his conscience being clear; once questioning the oil minister over 2.2 billion dollars missing in oil revenues, he accused him of theft, actually calling him a thief. As Ayatollah Talèghani's popularity grew so did his power, to the point that it equalled, if it did not actually exceed, that of Khomeini. Consequently the leader who saw his position in danger poisoned and killed him. If a man of such great popularity and power could be silenced without any resistance, then what chance did the rest of us have for justice and clemency, I thought?

Going to the southern edge of the city, walking away for a kilometre through terrain like a salt desert, I came to a 700-year old fortress. Paying the man at the door I entered. On the walls inside were paintings of human beings, mostly with swords in hands: have we always been fighting, I thought? Turning to the opposite wall I saw pictures of animals - Eric Von Däniken might make something out of all these. Spending a couple of hours there, I noticed, going round, that apart from the doorman I was the only one in that edifice. In third world countries people just paid no attention to their past. We didn't have a magnificent present either to be proud of, I thought. Leaving the place, I went back to the city to have something to eat.

At 8 o'clock that April evening, the sky got dark. There was nothing to amuse myself with, for the Ayatollah's men had closed all bars, pubs, discos and even the coffee shops in the country, since they were deemed immoral places. Late at night as it was, changing my mind, I decided to return home. At Yazd Terminal I got on the bus bound for Tehran.

On the way back I realized how nature had played the right cards for our country, where harsh punishments were meted out by a corrupt judiciary. Five kilos of narcotics meant the gallows, yet this stringent sentence could be mitigated by the authorities open to bribes. Again, inappropriate laws were subject to inadequate methods of investigation. Take my father as an example: imprisoned in Yazd, the system was not advanced enough to know that in another part of the country he was wanted for adultery, which made him liable to face the death sentence by stoning.

chapter fourteen

IT WAS MID-MORNING when I got home and I immediately sensed something was wrong. Soheila looked worried and I prepared for bad news. "What's wrong?" I asked her.

Instead of answering my question, she wanted to know where I had been - away for two days with no news.

I had told my uncle that I wouldn't be attending the shop for a while, then left straight from there, thinking he would inform them; but he hadn't.

Anyway, for a number of reasons I had decided to keep the rest of the family in the dark concerning my father's case. What good would it do, I thought, if I told them he was behind bars waiting to be sentenced to death? Should the news spread around, what a disgrace it would bring upon him and others of his family. I had persuaded my father to do the same, to keep it quiet from the family, and, like last time, just write to me. Lying about where I had been, I said I had gone to stay with a friend for a couple of days; then I asked Soheila again, "Now tell me what is wrong."

"Sepideh's been taken in," she said. It was like the last time when she told me about her husband's arrest, though this time she looked less worried, staring into empty space, as tears rolled down her cheeks. She said quietly, "We were shopping yesterday when a patrol car stopped; sentries came rushing out and started rounding up some women and loaded them into a minibus."

I didn't have to ask why. Nowadays everyone knew that sentries all over the country were arresting women for wearing nail varnish, lipstick, indecent dress as they saw it, and for quite a number of other reasons. "Last year alone," the spokesman for the judiciary once announced on TV, "15,000 women were arrested for looking non-Islamic." The real figure was probably twice as many. These women were taken to reform centres, kept there three to four days, ordered to sign an affidavit declaring themselves second class whores (those rated as first class were the ones selling their bodies; they usually faced long term imprisonments while the notorious ones were hanged), made to repent, then released. In fact, two of my cousins were subjected to same 'remedial action' not long ago: one because she had used red lipstick and the other because her Islamic dress was considered too tight, showing the curve of her ass.

Women were snatched walking alongside their husbands, fathers, brothers or whoever they might be with, if they didn't respect the laws laid down by the self-declared 'messenger of God', Khomeini and his keepers. Who would dare to speak up against this? Those who did ended up in the so-called 'Damned Cemetery', just outside Tehran, in mass graves.

"Did they give any reason for her arrest?" I asked.

Soheila answered, "She didn't have her head cover properly placed. They could see some bits of her hair in the front. That's what the man arresting her said." And, of course, displaying part of her hair they regarded non-Islamic. It spoke of vanity and was deemed a provocation for lust - something only her husband was entitled to enjoy in private.

The idea, according to Islam, was that a woman's body shouldn't become commonplace to man; otherwise it would not have the same mind stimulating effect when bedding her. The Koran stated: 'Cover your women and use your imagination concerning what lies under that cover; in this case one would choose to marry, something obligatory for every Muslim; then in sex, one would get the utmost pleasure.'

Listening to the BBC, I have heard it said many times, in regard to Islam, that 'a woman's body is something man cannot resist' - which is false information, for otherwise we would have had Muslims raping women on beaches all over the world. There are reports of rapes almost everywhere, and most to do with nudity; the rapist had seen a nude photo on TV or wherever, but hardly ever has one grabbed a woman on the beach, unable to resist the temptation, and raped her. In fact, I have seen women in their bikinis on beaches round Cyprus, some even topless, and it drew my attention for no longer than ten minutes, if that - and yet I had come straight out of Iran where females are covered from head to toe.

What kind of conclusion should one come to regarding women and cover? In my opinion, certainly nature has played the right cards in covering our women, since given the freedom to do as they please most went too far. Arguably it has worked in Western Europe, but then again surveys show that on average a person there reads one book a month whereas in Iran out of every 200 only one person reads books, and then only one book a year. In the previous regime people had money; many spent their holidays in Europe and, coming back, tried to imitate them, mostly women, not appreciating that they were living in a quite different environment, an illiterate society, so they were bound to fail, as they did; all that gave rise to one of the most common proverbs after the revolution: 'Imitation causes adversity.'

But coming back to my sister Sepideh - there was nothing I could do about it. Trying to comfort Soheila, I said, "This has happened to thousands of other women, so there is no need to worry. She'll be out in a couple of days' time." And with a lot of experience, I thought.

And indeed, two days later Sepideh was home. She looked healthy and apart from a few miserable moments when the authorities had spoken to her and the other inmates in a very harsh way, they had been enjoying themselves talking in groups. But then again, Sepideh was a very brave girl who took after our father, not like Soheila and me, under the influence of our witch mother who had always tried to bring us up like cowards so that she could use each of us for her own vile purposes.

I remember the day I started calling my mother 'a witch' in English. She got hold of a dictionary and looked up the word *vich*. It wasn't there, so she looked for the word *wich* - that was nowhere to be found either. Then, as she was going through the pages, I noticed the word *Welsh*. I pointed at it and said, "That's the one - pronounced *witch.*"

"Do I look like one of them?" she asked.

"Yes, you do. And behave like them," I told her.

This went on for a few days until one day her brother who knew some English came round. Quite unintentionally, the word easily tripping off my tongue by now when I spoke to my mother, I said "Witch" when I called her in the presence of my uncle, who gave a loud laugh. He must have known what it meant. Smiling, Mother turned back and, looking at her brother, said, "He thinks I look like them." Teasing her, he laughed, "Get a broom and fly!" Now she looked confused; trying to explain, she went on, "He thinks I look like the witch people who come from that part of Britain called Wales." Obviously that caused more laughter. Then my uncle explained to her, "That is Welsh - what you just said. He is calling you witch:

W.I.T.C.H." Paging through the dictionary she found the word, and a second later the dictionary went flying through the air towards me.

I hated my mother for whatever she stood for and I would have moved out of the flat if I could have afforded it. But times were bad: commodities were rationed and had to be obtained through coupons, and only families were allowed them. People living on their own had to obtain everything through the black market and with the money I was earning, that was unthinkable.

Life went on without much happening for almost another four months; Soheila and her two sons were still with us waiting to join Sohrab, who phoned every few weeks promising them their passage to the West would be 'next month'. Then I received another letter from my father which, among other news, gave me the date of his trial; it was now Monday and he was to appear before the court the following Saturday. He asked me not only to be present then, but also to go and see him on the visiting day, Wednesday, before the trial. His court case would probably take about 30 minutes and that included the time taken to get him into the courtroom, put him on the stand and then taken out again. I had seen many trials shown on TV. Usually twenty to thirty drug related convicts were sentenced in a day, in one courtroom alone, half of them to death. For the authorities these people were there merely to be discarded or disposed of, not as though they were fathers, sons, brothers, husbands or someone loved by their kin. Where were the UN's Human Rights Organizations?

On the Tuesday before my father's trial, I told my uncle I wouldn't be attending work for a few days and asked him to inform my family too. Later I phoned them to make sure he had, and at six in the evening I got on the bus bound for Yazd. As before, I arrived there at almost six the next morning. Again, I took my time walking from the station to the prison. Shortly after 9 o'clock the gates opened, the visitors invited in and searched, and again we all followed a sentry across the prison yard, ending up in the same visiting room. Once again I faced my father, seeing him after almost four months. He hadn't changed much: his beard had grown longer but couldn't have gone any whiter. Probably because his court case was close at hand, he looked worried but tried not to show it, forcing himself to smile. He knew as well as I did that this could be one of our last visits; if we couldn't bribe the judge, for some reason, or if the judge accepted the money but didn't keep his promise, then this could well be one of our last visits. Would nature play the right cards this time too, even if my father was hanged?

His girlfriend, Mahin, had been visiting him every Monday (the visiting day for women), travelling to-and-fro between Tehran and Yazd, not missing even one visit while he had been inside and she would be in the courtroom on his trial day.

My father who had learned a lot in the six months

of his captivity from the other prisoners, some of whom had paid three times to escape death, asked me to approach the judge on the same day after his trial, "sometime early in the afternoon when he has finished for the day and retires into his office". That was when he would be expecting to see people in my situation. My father said the judge would give me his price in his own way at which I was supposed to show surprise and exclaim, "As much as that!" - then enter negotiations with him and try to knock the price down. Around 10,000 dollars was what my father thought would probably be the final settlement. Mahin would have the money and before I entered the judge's office she'd hand it to me, because the judge would be asking for his money then; he would not make any promises, but then we had no choice but to rely on whatever hope he might hold out.

My father thought that if he ever got out of that prison (*alive*, I thought) he would sell his villa in the north, buy a shop and would start living an honest life. Drugs didn't pay: when those involved got caught, which they usually did in the end, they had to pay with their lives or, if lucky, with all they had earned; and with too many hands in the business nowadays, it wasn't paying much anymore anyway.

But didn't all say the same thing, I thought, while inside? Many prisoners on drug related charges were in for the second, third or even fourth time! They all repented, and in fact before leaving prison they were obliged to do so, but only a few stayed loyal to their words and certainly my father wasn't in that category. I don't know what his mind was working towards right then, but I'd judge him when he walked free, if he ever did.

The sentry from the end of the corridor shouted, "Time's up!"

"I'll meet you on Saturday then," I said, "and hopefully I'll be seeing you free quite soon after that."

"Once upon a time I gave you life, now my life's in your hands. Save it." He had learned a lot of beautiful sentiments while in prison.

I had learned a few too, through the BBC. "Be it unto me according to thy wish," I answered back.

Once outside I realized that this would be the mission of my life. A shiver went down my spine. I felt as if my own life was at stake.

There was always a limit to anybody's tolerance, and I had reached that limit. Walking through the streets I noted that I was talking to myself and sometimes loudly. It was a habit that had become quite normal among people in the country, and they all blamed the regime for it because it had caused so much anxiety since coming to power; but I had been growing worse over the last six months. I'd start fighting an imaginary adversary in my mind, regardless of my surrounding; I would imagine him (or her) in front of me, and start attacking the person verbally. Today, fighting that imaginary person, I threw a punch into the air. This wasn't abnormal either, especially in Tehran. (I had yet to see if this went on in Yazd too.) In Tehran, every now and then, one would see someone punching and kicking in the air, as if gone mad. The passers-by nowadays didn't take much notice; some just said a prayer and went their way. But I didn't want to end up like that though I knew I was on the way. My sanity was in question, I began to realize, and these three days of waiting would probably do more damage. Once over, I'd go to see a psychiatrist, I decided.

But the problem still remained: how was I going to get through these three days, with all that worry on my mind, feeling like a ton on my back, and stay sane? I thought about running away and leaving my father to the rope. He had lived his life; was 57 and not many people lived to be that old in Tehran or, in fact, any other city in Iran. Only a few living in remote villages lived to be 70, and hardly anyone got to 80 anywhere in the country. And, anyway, didn't everyone die in the end?

I started walking the streets of Yazd; every now and then someone approached me asking if I wanted to buy some opium. "Would you like a Lool, sir?" That was how they were sold, in Lools: thinner but longer than one's finger in shape, 22 grams in weight; the lighter and more yellow, the better the quality. Most people earned their living through dealing in this drug in the city of Yazd, and it was worse in Kerman. Half the fields in these two cities and towns around were apportioned to the cultivation of corn-poppy from which eventually opium was extracted. As long as these people paid their dues to the authorities, in cash or in opium (so I was informed speaking to them), they were left alone - and recently even protected, looked after and provided with good seeds. No wonder America has listed us as a drug-administering country.

In producing opium I have little doubt that we were, if not the first, the second major producer in the world. That figure holds for smoking it as well: almost forty per cent of male adults smoked opium in Tehran; this figure was worse in the north of the country around the Caspian Sea, I was told, because of the humidity there; and still worse, in the cities producing it, Kerman topping the list followed by Yazd. Of the remaining sixty per cent, money, or the lack of it, was the 'problem' that prevented people from buying the drug. Prisons were crowded with addicts, so the law enforcements didn't bother arresting someone just because he was an addict anymore.

The city of Yazd was a boring place, but somehow I managed to get through those three days.

On the Saturday morning. Mahin gave me the 10,000 dollars and I put it in my pocket. We were standing in front of the court building among 50 other people almost all in the same situation. It was 11 o'clock now and we had been waiting since 9 to be called in. My legs were shaking, my heart beating hard, feeling as if it wanted to come out of my mouth. Then we were called in. We entered the building and a sentry inside told us to wait in courtroom number 2 - a small room with a few chairs and a desk in it, quite similar to the one I had seen in Turkey, but under very different circumstances.

A few minutes later my father, handcuffed to a sentry, was brought in. Almost at the same time the judge, a cleric wearing a white turban and a black cloak, entered from another door and placed himself behind the desk. He appeared to be in his early thirties, almost too young for the job, I thought, and quite good looking. I have had enough experience of human nature, however, not to be deceived by appearances, and speculated that on the inside he might well be a monster who had sent hundreds to their deaths with the knowledge that some were not guilty. Who cared? Whether directly or indirectly involved in the case, people had learnt to keep quiet. Khomeini sent almost three million to their deaths in his war against Iraq - a war he started because of the animosity he had towards Saddam. Since then thousands were executed in Iran just because they did not share the views of this 'messenger of God'.

It is perhaps fitting, at this juncture, to inform those mainly Muslims who took to the streets in support of Saddam Hussein in his Gulf war against the Americans - to reveal the true nature of this monster. It is all too easy to justify his action in fighting our country since he was facing an enemy as evil as himself - but did his supporters know that to save his own skin, to be left alone by our side, the Iraqi leader at the time sent 2,000 MKO members back to Iran well aware they faced certain death?

Surely all these massacres could have been stopped, I thought. In the previous regime the Shah of Iran who left the country was responsible for the death of only a few thousand; had he killed half a million he would have kept his throne and saved the lives of three million, mostly youngsters. And that's only on our side: a difference of 2500000 lives, which could have been saved, and the rest of the country from mourning and hardship.

Therefore Mr Secretary General of the UN, don't keep saying that the first step towards a democratically elected government is by way of free elections; you know well this is not the case, or at least in regard to developing countries, no such election would work; look what happened when the people freely elected Khomeini! How could you call him democratic?

In a country where 95% of the people were at the best semi-literate, no such system would work. And by literacy I don't mean qualifications; most of our doctors and engineers didn't take much notice of traffic lights, and in fact while almost 75% of the people in the country could read and write properly, since leaving school they never bothered to read a page, causing their intellect to waste away. I can call to mind a good example to illustrate this: not long ago, following the spread of rumours over a few days, people were going up to their roofs in the belief that they could see Khomeini's visage on the face of the full moon! For the next two weeks this became the talk of the town, everyone having apparently seen this extraordinary event created by a divine supernatural power! Certainly this was reported by most of the customers at the shop. Some, the educated ones, even blamed America for having projected the image on the surface of the moon! An American backed regime, backed by the CIA, they claimed, would go to any lengths to keep Khomeini in power. Now, could anyone with a sound mind say that these people would elect the right government? They say your eyes are the doors to your brain, but it appears, somehow, it worked the other way round for us people (me included recently), especially when trying to give one a bad name or vice versa, praising the individual.

An audience of this calibre is fair game to the mullahs (clerics as they are called in Iran), expert rabble-rousers and masters of eloquence, and those gifted in the art of ranting, who were riding high. They say 'no dream lasts forever'; but this has been going on for a while now, and if their wrongdoing and cruelty lasted throughout my life, then wouldn't that mean forever - at least so far as I was concerned?

Back to the courtroom: a man was fighting for his life there, but that devil of a judge looked as if he had come to give his opinion on somebody's haircut.

Handcuffs removed, my father was made to stand in front of the desk, about a metre away from it, his back to us.

"What is your name?" the judge asked my father. On receiving the answer, he opened his briefcase, took a file out and put it on his desk, pushed the briefcase to the side and opened the file. Then he said, "You have been caught with 9 kilos of opium hidden in the petrol tank of your car..." With a mocking smile he looked at my father and carried on: "...and you are pleading not guilty." After a short pause he glanced back at his file and continued, "The charges against you are: in possession, carrying and with the intention to sell 9 kilos of opium - three charges. Have you got anything to say?"

Even I, who wasn't directly involved in the case, felt my brain freeze with fear - so how could a man in my father's situation be expected to defend himself? He needed someone to represent him, I thought. But that wasn't allowed, even though a man's life was at stake. Was this another card played correctly by nature? I cursed all human rights organizations again. Where were they now when most needed? I had only one guess: fixing oil prices between Khomeini and the CIA.

Somehow my father managed to answer: "The day before I was caught there was something wrong with my car so I took it to the garage to have it checked; someone there must have placed the opium in my car..." He went on in an attempt to explain what he believed must have happened. "The man placing the drugs no doubt chose my car because it had a number plate belonging to Tehran - they do that to make sure the owner is a stranger so would leave the city. Following it, once the car had passed through the checkpoints, he would try to steal the car to recover his load." Such things have happened. In fact, not long ago, four people were tried in front of cameras, shown on TV, for using a showroom car for the same purpose. The four accused had stashed opium in their own car, then offered it for sale at a garage, where it was displayed in a showroom at a price well below its value to attract a buyer visiting from Tehran. A car bought in this way, once through the checkpoints, was stolen by the original owner; and if stealing the car proved difficult to achieve, the smugglers still had the address of the buyer - so the four sent someone to approach the new owner, pretending interest in the car, offering him a much higher price than it was worth. They confessed to have sold many cars with opium, and sometimes heroin, stashed in them, and one way or another they always managed to get most of the cars back with their hidden payloads. In the few cars where the stashed drugs were discovered, the unfortunate buyers were innocently hanged.

My father tried hard to show that he had fallen prey to such mischievous behaviour, but it was obvious to the judge that in his case it was an attempt to shift the blame from oneself to others.

Cutting him short, the judge said, "I'm afraid, I don't think you are telling the truth." He looked at the open file on his desk and went on, "After a careful examination of your case and weighing the evidence against you, I'm left with no choice but to find you guilty." Found guilty, I thought with disbelief, so easily! A mere 15 minutes had constituted a 'careful examination' of my father's case. "Ridiculous!" I wanted to shout at that bastard. The judge gave me a glance as if he had heard my unspoken outburst, then, turning his eyes back to my father, carried on, "As you probably know, anybody found guilty in possession of five kilos of opium or more will receive a mandatory death sentence." His last two words almost caused my bowels to empty! Now looking really 'turned on' by his position of power - power to take somebody's life away at a whim - he permitted a faint grin of satisfaction to touch his face. The devil, the traces of his amputated horns hidden under the turban, stated clinically, "You have been caught with 9 kilos of opium, almost twice the limit...' Oh, how this monster savoured the moment and wished he could have hanged my father twice, I thought! He continued: "And you were found guilty against the said charges, mainly, as I mentioned earlier: in possession, carrying and with the intention to sell 9 kilos of opium. Therefore I am left with no option but to give you the same sentence...'

I could see my father wasn't listening anymore. The atmosphere of the courtroom was thick with fear. My chair started shaking and I felt numb all over. Mahin, next to me, was almost unconscious. Now, leaning on his desk, looking as if he was trying to get closer to my father, his eyes wide open staring at the victim, he was clearly enjoying playing the role of God towards the man standing in front of him. With a full grin, he said, "...you will be hanged by the neck until dead." This was final since prisoners were not usually allowed appeals.

"The sentence will be carried out within the next week," he informed my father, and delivered a Parthenon shot: "God have mercy on your soul."

I couldn't help recalling that it wasn't 9 but 14 kilos which my father had attempted to smuggle - which left 5 kilos unaccounted for. Given time and the freedom to ask questions, I knew I could find a very reasonable explanation for this missing lot. But as everyone knew, the answer was already there: the missing quantity of opium had been sold and the money almost certainly had found its way into the bank accounts of these rulers of this branch of law. So you are no better than my father, Mr Judge, I thought - the main charge against him (one, 'with the intention to sell'), applied to you as well, if you haven't already sold the missing 5 kilos. Therefore instead of one, have two ropes ready, Mr Devil, because, as you just said, 5 kilos, the missing amount from my father's lot, carried a mandatory death sentence. But then again, I suppose, such sentences didn't apply to the sons of God.

My father, back in handcuffs, was taken away and the Judge, returning the file to his briefcase, left through the same door he had come in. I sat there staring at the floor and feeling almost unable to move. Not long after another old man was brought in and the same judge entering, took his seat behind the same desk again. The old man was in for 2 kilos of opium and got 5 years for it. On receiving the verdict the brave old man, moving his hands, said, "Do you think your regime will last that long? I doubt it." Anyone who dared to make such a remark faced a death penalty or at least life imprisonment, but this judge seemed to be lenient. Writing something in the old man's file, he turned back and said to him, "I've put down a '1' in front of that '5' I've just given you and made it 15 years." The old man answered, "Make it 20, you are not going to last long..." The judge, cutting him short, shouted to the sentry: "Take him away before I send him to the gallows!"

This judge was of a lenient disposition - a good sign, I thought. It meant I could probably come to some sort of a settlement with him over my father.

My hopes were uplifted when about an hour later I was allowed to see my father just before he was due to be taken back to the main prison.

"The judge's name is Zargar," my father said, his spirits having become a little more buoyant. "He could be bought and we can rely on his words. Try to see him today."

At three o'clock that afternoon I entered Zargar's office for the greatest mission of my life. I was scared and cursed myself again for being a coward. He was behind his desk writing. I stood by the door waiting for his permission to advance. He gave me a glance and motioned me forward to sit down. I placed myself on the chair in front of his desk and waited again. He finished writing, closed the file in front of him and said, "Yes?"

"Good afternoon sir," I said. "You sentenced my father to death this morning. I have come to beg leniency on his behalf in any possible way."

"I'm afraid the sentence has been passed and there is nothing anyone can do to change the verdict." He looked at me sternly. "And if you are thinking of some dishonest way to alter the course of justice, it is not going to work; try it and you'll end up next to your father. Some of us you may find have loose values, treading on their pride, taking money, but let me tell you that I'm not the type to do so. I'm an honest person - I take my responsibility and my job seriously and in the eyes of God I will do nothing to undermine my integrity. Do you get the message? If not, then there's something wrong with you!" After a short pause, looking as if weighing my own integrity, he carried on, "In plain language, and for the last time, I can tell you that nothing can get your father off that rope, not even 15,000 dollars."

That, I presumed, was his price, but, as I had been told, may be subject to negotiation. Swiftly, acting on what my father had taught me, feigning surprise, I said, "As much as *that*?"

"How much did you think would get him off that rope, then?" he responded.

"It's his first offence, so I thought that about 5,000 would be enough."

Leaning forward on his desk, he said, "What are you talking about! Who said you can propose a bribe? Didn't I just tell you what would happen if you tried it?"

"This is not a bribe, sir," I said, "just a gift I felt was not out of place as an offering for the services you are rendering our country, and which in some ways may help my father too."

"5,000 dollars isn't enough," he said and went on to explain, "There are others I have to share this money with in order to get your father off that rope. No, I am an honest and responsible judge and 12,000 is the lowest I can go."

He was probably right about sharing the money with a few others, but a great portion of it went into his own pocket, of that I had no doubt. "Ten thousand is the highest I can go," I said, then got the money out of my pocket, in one bundle, all in one hundred dollar notes, and put it on the desk in front of him. I tapped my pockets, showing him I had no more.

That conjured up instant greed, as I had intended. A grin crinkled his face as he looked, fascinated, at the money. I suppose the sight of money always had the power to turn these people on, but by far the most exciting subject for these mullahs were women. He almost snatched the money, not able to stop himself, then got my father's file out of his briefcase, put it on the desk, opened it, got his pen out, and said, "Let me see; he has been caught with..." He wrote something in the file, simply changing the figure, reducing it to one-tenth by adding a zero in front of it, modifying the sentence as follows: "...0.9 kilo of opium, first time in, that carries a year imprisonment. He has done 5 months, so he will be out in 7 months' time." Grinning, he closed the file and replaced it in his briefcase.

Outside, a few minutes later, I jumped in the air: it was over! I had done my job! Now if the judge didn't keep his side of the bargain, which I found unlikely, there was nothing I could do until afterwards - and that I would decide accordingly when the time came. But for the time being, what had to be done had been done. I felt as if a lifelong burden had been lifted from my shoulders.

Now it was time to leave Yazd. Though I had to come back on Wednesday again and report the full story to my father, if he was still on the planet by then, the city had considerably bored me; I had stayed there for four days and it felt like a lifetime.

Back at home everything was in order, so it seemed. As always, Sepideh, book in hand, was reading poetry. Soheila was still waiting to join her husband; her older son was still at school, the younger one, 3-year-old Hoorash, showing every sign of bravery even at that young age, and mum in the kitchen cooking.

chapter fifteen

DURING MY ABSENCE, Soheila explained, a young man of normal appearance and holding a good job, introduced by a relative, had come to meet Sepideh - and on seeing her had offered to marry her if she was agreeable to the proposal. Accordingly, after talking to the young man in private, which was quite customary in the country, in one of the bedrooms and, of course, with the door left open, Sepideh, too, had found the man very pleasant and acceptable. But mum, forever jealous and suspicious, had kicked him out! This was the third person she had treated in this way within the last year. At the age of 55, looking almost 60, only 5 feet tall and quite ugly, she was no oil painting and it's a mystery to me why my father married her in the first place. Mum was in effect comparing herself with Sepideh - a young girl of 21, light brown hair down to her waist, 5'8" tall, with a very nice figure and quite pretty.

In hearing this I almost went berserk! The witch had

to be stopped! In a country where girls over the age of thirty could barely find themselves husbands, first because they were considered too old, and second due to the stringent financial condition that gripped the country, not many could afford to get married, with the result that many females reached their thirties unmarried, ultimately being turned loose in the streets, and at a time when all the pleasures had been stopped by the regime, the only one left being through marriage. The witch in effect was trying to withhold happiness and the attainment of a fulfilled life from her own daughter.

Yes, the witch had to be stopped! Provoking Sepideh, a few days later, through my prompting, she got hold of a glass and, regardless of the consequences, flung it at mum. It hit her in the face and gave her an inch-long cut under the right eye. Did it work? Judge for yourself: about four months later Sepideh became engaged.

The next Tuesday I got on the bus, destination Yazd. For the last few days I'd been living in a state of uneasiness: every time the phone rang I was expecting news of my father's hanging. Like the last few times I arrived in Yazd early in the morning and again started walking towards prison. Surely they would have informed us if he had been hanged, I kept telling myself, fighting despair. At the prison gate I gave my father's name, stuttering on the first letter, and when they told me to enter, I realized, taking a deep breath, he was still alive!

Thankfully, therefore, Judge Zargar had kept his word! A man loyal to his promises will soon find himself in a better position. This aphorism certainly worked concerning Zargar! Not long after Khomeini died and Khamèneh'E was appointed his successor, finding Zargar a man loyal to his promises, the new leader accepted the offer of his daughter's hand and as a result Zargar found himself in a 'better position'. In fact, at the time of writing these notes, Khamèneh'E is still the current leader and Zargar, his son-in-law, is second only to the chief of judiciary in the justice ministry. I wondered if I went to the new leader now and told him about that 10,000 dollars I had paid Zargar over a decade ago, what his reaction would be!

In the same visiting room, facing my father, I smiled, "So you're still around!"

"This is my second life," he said, returning my smile.

I didn't know he watched James Bond movies. "And believe me," I said, "you will live only twice and a short second one at that, if you don't learn your lesson while here." I did not realise then that in about four years' time these words would prove to be only too true.

He had been informed of the change in the verdict; one of the sentries had told him, but he wanted to know the full story. I explained everything to him, ending with the words, "...and in seven months' time you'll be out." The time would go very fast because days in prison pass much quicker than the ones outside - I knew that from my own experience; I thought of telling him this, but didn't, because then he would want to know how I knew. "And we'd better keep the whole thing a secret because of the disgrace it'll bring on the family," I advised. "And if anybody asks," I said, "I'll tell them you've gone to Pakistan."

Then I mentioned a subject that had been going through my mind ever since I realized he wouldn't be out for another seven months. I earnestly wanted to have the use of his summer house in the north to live a few quiet months away from everything around me, but I had to bring the subject up diplomatically, in a way that would not give him the idea that once I got inside I wouldn't get out. Therefore, quite casually, pretending the thought had just crossed my mind, I inquired about the place, adding, "And if it is not occupied, why not let me stay there until you came out?"

Two days later, quitting my job at the shop, I settled myself in my father's summer house. The house was located in the forest, about 500 metres from the sea and quite close to where I had my near-fatal encounter with the rope - a distance of some 30 km. In fact, the minibus that took me to my new locale passed through the very place; but then again, even had I walked the streets there in broad daylight, no one there would recognize me, since in the last six months I had aged more than ten years: my beard had turned white and my hair in the front was thinning.

The house was extensive with three large bedrooms, quite a big kitchen, two showers, a sizable sitting room, all fully furnished. It stood in the middle of a colossal garden which was fenced all around. All the windows in the house were protected by heavily lattice-like iron bars. With the lack of security at nights and sometimes even during the day this seemed quite essential. The nearest neighbouring house was about a couple of hundred metres away, and empty, since the owner lived in Tehran. In fact, most of these sporadically dispersed villas in the north of Iran were owned by people living in cities and were used only on holidays.

I settled myself in one of the two bedrooms facing the forest, the other bedroom and the kitchen facing the sea. The plan of the house was a rectangle, the three bedrooms situated at three of the corners, the kitchen occupying the fourth corner. These were separated from each other by the sitting room like a thick plus sign in the middle. From my bedroom window, on a clear day, I could see three to four mountain rangers, all covered with forest.

A couple of days later I bought a few rabbits, a couple of ducks and some chickens from a village nearby. I was planning to live on the meat provided by rabbits, eggs from the chickens and ducks, and vegetables from the garden; fruits of all kinds - oranges, apples, tangerines, lemons, persimmons, pomegranates, grapes and figs - were in abundance on the trees. To make a hutch for the rabbits, it took me almost a whole day to dig a hole two metres long, a metre wide and as deep in the garden; then, making walls of brick with concrete at the sides and bottom of the hole, I filled it up again. Now, if the rabbits dug down they would encounter these hard walls, thwarting any attempt to escape; but at the same time they could still live underground as they naturally did so, in burrows. Then I fenced the area, waist high, and covered the top with a metal plate. During this period of construction I kept the rabbits in a box and when I went to get them to place them in their new home they had doubled! I made a small run for the chickens and the ducks as well; no digging needed there, just a fence round the area and something on the top. They were laying almost five eggs a day.

Apart from the first few scary nights, waking up at any sound, the days went by quietly and I began to enjoy every moment of life in the beautiful surroundings. How I wished there was a planet like that with me the only human occupant! Living in such a peaceful environment, I felt relaxed - only too well aware that this heavenly interlude would come to an end shortly, when my father was released from prison. From Tehran, one of the most polluted cities in the world, I had come to live in a place where hardly any fumes existed. My lungs felt refreshed, as if I had emerged from a swamp and washed myself clean. I could train and work much harder now. The food was plentiful too: having almost one rabbit a day, I wondered if I would develop long ears and front teeth with an insatiable appetite for carrots!

Whenever I didn't have anything to do I went for a walk in the forest, but only in the daylight. Any other time it was dangerous, for the place was full of wild boars. During my stay there I saw quite a few of them, much bigger than the ones I had seen on TV programmes filmed in Africa, and almost always with their piglets. One would never imagine a piglet as small as the ones I had seen in such programmes could grow to become a fearsome creature that claimed quite a few lives in the north of Iran every year. Twice during my daylight walks I had to climb a tree to stay safe from some boar charges. These animals, I realized, had a very keen sense of smell; from 100 metres away they could smell one's presence, even if one were to hide behind a tree.

Some evenings it was pleasant walking at the seaside with no one around. I would enjoy just sitting on the beach, watching the spectacular sunset - an orange ball, the biggest I had ever seen, sinking into the blue sea. Then I would take the narrow dirt road back to the villa.

After such an idyllic day I would sit down to a cup of tea while listening to the BBC. Knitting my carpet, painting or doing some carpentry kept me occupied too. Soon it would be time to sleep; tomorrow would be another sublime day.

Up early in the mornings, I let the chickens and ducks out; entering the cage I would collect the eggs. Invariably, it seemed, my breakfast was always provided.

Ever since the country became embroiled in war, Mahin, who had stayed in the villa on a few occasions and, like most people, felt uncertain about the future, had stockpiled all kinds of foodstuff; a big freezer loaded with butter, bread, cheese, and almost everything that could be frozen. In another part of the kitchen she had stored almost a quarter ton of dried fruits. The nearest village which was about a kilometre away, provided my milk, a drink I couldn't go without. But recently going there to buy this milk I got to know some of the villagers and that was beginning to cause problems. They gossiped and you were expected to confirm their gossip, to the effect that the shopkeeper had the best milk and the next door neighbour put water in his. If you didn't nod your head in agreement he would show a bad face and probably no milk would be available to you the next time round; on the other hand, confirming such a gossip, you would soon find out he had told the neighbour that you thought he put water in his milk. Once I didn't go along with one of them gossiping and when he showed anger I went straight to the neighbour and told him exactly what he had told me about his daughter: "She is not virgin!" A few minutes later two groups, armed with sticks and stones, started fighting each other. I had to keep away from the village for a week. In this village of 70 families, though they were almost all married to close relations, there was at least one fight a month caused by gossip. It all resulted from the lack of entertainment or means of recreation, as I understood; people didn't have anything to do so they either gossiped or picked fights with one another.

There were problems in connection with the area too. The cities around the Caspian Sea once constituted the most popular tourist attraction in the country, but now after the revolution they have been the worst hit; women were not allowed to swim and men, once out of the water, had to cover themselves quickly. The people that populated this area didn't know what communism was all about, but were nevertheless influenced by Russia (at the time still a communist country) since it was so close, just the other side of the Caspian Sea. It was perhaps not surprising therefore that they should have shown a lot of sympathy towards that regime. By supporting the revolution, to start with, they expected to be allowed to break free and have their own communist state - but they couldn't have had it more wrong; the government, finding out about their intentions towards secessionism, has since maintained a very close watch over these people which has taken a severe toll on them: more than anywhere else in the country, they have been forced to send their youngsters to war and therefore they scored the highest casualty in the land. Almost two out of three families had a black flag hanging outside their houses above the entrance door - the sign that one of their family members had been martyred. They definitely didn't like the regime ruling the country and quite often talked about it openly. But then again if they said anything against the regime it was alright, yet on my side it would be all over the village the next day and I would be earmarked as a counter revolutionary and not looked upon favourably. God knows these people deserved what they got, if not worse.

chapter sixteen

I HAD A VERY VIVID DREAM at the villa one night. In my dream I was woken by a high-pitched humming type of sound one hears when a mosquito approaches one's ear. It was coming from the forest side of the house. Going to the window, pulling the curtains aside, looking for its source, I found it; with my eyes and mouth wide open, I saw this flying machine, about 10 to 20 metres above the ground just over the edge of the garden. I stood there looking at it, transfixed, thinking that at last someone had come to take me to a distant desired planet. The craft was like the ones I had seen in movies and quite often in cartoons: an upside-down saucer with a very thick rim at the top, and a domed roof on top of that. Leaving my bedroom I went outside to have a better look; it was a silvery colour, a faint orange light coming from its underside. A row of brightly lit windows encircled the rim and behind one of these windows I saw two people looking down at me.

Scared, but trying to show bravery, I went closer, keeping calm. At this point I have to mention that most of the details of this dream came to me not at the time, but days after. Then the craft descended to a height of about five metres. A hole opened at its bottom and the orange light was replaced by a white bright light while a telescopic ladder came down through this hole.

I began to panic, but, I thought, they were intelligent, and if I kept calm, they wouldn't harm me; I was willing to go with them, wherever - wouldn't it be nice to see other planets, a chance of a lifetime! I went to this ladder and climbed up, using my hands only with no help from my legs. I wanted to show them that I was strong and they'd better not risk trying to hurt me. Once inside I saw six people all wearing tight shiny silver coloured uniforms that covered their heads as well but not their faces, which were round, each with a small circular hole in place of the mouth, with two big and beautiful transparent eyes cornered at the sides and round on the inside. They had neither eyebrows nor noses; and where the ears were supposed to be, the head cover had bulged out a bit, so I concluded they had some kind of ears. They all had the same skin-colour, white, and almost all of them were of the same height, a little bit shorter than me, apart from one who was shorter than the rest and had a big bulging chest - a female, I thought, and the rest males.

"Correct," I sensed rather than heard one of them say, who pointed with his four-fingered hand, also covered by the same uniform, towards her. He carried on, "She is the only woman on this ship." I was amazed! They could read my mind and spoke, if I could call it that, without sound; as they were all standing close to each other, only when moving his hand I guessed who was talking; there were no mouth movements either, but still the words were actual and somehow put into my head. How did he do it? Later when I asked him, he explained that brainwaves could be transferred from one person to another, and as I wasn't that advanced I couldn't control my brainwaves and therefore anything I thought about was picked up by them. *I'd better not think naughty thoughts, especially about that female*, I told myself, *otherwise they will pick that up too*; then I heard, or rather, felt them laughing.

The only female in the ship came forward, took my hand and put it on her bulging chest. It felt unspeakably soft, very pleasant to the touch, but in front of all these occupants, embarrassed, I pulled my hand away; they laughed again.

The ship was much bigger inside than it looked from outside. I made out the diameter of its interior to be about ten metres. Instruments with flashing lights of all colours in the shape of small squares on their screens were to be seen around. There were six armchairs, all of the same white colour, one at the centre of the floor, and the remaining five positioned in front of these instruments at intervals of about two metres (each with one thick cylindrical leg, thin in the middle and symmetrically thickening to the ends, fixed to the floor) until it came to a part of the ship where there was nothing but a flight of steps going up. With the railing on the left, the right side ended on the wall; if the left hand were to be kept on this railing going up, one came to a landing about less than a metre wide, going round half the ship in an anti-clockwise direction, and with one's left hand still on the railing, rectangular-shaped windows would be seen on the right. Looking further up I noticed the ceiling wasn't domed inside, unlike the way it looked from the outside; it was flat and I guessed its height to be about four metres from the floor. The place was bright with a white light that emanated from the walls; somehow they were glowing, yet I didn't understand how. Then, apart from the one who had talked and later introduced himself as the captain of the ship, they all went back to their seats in front of the instruments and started pressing what looked like light squares in some kind of combinations.

They asked me if I had any questions. Not all that familiar with the subject of space or space travel - I had seen a couple of movies on UFOs and aliens and heard a few lines on the radio about them, but apart from that I was ignorant of the subject - only a few preliminary questions came to mind.

"Where do you come from?" I asked.

"A system 25 of your light years away," one of them answered.

"How did you cover this vast distance to get here?"

"There are time-location tunnels everywhere in the universe, cutting distances short. Entering the tunnel leading to your system, then leaving it at the right time, we came close, within a few light seconds, to your system at the right date."

I said, "I understand when you refer to our light years and seconds, but what do you mean by the right date?"

He began, "It is too complicated...", and stopped.

Did that mean they could enter our planet in the past or future, any year they wanted to? I thought this but never received an answer. Then I asked, "How come your ship looks bigger inside than seen from the outside?"

He answered, "An extra dimension is added to it."

When I showed puzzlement and began to question how, he cut me short and I stopped involuntarily. Then I suppose, trying to change the subject, he asked, "Do you want me to turn the gravity of the ship down a bit? Because I know this is more than you are used to on the earth."

In fact, since entering the ship and trying to move, I had found myself feeling heavy and had attributed the cause to some other reasons than gravity, which I knew was almost the same everywhere on the surface of the planet within the atmosphere. "No, I quite like it. This is like exercising," I answered. To them this gravity appeared normal; they walked in style and erect without showing any difficulty. "So you must come from a planet heavier than ours?" I ventured.

"Yes, almost twice the size," one of them said.

Then, by way of telling me why they were there and

why they could not take me with them, he asked the female of the ship to come forward; talking to me, he said, "Would you take her to your house and show her around? She is with us to carry out a few experiments and will do so there while we carry on here."

"By all means," I answered. We went down the ladder, this time with me using my legs as well. Down on the ground I felt lighter while taking the first few steps; she on the other hand was almost jumping in the air walking; our gravity seemed too low for her. We entered the villa and she went to my bedroom while I followed her. Was she going to start her round from there, I wondered? No answer, only a smile that I felt rather than saw appear on her face. I turned the light on and she turned it off. The curtains were pulled back and the light from the craft, now dim, still shone through the window. I could make out a few things, though not clearly. Then she came to me, put her hands round my waist. I did the same, as though my willpower had been drained from me, and we held each other. She came up to my chin and she felt indescribably lovely. I bent down and kissed her face. It was much softer and more pleasant than any earthly face I had ever kissed. Her breasts felt full, pressed against my body. Now my eyes had become accustomed to the dark; I pushed her head cover back and noticed that she was totally bald, yet somehow it suited that round face and those striking eyes. Looking at her ears, they, too, were like two pieces of fat sticking to the sides of her head. Freeing herself, she took a step back, then through an opening of her suit at the neck, she pulled back a short zip on her right shoulder which now showed through her suit. Then she started to remove her suit, or uniform, asking me to do the same - in other words, to get naked and I was totally subservient to her will.

As she was undressing I noticed that she had only one breast across her chest with only one nipple, on her right side; there was no belly button either. We were both naked, and I saw that she didn't have a strand of hair on her whole body - unlike me, who was covered with it. I looked between her legs: instead of the usual slit that an earthly woman possessed there, she had a hole, and where I could only just see it. Was that her anus or her private part, I thought? "My private part," she brainwaved to me. "It looks quite different from the ones I have seen," I brainwaved back. "You'll find mine more pleasing," she expressed through thought. Then, extending her hands, I took them; she had four fingers to a hand and somehow the arrangements seemed different - instead of a little finger she had another thumb and where the middle finger was supposed to be there was an empty space, all with more joints; and when she held me, her grip was much stronger than mine. There were no nails on any of the fingers. Never mind the fingers, I thought as I pulled her towards me and we clung together, now both naked. It was the softest and most pleasant body I had ever held. I was about to come, just holding her. We went to bed: rolling over one another, she took hold of my erect penis, held it in front of that hole between her legs and asked me to push it in. I entered, and it was exquisite, nothing like I had ever felt before - better, in fact, than the first time I ever made love in my life at the age of 15 to a woman of 28, which until then I always thought was the best I had ever experienced. Every single cell in my body was enjoying this and it didn't take long before I came. Surprisingly my penis staying erect, still inside her, and a minute later, so it seemed, I came again. All settled, this time she made me pull out; almost feeling paralysed, not able to move, I fell asleep.

When I woke up in the morning I found myself naked, an unusual way for me to sleep, and when I tried to move, my right foot was hurting. During the night, in my dream, I remembered, for some reason, going outside; before climbing down the four steps from the balcony to the garden, my foot had contacted a flower pot which fell onto a paved path in the garden and broke. But that was in my dream and so there was surely no cause for my foot to hurt! I put on my pants, shorts and t-shirt, the way I usually did, and went outside to investigate. There was a broken flower pot on the paved path in the garden. My first guess was that I must have been sleepwalking the night before. Picking up the broken pieces of the flower pot, I concluded that I had had a very pleasant dream. But the pleasure didn't last long. Back inside, I hadn't finished my breakfast before I started to vomit and feel giddy, like the way one's head feels after drinking too much alcohol - though I hadn't had a drop of the liquid for weeks. I stayed like this for almost the whole day and going to bed at night I was still giddy and confused. The early part of the next day I did not feel as bad as the day before, then gradually I started to feel better.

A few days later, when bits and pieces of this dream came back to my mind, I began to think that, perhaps after all, it wasn't just a dream.

Weeks went by and walking in the forest one day I met a strange looking old man who seemed to be wandering aimlessly around. He was shorter than me, of medium build, with sea blue eyes. He wore a long dark cloak, his white thick hair plaited at the back down to his waist, and in the front a long white beard covered his chest. Looking at me he smiled. To show him respect due to his age, I said, "Hello."

The old man returned my greeting. Then coming closer, I noticed he was carrying a large sized copy of the Koran in his hand.

In need of someone's company and finding him a learned old man, not a religious fanatic, I invited him to my place. Over a cup of tea he told me that he lived in the mountains and spent most nights in caves. At least we had one adventurer in the country, I thought. He talked of caves with drawings on the walls inside them. I had no doubt he spoke the truth since, as I guessed, there were many of them around the country waiting to be discovered. But by whom? In a third world country like Iran, who cared about caves with drawings inside them? As the saying goes: 'We wait for the British and Americans to come to discover our caves and conquer our summits.'

Then our conversation took a different turn and we started talking about the stars. With hardly any artificial lights around, he was right, the place was ideal for astronomy. He told me about other worlds with creatures much more intelligent than us on them. Then he opened his copy of the Koran and showed me a verse saying there were another 18,000 inhabited earths in our own galaxy alone. I knew the Koran was full of amazing revelations, but for someone to have thought of other worlds, and that 1400 years ago, was more than amazing. The old mad made me think of my dream, or whatever it was that had happened. I found the old man's company interesting; he stayed with me for over an hour, and before leaving, from the pouch he had hanging from the rope round his waist, he took a handful of fresh leaves and, giving them to me, said, "Though looking healthy and athletic" (pointing at the weights I had in the room on the floor before carrying on) "at a very young age a bad sickness has left you with almost no immune system; so if you ever get real bad, take a few of these leaves and it'll cure you." At the age of three cholera had indeed left me with a very weak immune system so that even a small cold kept me in bed for over a week. At the time the doctors had told my parents not to expect their son to live, so they had prayed and promised God that if I ever pulled through alive they would give five bottles of milk away to the poor every year. Surprisingly I recovered and since then mum hasn't missed a single year in which she gave five bottles of milk away. But how did this cave man know about that? However, just to show respect for his beliefs, I got an envelope and put the leaves in it. "I will definitely remember that," I said. Then he left, never to be seen again.

Not long afterwards, one day, I was down with a cold, as usual accompanied with a bad headache, runny nose, pain all over my body, unable to move, trying to get my hands on anything that would help ease my suffering apart from man-made medicines which I never took. (I usually had some fruit and that hardly ever did any good.) Then I remembered the leaves the old man had given me; they had become quite dried out by now, but I got two slices of bread and put a few of the leaves between them, and started eating it like a sandwich. I couldn't believe the effect this had on me! Ten minutes later the cold was gone, and five minutes after that I was running about. In fact for the next four years I didn't suffer a cold, and that was at a time when I used to go down with one cold every six months. My cold cured, I felt one of the biggest problems of my life had been shifted out of my way.

A few years later, soon after being sent back from Japan and going to the north by the Caspian Sea, I looked for the old man. I asked the locals who knew of him, some calling him the mad old man; he had been seen sometimes, some said, at a distance of 500km away. I remained in the forest for two more days but I never saw him.

Months went by pleasantly enough, until one day, sitting on the balcony in the back garden, looking at the forest, I heard footsteps approaching from behind; turning, I saw my father there. He had been released from prison a few days earlier. Relieved and happy to be free, he had come to sell the villa and, with the money thus obtained, planned to start a new business venture as well as embark on a new and honest life. He looked positive and determined. Obviously the life in prison had taught him a good lesson. Or had it? In about three years' time I was to find out my expectations were wrong.

chapter seventeen

AFTER SEVEN MONTHS of peaceful living in my father's holiday home where I had enjoyed every day of my sojourn, it was time to leave my little haven. I packed my belongings, which didn't amount to much, and put them into my father's new car. His Peugeot had been confiscated, so he had bought himself a Hillman. On the way back, sad and quiet, my eyes filled with tears. I didn't want to leave.

When we got to Tehran, with nowhere else to go, I asked to be dropped at the same old place where I had been staying seven months earlier with the rest of my family. Entering the flat, they were all there, almost on the very spots where I had left them. I felt like a pawn taken back to the same square on the chessboard, the rest of the pawns having been moved only slightly - though there would be a lot of moves soon to come.

Going to see my uncle the next day, I started working back at his shop; I felt stultified by the old hated surroundings. While going through the same routine and engaged, one day, during some busy training at the shop, my father walked in. I hadn't seen him for almost a month by then, not since the day he drove me back from the north. Looking prosperous and happy in a three-piece tailor-made suit, he informed us that he had sold his villa in the north. He had got 15,000 dollars for it, a high price at the time, I thought; the good old lad that he was, he generously gave me 2,000 dollars, stayed for a cup of tea, then left.

Since I was thinking of leaving the country for Japan, this money was of a great help. With it, a few days later, after standing in the queue for two days and nights, sleeping on the pavement, I managed to buy myself an air ticket, destination Tokyo. It looked as if everyone in the country was leaving for Japan. Outside travel agencies' queues stretched for miles. Taxi drivers, shopkeepers, bankers, bakers, factory workers, almost everyone in the streets, talked about Japan, where foreign workers were in demand and the pay was unbelievably good - so they all had heard. I looked forward to this trip, and if things went according to plan, no hindrances or cancellations, I would be flying a week after Sepideh's wedding, which was in three weeks' time.

Meanwhile, Soheila, too, had received the necessary papers from her husband Sohrab to obtain her visa to enter America. But since there was no American embassy in Iran, she was flying to Greece first, where

Sohrab would join them, coming over from America - something necessary if they wanted things done fast. He would try to secure this visa for his family at the American embassy there, in Athens.

Did it all work out for them? At the time of writing these notes, couple of decades later, I am pleased to say Sohrab, Soheila and their two sons have been living together happily in the state of California. They phone me every now and then asking me to join them. I've tried many times to do so, having tried to obtain my visa through American embassies in different countries, but without success. In fact, I tried my luck in Japan too: though armed with an invitation letter sent to me by Sohrab addressed to the embassy stating he would pay for all my expenses and guaranteeing my departure at the end of my visa, they still refused me.

At last Sepideh's wedding day arrived; a number of guests were invited and a great big cake ordered. Her husband to-be, a young man of 25, tall and quite handsome, seemed to be of a good nature too. Sepideh to all appearances had been lucky: the man drove his own car and had a place of his own; wedding over, they'd be moving to his place.

Oh darling Sepideh, how could things go so wrong! Even now, after all these years as I try to write about that wedding day, my eyes are filled with tears and I don't want to remember.

That day, Sepideh, like the rest of us, arose early to have a shower, usually taking 10 to 15 minutes to have one; this time it took her almost twice as long, and Soheila knocked on the bathroom door asking her to hurry for we were all waiting to have showers too. When she got no answer, she knocked again, this time louder. No answer again. Now worried, we all gathered behind the bathroom door. I pushed them away and knocked. Nothing - only the sound of the shower running; so I kicked the door open and went in. Sepideh was lying on the floor unconscious and the freezing cold water from the shower was pouring down on her.

I turned the shower off and asked for a blanket. Mum and Soheila were screaming behind the door. Clearly they were not in a position to help, but Hoorash, who had proved himself many times to have been born brave, gave me a blanket. I wrapped Sepideh in the blanket, picked her up in my arms, and rushed downstairs. In the street outside a friend was driving by; I stopped him, lay Sepideh down on the back seat of his car and asked him to rush her to the nearest hospital. With all the ambulances sent to the war zones, this was the only way to get patients to hospitals for emergency treatment.

My guess was that the sudden rush of cold water from the shower on her body had caused her to suffer a heart attack. The bathroom shower system, all fixed to the wall, consisted of two parts: the shower on the top, the tap at waist height. A lever in the middle, pushed up and down, changed the supply from the bath to the shower. Many times I had entered the bathroom, not noticing I had the lever on the shower, and turning the water on, it came pouring down, cold as it was to start with; standing underneath it, it took the breath out of me. And also I remembered that recently Sepideh had been complaining about the difficulty she was facing with her breathing in the mornings.

About twenty minutes later we reached one of the best hospitals in the country. At the entrance a nurse with a stretcher, taking her time, came forward and I put Sepideh on it, still unconscious. Now they wouldn't do anything unless I left a 100-dollars deposit at the reception. Then it took them almost ten minutes to call Sepideh a doctor; and this was one of the best hospitals in the country! Complaining wouldn't work; the answer as usual would be: 'Priority is given to war casualties, those who have been fighting for Islam, not to ordinary people.' Islam was a defending and attacking tool in the hands of not only the people in authority, but in the hands of anyone who found it useful to gain an upper hand. I had never seen such misuse of justice, and such instances of two-faced hypocrisy under the sun. And often words of complaint were somehow twisted and shaped into something said against Islam, causing more trouble. I had decided to avoid grumbling long ago, until the day I'd have my own bloody rules to lord over these people.

The doctor examined Sepideh, then gave an order to the nurse. On her stretcher, she was pushed along the corridors and I followed. We passed through a few swing doors, the last one marked 'Emergency Room.' They went in, but I wasn't allowed beyond the doors.

Now I thought it was time to let the rest know where I was. Using the public phone on the wall just outside the Emergency Room, I made two phone calls, one home, the other to my father. I explained what had happened, where I was and that I did not know what to expect. Both replied, saying they would be at the hospital in no time. Putting the phone down, my legs not able to keep me standing anymore, I sat down on one of the benches, feeling drained and empty in that corridor, close to the door. Ten minutes passed and still no news. My heart was beating hard and I felt I would be sick any minute. Things had happened so fast. Feeling lost, I chastened myself with the thought that I should have been ready for unexpected situations. Then suddenly the Emergency Room swing doors were pushed open and the same doctor came out; looking into his eyes, I froze with foreboding, and knew instantly that something was very wrong.

He came forward and said, "Sorry, we tried, but she was gone long ago…"

I wasn't listening anymore and the doctor just walked away. Sepideh in the next room was lying dead - that was all I thought about and could see. I tried to move from there but felt numb all over. Could this be only a nightmare? I pinched my leg and knew this was real. My brain wasn't functioning normally. I sat there staring into empty space, thinking our beloved Sepideh was gone, our sweet gentle Sepideh.

Long afterwards it dawned on me that I was the one

who had to break this devastating news to the others, who by now must have arrived, waiting outside. With a Herculean effort I picked myself up and tried to walk. I hadn't gone a couple of steps before I felt sick. I went to the toilet and vomited. Coming out, an idea hit me: I could just leave through the window and in a few days' time I'd be in Japan, never to come back again; or even if I did return one day in a few years' time, everything would have been sorted out and people wouldn't even remember there had ever been a girl called Sepideh. It was like dreaming, as I often did, of undertakings beyond my capability. A few minutes later I opened the entrance door and stepped outside. My aunts and uncles, on my mother's side, were there too. One look at me and the women started screaming and the men went all white and quiet. I broke down in tears.

The guests informed, the wedding was cancelled, and the next day they attended Sepideh's funeral. The autopsy confirmed my guess: heart attack due to the sudden rush of cold water contacting the body. She was buried in the main cemetery just outside Tehran. My father asked one of the clergy to attend and say the prayers for Sepideh's soul. The old man went on: "…and God claimed her young and she is in the best place now…" - and I thought, God has been claiming more than a few million of the young from this country recently. What was he doing up there?

The would-be bridegroom, hearing the news, gave a hysterical laugh and almost went crazy. He attended

Sepideh's funeral crying non-stop, then left, once more a stranger, never to be seen again. Some years later, quite accidentally, meeting his father on the road, he told me that a few weeks after Sepideh's incident his son sold everything he had and somehow got himself to Australia, where he got married and has been living since with his Australian wife and two kids. Fate, I thought, may have played the right cards for him after all.

Four days after Sepideh was buried, Soheila left for Athens. Getting on the plane she was full of tears and covered in black; what a departure and then a reunion it would be with Sohrab after almost a year and half of separation. For mum, back in the flat crying, it was too late to be remorseful now for her attitude towards Sepideh. I asked her to close the door of her room for I didn't want to hear her - I needed rest and silence. Regarding Soheila's younger son, who spent most evenings in my room, I felt his loss, just as much as I missed Sepideh. It was an extremely sad moment in my life and it looked as if the world had reached its end. Three days later I left the country too.

chapter eighteen

ON A DULL THURSDAY AFTERNOON, after a long twelve hours' flight with only one stop, at Beijing airport, I arrived at Narita International Airport just outside Tokyo. Following the crowd, I came to a big hall where at one side people standing in queues were being issued with visas by immigration officers sitting in some kind of glass cubicles. Iranians formed queues of their own: passengers from an Airbus 747, tickets sold to the last seat, some said toilet seats included, were there, over 400 of them. And all had come to work, though illegally, since to do so in Japan, an appropriate permit had to be obtained before entering the country. The immigration officers were all well aware of this fact, yet turned a blind eye and only one out of ten were sent back by the same flight. The rest, as long as they kept quiet about their purpose entering the country and only mentioned they were there on holiday, and in possession of 2,000 dollars each, were given a three month's visa - reduced to 15 days a few months later, and stopped altogether a year after that, when no Iranians were allowed into Japan.

By the time the queue got to me, words having been exchanged, three had been deported. The immigration officer didn't look friendly; I put my passport on the counter and as he was taking it, he asked, "Why are you here?"

I answered, "To spend my holiday, sir."

Pressing a few buttons on his computer, he said, "Have you been in Japan before, illegally?"

What kind of stupid question was that, I thought! "No, sir. This is my very first time in this country."

Then he wanted to know how much money I had on me.

"2,300 US dollars, sir," I said.

Not bothering to check it, he handed me back my passport and asked for the next one in the queue to come forward.

Going down the stairs towards the baggage carousel to get my bag, taking a deep breath, I opened my passport and noticed he had given me a three months visa. A day's visa, I thought, would have done - for once inside I never intended to leave the country.

I collected my knapsack which was only half full, light so that I could get myself around fast. Coming to customs, only my knapsack was superficially checked and not my person. After that I came to a visiting hall of colossal size. I had heard that in here I could find some Iranians or Pakistanis who, for the price of 500 US dollars, were offering jobs to the newly arrived people.

Among us these people were known as Job Fixers, and one had to be very careful dealing with them, because sometimes one paid but never got a job. It was a risky situation and recently due to the flock of foreign workers entering Japan, there was a job shortage, and so, with people desperate to find jobs, the situation had created a very suitable atmosphere for the opportunists.

Looking around I couldn't find any job fixers or identify other Iranians in the same situation. Then, quite accidentally, I met this Englishman who had lived in Japan for a number of years and knew his way around well. He told me that people offering jobs had been stopped from entering the airport and were now all operating from a park called Ueno; this, as I later found out, was the centre for all illegal activities in Japan, mostly carried out by foreigners. The man also told me that if I couldn't secure myself a job through people in that park - and hardly any job fixer could be trusted there - I might be able to find one in a place called Kawaguchi, on the outskirts of Tokyo, where the factories were located. I thanked him, but not enough, for I didn't know what a vital piece of information he had given me.

Outside the airport buses were taking people to the nearest underground station. I got on one of them, but shortly afterwards took a train instead which, after some time, I got to Ueno station which was within walking distance to Ueno park. I came out of the station and had my first view of a city which has always been so much in the news. Jaunting around, I decided sight-seeing could be left for later - there would be plenty of time for that in time. With only just over two thousand dollars on me in one of the most expensive cities in the world, the priority was to find a job.

Spending a couple of hours in Ueno park, I didn't come across even one job fixer. The place was crowded with hundreds of Iranians, Pakistanis, Sri Lankans, Nigerians, and some even from Brazil - all milling about and looking for jobs, some even approaching me thinking I might be able to help them. In the Iranian corner, many were into the business of selling forged telephone cards; later, contacting Soheila in America, I found this very cost effective. A telephone card bought for 10,000 yens in the shops could be obtained at one-tenth that price in the park, doing the same job. And only 10,000 yen cards were forged; the other two, 1000 and 5000 yen cards, I supposed, weren't worth the money saved; like the 100 dollar bill, forging less valued notes, as I had heard, wouldn't cover the costs of forging! These cards were being produced by Japanese Yakoosa (Mafia) and were distributed among people, above all, through Iranians. Yakoosa was a name to be reckoned with! People feared them and at the top they were almost running the police force in the country. Peddlers had to buy their permission from them in the area they were working. Over a year later when I stayed at a guest house in the middle of Tokyo, sharing a room with a Peruvian selling ornaments in the shape of lady birds, 1000 yens each (at 50% profit, imported from his country), he told me that he had paid 700,000 yens to a Mafia member in order to be allowed to stand by one of the Shinagawa underground station entrances to do his business for three months. It was worth it, he told me, for he was selling 60 lady birds a day, making roughly 900,000 yens a month.

With my knapsack over my shoulder I left the park and hit the streets of Tokyo. Leaving Iran where everything was black, white or dark blue, once more, like the time I entered Istanbul, things looked colourful. I paced the streets until I got hungry and thanks to that I experienced my second setback. I entered a shop, attracted by the sign above it that read 'Curry and Rice'. I barely closed the door behind me when the man sitting behind the counter stood up, crossed his hands and shouted, "Hoy, damè!" Obviously by saying HOY he meant to draw my attention in an insulting manner; but the word, *damè*, I didn't understand. That didn't matter, for his crossed hands and reaction said it all: Do Not Enter! A few standing in the queue to get their plates and many sitting round a big table eating, all kept to themselves. Were they embarrassed? Later I realised that the Japanese didn't have that sort of feeling. Though this was the shopkeeper's private place which gave him the right to ask me not to enter, this cunt didn't have the right to talk to me like that! I was thinking of telling him to fuck off, but not knowing what kind of people they were, I might end up in a fight and that on my first day wouldn't have looked good; so, saying not a word, I decided to leave. Soon I came to realise that, though Japan is a developed country, its citizens were not an exceptionally cultured people.

Long afterwards when I thought about this incident, I realised what a wise decision I had made in leaving that place without causing trouble. Police getting involved in disputes between a Japanese citizen and a foreign national would never want to know about the cause of the trouble; the Japanese were always in the right and the foreigners in the wrong - that's just the way it was. And if this foreigner didn't have a visa, a couple of days later he would find himself on a plane back to his country. In some cases even a visa holder, without any kind of trial, right or wrong, was deported.

Foreigners with dark skins were not allowed in restaurants or places of entertainment, with the exception of a few places where the manager had lived in England or America and so been westernized. Foreigners with blond hair and no dark eyes were treated differently; on entering a place, they were even respected. It was Hitler's laws reinstated! Also, foreigners accompanied by Japanese, though not welcomed, weren't stopped entering most places.

Now, was I ever stopped entering a pub, restaurant or a place of entertainment during my ten years' stay in England? NO, not even once! However, I did get into trouble with some British tough guys once and the police were called, but in sorting out the problem, did the police display any prejudice against me for being a foreigner? NO, they did not! Did the British ever treat me differently from the way they treated themselves during my ten years stay there? NO, they did not.

I was feeling quite hungry now. Going around I came to a McDonalds. Being under the influence of Americans, surely, I thought, they wouldn't refuse to serve dark foreigners! With a lot of uncertainty I entered and stood in the queue; so far no problem. My turn came and the Japanese girl serving, not taking any notice of me being a foreigner, handed me what I asked for.

Coming out of McDonalds, it was getting late and also, having spent the preceding night in the plane, I was feeling tired. From the information I had gathered about Japan before entering that country, I was aware that some people spent the night in saunas and that usually in most areas there were a few of them about. When I entered the first one I found, the manager from behind his small reception desk refused me, his hands crossed. Normal procedure, I thought. Entering the second one, going up the stairs, turning right, I met a pleasant young lady sitting behind a reception counter. She didn't know much English, which wasn't surprising since not many did in Japan. Using body language and at the same time speaking slowly, word for word, I said, "I want to sleep here tonight."

"Nighto eslip…" She hadn't finished when a manager, a middle-aged man, came through the door behind her. Turning back she looked quite relieved to see him; not me, for, on the contrary, I felt tense: his appearance was like another No Entry sign to me! Never mind, I thought, if it came to that I could always go back to Ueno park and, like those hundreds there, spend the night there too. The man, speaking good English, asked me, "May I help you?" I repeated what I had told the lady and in a few more sentences, I also told him that it was my first night in Japan - not mentioning that I had already been refused entry by one sauna. The man proved me wrong; he wasn't bad natured after all and, in fact, trying to be helpful, he told me in a few short sentences all about saunas in Japan. I paid and, after leaving my valuables at the desk as he advised me, got my towels and went inside for my first sauna adventure in Japan. I took my clothes off, put them in a locker, closed its door, took the key out of the lock which at the same time locked it, and put the elastic band attached to the key round my wrist. Going through some swing doors I came to the shower room. Everything was spotless and beautifully clean. There were about twenty hand showers at waist height on the surrounding walls and all powerful. At a level below each shower there was a narrow shelf protruding from the wall on top of which one could find all kinds of shampoos, soaps, shaving stuff and creams, as well as a disposable toothbrush. Beyond this room there was a medium size pool filled with hot water - so hot that only the Japanese used to the hottest sun on the planet could enter. Next to this pool there was a sizable steam room.

I had a long hot shower, dried myself, put the Kimono (Japanese dress) on that I was given at the reception, and left to discover the other promising parts the manager had told me about. During my three years stay in Japan, I used saunas many times, but, for some reason, I never entered the pool or the steam room, always only making use of the shower.

Going up the stairs and then through some double doors, on the second floor I came to a medium size saloon brightly lit and crowded with people. In this saloon there was a big screen TV at each corner showing different channels; in rows facing these TVs were beautiful automatic beds, the ones with buttons on the side for adjusting the head or leg supports. At one side of this saloon there was a food and drink bar, in front of it people sitting on the floor behind low-level tables, in Japanese style, eating noodles and drinking Saki, an alcoholic drink made from rice which was taken in great quantities by almost all male Japanese seven days a week.

Leaving this floor, using the stairs, I went up to the third and last floor. Again, going through some double doors, I came to a bigger saloon here, dimly lit and very quiet. Beds of the same type, arranged in perfect rows, about a metre away from each other, were all facing a small cinema screen showing an American movie. I placed myself on one of the beds and while watching, exhausted as I was, soon went to sleep.

Early the next morning I left for Kawaguchi, where that Englishman at the airport had told me I might be able to find a job. Using the underground and changing trains only once, I got to Kawaguchi station. Coming out, the place looked just like any other in the area: just shops and streets around. Had I come to the wrong place? Asking someone who spoke some English - those who could were more than willing to display their proficiency! - I was told that there was an industrial estate in Kawaguchi, a couple of miles away from the station. I got on the bus and went there. Getting off at the end of the line I found myself in the middle of a very big industrial estate. There were many factories around with workers, some looking foreign, going to work. How I envied them, jobless as I was! As it was still too early to go around asking, "Arbaito Iroo?" (worker needed?), I got myself a couple of sandwiches from one of the shops there and went to a park nearby to have my breakfast. Eating over and prepared mentally for whatever fate might befall me, I started going round, at about 9 o' clock that Friday morning, trying to find myself a job. At the first five places I called at I was shown a 'no entry' sign. Only at one of these places a man who was in charge and could speak English well told me to come back the following Monday when Sacho (the boss or owner of the place) would be present; the man said he would then be able to put a few words forward on my behalf, which might improve my chances of being employed there. He had lived in London for many years and realizing that I had lived in England too, tried to be helpful. "If I don't find anything then, you'll see me on Monday," I told him and left to try my luck elsewhere.

At ten o'clock I stood in front of this huge warehouse looking place, inside of which two lift trucks were moving things about and a few workers busy putting bundles of books inside cardboard boxes. Just outside this place, on the right and connected to it, there was a big room with a door that bore the word OFFICE displayed in large and clear letters. I was thinking of entering this office and asking them if they needed anybody, when its door opened and a small middle-aged woman came out. She looked at me, and in that opportune moment I said to her, "Arbaito Iroo?" With a motion of her hand she asked me to wait, then went back inside again, leaving the door open. A moment later a young man of about 30 with glasses put his head out of the door and asked me into the office. Two young girls, two middle-aged women and a man of about fifty, were already there working; as I entered, they stopped, all staring at me - a Japanese habit on seeing a foreigner. The young man, thin, a couple of inches taller than me, sporting a moustache and a wisp of beard on his chin, looked cheerful and introduced himself as the Boss of the place. Though he spoke a brand of English I had never heard before, I managed somehow to understand him. The rest didn't know a word of English, but whenever we said something funny and laughed, they laughed along too. The Boss, or just Boss, as I called him from then on, told me my job would be packaging, a hard job, but I looked strong enough to manage. He would give me 800 yens per hour, 5% tax deducted, and I would be paid monthly. The work started at 7.30 in the morning and finished when there was no more work to do, and that meant usually anytime between 5 in the afternoon and 12 at night. He didn't care whether I had a visa or not. In fact, as long as one kept out of trouble, even the police didn't bother to check one's visa; no random searches were carried out, unlike England where the police would come looking for one once one's visa had expired.

Boss put my name on a time card and clocked it. At 10:30 on that Friday morning I began my first working day in Japan for Kobayashi Packaging Factory.

There was another foreigner working there too. He was from Ghana, 20 years of age, tall, well-built and fortunately spoke English. This good looking young man was called Tony; he was full of life, and at this young age had lived in so many different countries. Apart from English, he spoke a few other languages and had seven girlfriends, one for each day of the week and, as he put it, "if the week was ten days long I would still manage to fill in those three extra days with different ones!" Tony had lived in Japan for over a year, the first three months attending language school, and so spoke Japanese quite well; the fact that his mother tongue was English gave me a lot of morale, since, firstly, here was someone I could understand; and, secondly, he made it easier for me to make contact and communicate with the other workers, all Japanese, numbering some 15 people; apart from Boss, none spoke a word of English in that factory. I had been lucky! While hundreds of foreigners were still looking for a job, I had found one on the first day of searching, not even having to pay a job fixer. Thank you, Mr Englishman, for your vital information which enabled me to find a job! That first day I finished late in the evening and went back to the same sauna to sleep.

Days went by slowly. I was putting bundles of holiday leaflets, advertising papers, books and almost anything made of paper into boxes, closing and taping them. Another person picked up these boxes one by one and fed them to a machine called a banding machine; then, by pressing a button on the side of this machine, a hard plastic strip became fixed around the box along the middle of its length; then, turning the box from its length to its width, pressing the button again caused another strip of plastic to be fixed around the box, at right angles to the first, and in this way the box was fully secured. The next person picked this box up from the machine and put it on a wooden pallet. When there were enough of these boxes on one pallet, a forklift picked it up and took it to a truck waiting outside. Sometimes there was only Tony and me doing the whole thing; first we filled the boxes, rolled the banding machine towards them, me doing the banding and Tony putting them on the pallet; every now and then we changed places. On average each box weighed something between 10 to 20 kilos and in one working day sometimes we went through 1,000 of these boxes, apart from other work we had to do. I was certainly getting enough exercise!

Work finished, usually after ten at night, I went back to the same sauna in Ueno to sleep. This was beginning to prove costly, so one day after having a short chat with Tony, and also finding out that it was the factory's job to find workers a place of stay, and since I had shown myself worthy of the money I was earning, I decided to have a word with Boss on the subject of accommodation. I would ask him to find me a place, if only to stay at nights, for during the rest of the time I was working. On the first day when he had engaged my services, he had asked me where I was staying, and, lying, I had told him I was staying with some friends, thinking that someone with no fixed address wouldn't have had much chance of being employed. Now I decided to tell him the same thing, once again being economical with the truth to bring my situation more in line with the actual truth. So that day when we finished work, I clocked out, then, excusing myself, asked if I could have a word with him. Standing just outside the office, I began by referring to what we had talked about on the first day he had asked me into his office. I reminded him of my statement that I had been staying with friends, and added, "That was only on a temporary basis, Boss, and for the last few days I've been staying at a sauna in Ueno, costing me a lot of money..." Then I asked him if he knew of a room I could rent, since rooms usually cost a lot less than saunas. When he gave a negative answer, I came out with what I'd been aiming for through our conversation. By now I had found out that almost all foreign workers lived at the place where they worked. Nodding my head towards the room above the office, the place where we had our lunch and sometimes watched TV, I said to him, "I wouldn't mind staying there." Turning his head round and looking up as though inspecting the room through X-ray eyes, he didn't seem surprised at my proposal, as I had expected; he had stayed there himself at one time, for over a week, he mentioned, with a number of employees, when there'd been too much work in the past to finish before it was very late at night. But trusting someone he had only recently met to be let loose in the entire factory, and that a foreigner, seemed a hard pill for him to swallow. "I'll have to ask Sacho about that," he said; then, suddenly changing his mind - something these inscrutable Japanese were quite capable of - he conceded, "but you can stay." I didn't show much excitement, though I had a job holding myself from jumping into the air - for by now I had learned that among the Japanese an effusive display of happiness when a favour was granted was to invite a withdrawal of the favour.

"Thanks Boss!" That's all I said.

Then, just before leaving, he turned back and mentioned, "If you make fire you'll be fired."

That night when everyone was gone I went to the

office and locked the door from the inside. The factory entrance had already been shut by means of a huge corrugated door which at the touch of a button slowly unrolled from the top. After a quick wash at the sink I went upstairs to my night room and watched some TV. Tired, I spread a couple of blankets on the floor and, lying down, I was asleep in no time.

From that day on I started to save some real money: I didn't have to pay for saunas, trains and buses anymore. The room was saving me around 3,000 yens, at the time almost equal to 30 US dollars per day. Also, there was no need for me to get up at 5:30 in the mornings anymore to be ready for work in time. In fact, I got up at 7, had my breakfast at the coffee shop across the road and still had time on my hands before starting the day's work.

I lived at the factory until payday, at the end of the month. That day Sacho himself came down to hand us our money; plus a free lunch everyone received, offered by him. It was an exciting day and as he was handing me my pay, he said, "Nippori Aparto." Nippori was part of Tokyo, next to Ueno, only about 1km separating the two stations, where the head office of the factory was situated, and also, as I later found out, the place of Sacho's residence, and Aparto just meant Apartment. But what message was he trying to convey? I didn't understand the significance of it at the time, and so, excited with the pay, didn't think much of it soon afterwards either; maybe it was just a remark thrown casually into the air.

That day when work finished Boss asked me to pack my stuff - I would be going with him somewhere. Now I was beginning to realise what Sacho might have meant by saying, 'Nippori Aparto'. With my knapsack over my shoulder, clocking out, I followed Boss into the factory truck he always drove after work finished - a small sized vehicle and the last one we loaded with boxes at the factory. On the way he told me that he drove the truck to the main office every night, almost a thirty-minute drive, left it there, went home, to come back the next morning to empty it of boxes which, for whatever reason, were left there. That finished, he drove the truck back to the factory. "From now on you will accompany me on this trip because you've been given an apartment in Nippori," he said.

On the second floor of a three-storey building Boss opened a door and we entered. Right in front of us there was a narrow corridor about a metre in width, five metres in length and a ceiling so low that, stretching my hand above my head, I could touch it. For the first metre the corridor was twice as wide - enough for a sink to have been placed just next to the door on the left with two water taps over it; one with cold and the other one connected to a small gas water heater placed above it. This corridor led to two doors, one facing us at the end of it and the other one on the left. Boss had told me that it was a two-bedroom flat: I had the use of one room while the other one belonged to another factory worker who was in the hospital at that time. But what about the bathroom? "No old places have one. People use *sentako* (the public bath) to wash. There are many of them around," he explained. And the toilet? "No old places have one" - and again he explained and told me that there was a toilet downstairs common to everyone in the building that I could also use. I didn't bother to ask about the kitchen and sitting room. Pointing at the door on the left, he said, "This one is yours." He opened it and, taking our shoes off, we both went in. It was a small room, about 3x3 metres with the same low ceiling. The place looked good but I tried to appear indifferent. He saw the expression on my face and as there was no need for him to stay any longer, said something like, "Keep it clean", gave me the key and left.

I put my knapsack down and opened the window which almost covered one entire side of the room, from just above the floor up to a foot below the ceiling. The window opened to the narrow street outside - an area with old houses around. I looked to see if there were any shops close by; there were none. But later when I explored my surroundings I found a few within walking distance, including an American chain shop 7,11.

I turned my attention back to the room. It had a green carpet and a small fridge in one corner, and a new thin, folded mattress with clean sheets and blankets in the other corner, on the floor. "The Japanese don't use beds," I had heard Boss say, something verified in the movies I had seen. "Neither do they have furniture in their houses," I was told, apart from a low table they ate on. Not much else to do in the room and, feeling hungry, I went out to have something to eat; when I returned it was close to midnight so I made my bed and went to sleep.

The next evening Sacho, who lived within walking distance from the flat, came round and said the rent for the room would be 20,000 yens per month, and that it would be deducted from my salary.

A few days later I opened an account in the Fuji bank, a great big white building halfway between Ueno and my lodging, and I deposited my pay there. Also, changing my remaining dollars to yens, I added that to my account. These deposits and my balance were all printed in my bank book, and I was issued one cash card with a four digit pin number. From then on I was able to make withdrawals from and deposit my pay into my account anywhere in Japan, using Fuji bank cash machines.

But soon I began to encounter problems. The country called Japan, known as one of the most advanced places in other parts of the world, didn't seem to have been occupied by a highly civilized people. Getting up in the mornings for work was like getting ready to enter the lion's den, if not worse. At the factory, which I called the torture chamber, Tony and I were being treated like slaves; they shouted at us and sometimes shoved us. Everything we did seemed wrong, expressed in very coarse language; we noticed that if the same actions were carried out in exactly the same way by one of themselves, it was perfectly okay. If we tried to appear indifferent, they provoked us by displaying more sadistic behaviour; on the other hand, if we betrayed any reaction, we were threatened with *koobi* (being fired). Ueno park was full of foreigners who at one time had a job, who were pushed hard at work, and who, when protesting or showing dissatisfaction, had faced *koobi*; working illegally, what rights did they have? Some even talked of bosses carrying sticks, hitting them any time they had inadvertently transgressed. Though I never came across a boss who had hit me, I wouldn't dismiss the idea out of hand; some were quite capable of such conduct, I'm sure, because if Tony and I hadn't stood firm often enough to some of them when the going got really tough, they would have probably started kicking and punching us. Knowing our position gave them a little bit of ground which they never failed to take advantage of if given the chance. They hardly called us by our names; to show that we were of a lower class, especially when one of the women was around, they either called us *Hoy* or *Baka* (meaning 'stupid'), the most commonly used words in Japan. *Gajin damè* ('foreigners no good') - we heard that being said quite often. They abused us and it came to a point where we didn't care anymore if we got *koobi*. We dared to show that we could treat them in the same way, and so started crossing the line. Boss kept telling us, "Kiyo wa shigoto wari koobi dayo" ("Work finished today, you will be fired)" - but changed his mind by the end of the day. We realised that he too, like the rest of them, could be intimidated. Our threat of arson did not fall on deaf ears, bearing in mind the factory was filled with paper; and in the same vein, sufficiently provoked, we showed them our cutters, the tools we had been given to open the boxes, and looking into their eyes, would say, "Shindè!" ("Death!")

Bodily, they were all weaker than Tony and me, and vulnerable to intimidation; on the other hand, most had a big mouth, and unfortunately we were not in a position to shut it once and for all. For the twentieth time Tony said, "When I get back to my country and I see a Japanese on the road I'll have a go at him!" All coloured workers on buses, trains and everywhere I went were saying the same thing; most complained of the treatment they received in the workplace. For the umpteenth time I thanked providence for allowing the right outcome - the defeat of Japan - in the Second World War, and cursed America and Britain for letting these people go free after Japan had lost the war. No way, no way, would they have let anyone free if the outcome of the war had been the other way round! Without question they would have made slaves out of us all.

Sunday was our day off. On that day I got up late and after a quick wash at the sink, left the flat and walked down to Ueno and then to Akihabara, the main centre for electronic equipment in Japan, and probably, apart from America, the largest in the world for that kind of house goods. I stayed in Akihabara until late, window shopping, and then took the underground back home.

One Sunday as I was leaving the building I met a foreign looking woman who seemed to be wandering about in the area. We spoke for a while, like two foreigners drawn to each other, and I invited her to my flat for a drink which, reluctantly it seemed, she accepted. Her name was Afrooz, from India. She was 32 years old, of medium build and appearance, her white teeth very noticeable when she smiled! She had dark hair, dark eyes, but was not as dark skinned as Indians usually were. She looked sad but I found her company quite pleasant. She had just lost her job that same day, she told me, and was going to a friend to stay with until she found another one. Back in her country she had an old father, a middle-aged mother, eight brothers and sisters, and she was the only breadwinner of the family; she was also supporting two brothers at university. With that many to provide for, I thought, how did she manage to lose her job - especially at a time when another job was so difficult to find? Even I, in a far less serious situation and only myself to support, tried my best, in spite of all the abuse I had to put up with, to keep my job.

Also, losing her job on a Sunday was a bit strange and gave me food for thought. Then I remembered an Iranian woman I met a few weeks earlier, one late night, who was almost in the same situation. She had been given a job and instead of giving her work her boss had asked her for sex. When she refused, he had tried to rape her; she had fought him off and as a result had got *koobi*.

I wondered, had Afrooz been through the same ordeal? By now, after three months of working side by side with Japanese men, I felt they were quite capable of trying to rape a female foreign worker if they got the chance. I deliberately looked Afrooz straight in the eye and asked her kindly but quite emphatically, "How did you come to lose your job on a Sunday?" She tried to dismiss my question with a swiftly made-up answer, but I realized that, with my eyes still fixed on hers, that she was avoiding the truth. For a moment she stared into empty space; then she took off her blouse under which she had a vest on, and I saw the bruises that covered her arms and chest where the vest wasn't covering her body. She told me what I had already guessed but never wanted to have confirmed. Her boss raped her almost a week after she started working for him and on this particular Sunday he went back to the factory, where she'd been given a room, to have her again; she had resisted, and so was rewarded with *koobi*. There was no question of going to the police. For one thing, she didn't have a visa. Even if she did go to the police and told them about it, not much usually happened; she would most probably find herself on the next plane back to India. The police seemed reluctant to hear from these people, especially when they were complaining against a Japanese citizen. Afrooz had seen it happen to a Bangladeshi friend of hers who was sent back on the next plane.

Afrooz stayed with me and within the following month I met quite a few of her girlfriends, mainly from India,

Pakistan, Bangladesh and Sri Lanka, of which almost 50% had been through the same situation, but most, scared to lose their jobs, hadn't fought hard enough.

Writing these notes, an incident comes to mind that seems relevant here. A few years ago, listening to the BBC, it became apparent that for at least a few months the news was centred on three American servicemen who had raped a Japanese schoolgirl on the island of Okinawa. A horrible crime, by any standard, and the servicemen were punished according to the law. Then the next thing I heard, Okinawa residents had asked Americans to leave the island. Just imagine what would have happened if the shoe was on the other foot and the Japanese had won World War II and three Japanese servicemen from army units based in Hawaii had raped an American schoolgirl! The incident wouldn't have made it to the news rooms, never mind the local residents being in a position to ask the Japanese to leave.

Over a week later Afrooz found herself a job in a factory packing biscuits. Although I had gone to the place and introduced myself as her husband, the boss there nevertheless tried somehow to have it off with her. It made me mad to hear that, but Afrooz wouldn't let me go round and confront him.

By now I had grown very fond of Afrooz. We made love almost three weeks after we first met. She was full of passion and was eagerly in need of a man who could hold her tight with a lot of love, and I was just the right person to satisfy this need.

Back in the factory one day Tony and I were working when one of the workers, passing us, deliberately shoved Tony out of the way in spite of there being a lot of room to get by - then, as if nothing had happened, just walked away. Tony, who had been on edge for the last couple of days, took a few running steps and caught up with the man, turned him round and punched him. The man, holding his stomach and face, went down. What would happen now, I asked myself, looking aghast at Tony! Half an hour later in his office, Boss told Tony to clock out and leave. We both had expected this but what about the other bloke? He was after all guilty to some extent and had to face some sort of punishment, I thought - but no, he got away without even a reprimand.

While Tony was changing upstairs and packing his few belongings, Boss had a change of heart and when Tony came down he told him to stay away for just a week - to let things cool down - after which he could return.

During the time Tony was absent the situation grew tenser - not only in our factory but also in other places of work where they had foreign employees. The country was just beginning to experience foreigners, never mind coming into close contact with them in the workplace. The diverse cultures just couldn't get along. The *Japan Times* was full of reports of fights between locals and foreign workers. "A Japanese was stabbed by a Pakistani at work, when he told him to *hayacu* (hurry up)." "A foreign worker smashed a club on his boss's head." News of this type was on the increase and getting round fast. The Japanese realised that foreigners were running out of patience with them; and some, losing their tempers, could even become quite aggressive. Long afterwards, gradually, the situation began to stabilise; it didn't get better but at least it didn't get worse either. A Japanese worker employed only a week earlier would try to order us about and then '*hayacu*'. They seemed to enjoy abusing and ordering foreigners about. Evidently Japan wasn't yet ready to have workers from outside placed among locals. Perhaps because of the publicity they got round the world, they counted themselves highly civilized and therefore others were *baka* (stupid); compared with the British, I wouldn't call them civilized or even half as intelligent.

Tony came back, not to work but to collect his pay and settle some scores. Perhaps not surprisingly in his week off he had found himself another job. Like a lion looking for prey, he watched them, but they were all very cautious not to respond to his stares. Then at the right moment, finding his chance, he kicked and punched two Japanese workers, head butted another, and chased one with his cutter in his hand, calling, "Shindè!" ("Death!") He got his pay, left, and sadly I never saw him again.

With Tony gone I found myself alone and realised that my days were numbered at the factory. It was only me against all of them now. I felt like a prisoner who had the chance of freedom but once free had no choice but to find himself another prison - with conditions, probably, just as bad. So I decided to hang on as long as I could, but when the time came, like Tony, I would settle some scores and then leave proudly.

Meanwhile Afrooz found herself a job in a glass factory owned by a decent boss and was given a room there. She didn't want to accept the room and told me she was quite happy staying with me. But I insisted that she should take it. I thought: once I lost my job my room would go with it, therefore it seemed wise to accept the room she had been offered. It was a small but beautiful room which I saw when I called round at her work. She introduced me as her husband to her boss, which in effect I was in all but name. Surprisingly, he seemed happy to see me there, and had no problem with me sometimes staying overnight. After all, not everyone was bad in Japan, and certainly not the women - their attitude towards foreigners was for most parts the opposite of their men.

Almost four weeks after Tony had left I landed my strongest left hook on one of the most bothersome fellows in the factory. He flew into the air, hit the surrounding boxes, and fell to the floor. Some of the boxes landed on top of him and for some time he lay there without moving. Another worker standing nearby did not dare to get involved; but then again, everything happened so fast he couldn't do anything apart from calling for help, which brought the rest of the workers running to the man's rescue. It took them almost ten minutes to bring him around; and when he did regain consciousness, he was confused, unaware of where he was. I was pleased that the score was successfully settled with this man since it had been on the top of my list! I followed Boss into the office and before I could say anything he turned back and said, "KOOBI!" - the message was loud and clear. He wasn't in the mood to listen to me, so I went upstairs, changed and came down, clocked out, stood by the doorway and said, "Ashta watashi wa kairoo, okanè." ("I come back tomorrow, money.") He owed me more than two weeks' pay.

I went back to the factory flat in Nippori, not mine anymore, got my belongings, put them in my knapsack and left to see Afrooz whom I hadn't seen for the last couple of days. It had seemed like a lifetime since I last saw her. For the last few days my factory flat had become a veritable torture chamber. The other room there, until recently empty with its occupant in the hospital with little hope of survival after three operations, unfortunately recovered and came back to occupy his room. A couple of days later as I was washing my hands at the sink he opened his door and told me I was wasting too much water. I had seen him letting the water run non-stop when washing his hair and then brushing it; and when I mentioned this to him, he said, "Watashi wa Nihonjin to anata wa gaijin daya." ("I am Japanese and you are a foreigner.") Now what would one do with a stupid person like that? If I confronted him and it led to a fight, I would lose my job and the flat, and if I remained silent he would be encouraged to go further with his abuse. I left the flat with the water running full speed.

Afrooz worked from eight in the morning till five in the afternoon, but most days worked overtime until nine. When she saw me with my knapsack she needed no explanation for my appearance. "Never mind, you'll find another job," she smiled. I always found her encouraging; and though a woman, she could teach me a few things when it came to bravery.

Early the next morning, before going up to Kobayashi factory to get my money, I phoned Boss up and told him I was on my way. He had the money ready and asked me to be there on time. When I put the phone down I thought: if he had my money, what difference did it make whether I got there on time or an hour or two later? Perhaps he was going somewhere. But during my seven months working there not even once had he left the factory before work finished; and in any case, he could leave the money with someone else in the office. Or perhaps he had some evil plan, I thought, like calling the police, which I wouldn't dismiss off-hand with these people. They were quite capable of faking a charge against a foreigner and knowing that he would get deported, who would think of consequences? Anyhow, I resolved to be very cautious when approaching the factory.

About half an hour before I was supposed to see Boss, I entered the coffee shop across the road from the factory, got myself a cup of coffee, took a seat by the window where I could have the factory under my surveillance, and watched. Drinking my coffee, I took my time and it paid off: a policeman riding his bicycle, passing by the coffee shop, stopped in front of Kobayashi factory, parked his bicycle outside and entered the office. Though I had anticipated a trap, I didn't think Boss would actually put it into action. The way Tony had left, I supposed, suggested that he had sufficient cause for concern to be cautious and take no chances. I finished my coffee and left to make another call.

It was Boss I called. His secretary answered and called him to the phone. I said, "Sorry Boss, I can't make it today. I'll come tomorrow."

"Okay," he said, "but before you come don't forget to phone me first."

Replacing the receiver on its cradle, I went back to the coffee shop, bought another cup of coffee and took the same seat. Sipping my coffee and looking out of the window I saw the policeman accompanying Boss coming out of the factory office; after a short chat, standing on the pavement, they shook hands and parted. The policeman cycled away and Boss went back to the office. I finished my coffee, left the shop and started for the factory about 50 metres distance. If Boss tried anything stupid like calling the police, I would get my cutter out and slash his jugular vein, or have one of his eyes out! I approached the office quietly and, standing by the door, looked through the window. I saw him behind his desk, head down writing; the two young girls and one of the women were also there, in the office with him, behind other desks, busy sorting labels out. In one swift movement I opened the door and entered, closing the door quietly behind me. Boss looked up at me and all the colour drained from his face. He looked as though he had seen a ghost.

"Ohayo gosaiymasu" ("Good morning"), I said, displaying a sarcastic smile. "Dayjobo deska?" ("Everything okay?") "Watash no okanè koodeh sai." ("My money, please.")

Staring at me as though trying to convince himself that it wasn't me he was seeing there, and looking lost for words, he managed, with a lot of effort, to say, "Ashta." ("Tomorrow.")

Now I had a surprise for him too. I got the cutter out of my pocket and said, "Anonè" (by the way), "Boss, corè kojo no cutta watashi wa wasýrèta ageroo." ("I forgot to give back the factory cutter.") Then pushing the blade half out and staring into his eyes in a threatening manner, I carried on, "Watashi wa ashta deky nai." ("I can't make it tomorrow.") "Watashi no okanè ima iroo." ("I want my money now.") The women, looking very scared, kept quiet in their seats. He, too, suddenly dumbfounded, submissively dropped his stare, pulled out the top drawer on the right side of his desk, got an envelope and threw it to me. I caught the envelope in the air and looked inside. The money was there. I gave him a winning smile and said, "Arigato gozai mashta, Boss!" ("Thanks very much, Boss!") Then throwing the cutter on his table and changing my smile to a scornful one, I carried on, "Matta aii masho." ("See you again.") Not a word said, he kept staring at me. I left the office and, once outside, I shouted, "Kibo shi naii!" ("I hope not!")" So after over seven months of working for Kobayashi factory, I said goodbye to it.

chapter nineteen

A FEW DAYS LATER through one of Afrooz's friends I found a job servicing ski lifts in ski areas round the country. It promised to be an exciting job, travelling from one place to another, but it was a sad moment leaving Afrooz behind.

Now I had a new Boss; he was in his fifties, with thick greyish hair, wearing glasses, a bit taller than me and almost weak in appearance; he had been building and repairing ski lifts around the country for the last thirty years and told me that almost everyone skied in Japan. Ski was one of the most popular sports in the country and there were over 700 ski areas people crowded into during the winter. But now it was summer, the ski season over, the snow had melted away and so maintenance could start.

Leaving Tokyo for the first time, driving north, a few hours later we reached a place called Minakami - a medium size ski area next to the city.

There was only one more person, apart from the Boss, that I was working with on this job. His name was Okasawa. In his late thirties, although he looked 25, he was tall, well-built and he also wore glasses. I felt fortunate because now in times of trouble I had to face only two people.

The Minakami ski area had six ski runs. The longest was covered by a four-passenger chairlift; this was the case in almost every ski area we went to, as I later found out - in fact only one four-passenger chairlift was to be seen in any one area. Two of the runs had two-passenger chairlifts, and the remaining three runs, single ones. We started on one of the two-passenger chairlifts they called 'Romance' - perhaps because a boy was supposed to sit next to a girl going up. When we finished working on this lift we would be leaving, the Boss informed us, because this was the only lift in the area under the supervision of the company he was working for. Six lifts were built by almost as many different companies. I didn't know anything about the job but soon learned. We took some of the chairs down from a cable 4cm thick and almost a kilometre long, and repaired them. Some of the tires round the wheels on top of the posts had worn out, so we changed them and greased the bearings. Working on top of these posts, some as high as ten metres, was dangerous, but then again, the pay was good: I was getting 10,000 yens (90 US dollars) per day, for eight hours' work, plus three meals a day, all paid by the Boss.

For overnight accommodation each area boasted a very big 4-star hotel of its own with tennis and badminton courts, table tennis, indoor swimming pool, sauna and above all a weights room where I usually spent a lot of time once work was finished. And since the ski season was over, most rooms in the hotel were empty, which, thankfully, meant that we were given separate rooms - all paid for by the Boss. Breakfast and dinner were served at the hotel restaurant, but for lunch we were given *bento* (packed food) to have where we worked in the mountains. Back from work in the evenings, in my hotel room, I noticed my towel, bed sheet, pillowcase and kimono had been replaced with clean ones. The living was *saiko* (a word the Japanese used when everything went exceptionally well or smoothly), yet the Boss and Okasawa were no different from those Japanese I had worked with in Kobayashi factory; there I had been treated like a slave and I had resisted that - and that had caused trouble; but fortunately in my new situation there were only two of them I had to face, and then again, by now, after seven months of working side by side with them, I had learned how to handle most situations.

We stayed in Minakami for three weeks and then left for a place called Tsumagui, where we had more lifts to work on which needed repairing. A few days later another worker, apparently someone who had been working with the Boss on and off for many years, joined us. Because a third Japanese was joining the team, I thought trouble might be afoot - but I couldn't have been more wrong. The new man, called Hammamula, proved to be a different personality altogether. He was about my age, slightly taller and slimmer than me, and one of the strongest men I had ever met, as I found out later. He talked to me in the same way as he did with Okasawa and the Boss, and contrary to most Japanese, he was humble. I got on really well with him and we spent most evenings playing games and sometimes going to the town to look around and chase after Geisha girls! Unfortunately Hammamula didn't remain with us long, only a month, for he had to go back to his job as a porter. But before leaving, giving me his address, he told me that I could stay with him if I ever got the chance of a holiday. And I did. Three months later when we finished in Tsumagui we were given a week off during which I spent three days with Afrooz and the rest working as a porter alongside Hammamula plus eight others, in Lake Ozè National Park - one of the most beautiful spots of its kind in Japan and probably half the world. People from all over the globe came to see this park, and in fact I was told that about 10,000 visitors toured Lake Ozè National Park daily. The place was vast and to see the whole park took more than a day.

Hikers entering the park used two wooden paths, or boardwalks, half a metre wide and as much apart - one was meant for going, the other for coming back though people generally chose both paths travelling either way; it was a 12km walk that took the walkers through forests with mountain views, passing over a couple of rivers, swamps and fields with flowers all over the place. Occasionally a side path would branch off the main path and take visitors to the other parts of the park, though I never wandered from the main track. With my poor English and limited descriptive skills I find it hard to convey the stunning beauty of this park, but to appreciate its breathtaking splendour I strongly recommend tourists travelling through Japan to visit this park. In those four days working there I took innumerable photos with my camera.

Along this path there were comfort houses providing food and drink for the visitors and occasionally a bed if they wanted to stay overnight. Supplies to some of these houses, which ran out rapidly and had to be replaced fast, were brought in daily by porters; these supplies were carried in great quantities, using a ladder-like structure they called *shoiiko*, made of wood, about 180cm high and half a metre wide. Food and drink came in boxes, which were placed on the *shoiiko*, fixed to it using ropes; the loaded *shoiiko* was carried by means of its shoulder straps - like a knapsack. It was the most laborious job I ever came across.

The first group of houses, Shibuts Sansoii, was situated 4km away from the 'starting point', so called since everyone began walking from there. No animals were allowed in the park, a notice said in large and clear writing, in English, and above that, I supposed, the equivalent in Japanese - a language I hadn't managed to learn, after all these months, apart from a few letters and phrases.

There were about ten houses at Shibuts Sansoii and they were very busy. Nearly 3km further away was Riyogo Goya with the same number of houses. Miyar Ashi with twice the number of houses was 3km further away from Riyogo Goya, and at last, Ichiban Toii, with only five houses, ended the journey 12 kilometres from the starting point.

Not all the houses were supplied by porters in Hammamula's group, and in fact I saw only about a handful of other individual porters, every now and then, along the path. Hammamula told me that most houses got all of their supplies at the start of the season by helicopter, at great cost.

Hammamula lived in the village of Katashina with his wife Kiyoko and 4-year old daughter Kimè. Every morning at 5:30 he took his microbus and went round collecting porters. There were nine of them working in the park, including a 75-year-old woman, and they all lived close by. The park wasn't far away either. By the time they also collected the boxes from the Boss's house and arranged them in the microbus, spending almost 45 minutes doing so, and then driving off again, it would be 7 o' clock before the starting point was reached. A big car park located there was usually full and sometimes on weekdays one could see a few cars parked also on both sides of the road leading to this car park. At weekends the car park was full to capacity with cars parked on both sides of the road for at least a mile down the road. That was when most people at weekends came by tour operators and therefore brought in by coaches that would drop their passengers at the entrance, then return in the evening to pick them up. At one corner of this car park a single space, roped around and kept vacant, was reserved for the porters. In here the boxes were unloaded, grouped according to the houses they were destined for and then given to the porters who took turns going to these different places.

One day, as I recall, the strongest porter, Sakèkibàra, with 140kg of food, drink and other necessities loaded on his *shoiiko* over his shoulders, set off for Shibuts Sansoii. Hammamula, the second strongest, with 110kg, and a woman with 50kg, also departed for the same place. The rest, taking their *shoiikos*, quite reluctantly started moving and by 7:30 they were all gone.

The further these porters went the less weight they carried. A couple of days later Sakèkibàra took 110kg and Hammamula 90kg going to Ichiban Toii, the furthest of the houses. But, then again, the further one went the better money one earned. For each kilo carried, Shibuts paid out 70, Riyogo Goya 110, Miyar Ashi 140 and Ichiban Toii 170 yens. Therefore every time Sakèkibàra went to Ichiban Toii he received 18,700 yens - very good money, but still a torturous job. How can a man take 110kg and walk 12km? Back in Iran I told a couple of relatives about this and they were amazed. Even without carrying anything, just walking the long distance would be tiring. With all my training, on day one, I took 50kg, which felt very heavy, and had to carry that to Miyar Ashi, 10km away. A very good looking peasant young man of 26 by the name of Harooki, who took 70kg and never stopped calling me Mr Cyrus, was going to the same place, and I followed him.

For the first kilometre at intervals of 100 metres of flat boardwalk there were neatly made wooden steps we took going downward, to the next level stretch; there were about 50 of these steps and by the end of this kilometre I estimated that we had descended some 200 metres. After that, for the rest of the journey, the path, though twisting here and there, was flat with no steps either up or down.

Everyone walked at a normal pace and rested every 200 to 300 metres for about a couple of minutes; it didn't take long before the gaps between the porters began to widen. On my first day Harooki took it easy. Soon I was wet with sweat which started dripping down from my head. The scenery was beautiful but the weight over my shoulders was challenging any pleasure derived from the surroundings. Somehow we got through the first part of the journey and at about 9 o'clock Harooki and I reached Shibuts Sansoii. Most porters were there already, gathered in the house Tanabi; I could see their *shoiikos* outside. We left ours next to theirs and went in. They were all in the kitchen drinking coffee and eating sandwiches. The owner, an old lady, also offered me a sandwich and a cup of coffee and the same was given to Harooki.

By now I had learned a lot of Japanese and could keep up a limited conversation, which it seemed was all I needed; therefore it didn't matter that all the porters in the group couldn't manage more than just a few words in English - some of them not even that, with the exception of Sakèkibàra who could speak English well and who I found to be a very nice person. It didn't take long before I realized all these porters were like Hammamula: humble, doing their best to treat me like one of themselves.

One by one, about 15 minutes later, porters started to leave the house. Sakèkibàra, Hammamula and the woman had finished for the day, but the rest still had a long journey ahead of them.

Now all of the porters, *shoiiko* over their shoulders, were en route, and I followed Harooki again, the last one in the line of porters. It didn't take long before I was wet with sweat again and I cursed myself for undertaking such a hard job. Surely there was an easier way to carry this pile, I thought.

A couple of hours later we got to Riyogo Goya, the end of the journey for another three porters. Here Harooki and I stayed for only five minutes, had a cup of *ocha* (Japanese green tea) in one of the houses, then left to finish the last part of our journey. We had lost the sight of the other two porters going to Ichiban Toii. I only knew that they were ahead of us.

Around one o'clock we got to Miyar Ashi. What a wonderful moment! Taking the pile off my shoulders and knowing I had to carry it no longer, even though just for the day, I was overjoyed and felt as if I had completed a great task. Now, walking again without my load, I was jumping in the air! We handed the boxes to the house Yashiro Goya there; the owner's wife had spent a few years in America and spoke some English, and for this reason, I believe, gave us a good lunch plus salad. Harooki told me it was the first time she had been that generous! When we finished the repast we started on the return journey.

At Shibuts Sansoii the porters met again, in the same house, Tanabi. There were two more houses in the same area receiving supplies from the porters, but the group all preferred to gather in Tanabi; it was owned by an old lady who had created a friendly atmosphere, something lacking in most other houses.

I felt relaxed talking to these people, unlike the time when I worked in Kobayashi factory or alongside my present lift Boss and Okasawa. Though a much harder job with less pay, I would have preferred to stay here rather than go back to the ski lift job. Unfortunately there were problems, however. First, there was the matter of accommodation: as a porter I was staying with Hammamula and his family, and though they did everything to make me feel at home, I nevertheless soon began to feel uneasy taking advantage of their kind hospitality; also, finding another place to stay would be very difficult, if not impossible. And second, my lift Boss had asked Hammamula to send me back to him at the end of the week, a request Hammamula wouldn't hesitate to obey. And when I thought of quitting my job with my lift Boss, telling Hammamula about it and asking him if he would let me stay on for a while longer, he shook his head and told me that it would be a breach of Japanese customs and conjure up bad feelings between two friends, meaning himself and the lift Boss; it would be tantamount to robbing the lift Boss of his worker.

Never mind, I thought, I would return and try to be patient working with my lift Boss and Okasawa. It took courage to tolerate the intolerable.

We had coffee at Tanabi, followed by a short chat and then left for the starting point. Sakèkibàra and Hammamula had gone back to the town to play *pachinko* (a fruit machine-like game that was a daily part of Japanese life). At 5 o'clock Hammamula would be at the car park waiting to take the porters back. We still had time and with only a light load in our *shoiikos* everyone took it easy. Harooki, most relaxed of all, kissed his girlfriend non-stop on the return journey!

When we reached the starting point and the car park, Hammamula was already there waiting. We got in his microbus and he started off. On the way back the porters called at the Boss's house, had a drink there and I took some more photos. I was having a great time with these people. Then we left and Hammamula got everyone home.

At his house Hammamula took his shoes off, told me to do the same and we entered. He kissed his daughter Kimè, gave his wife Kiyoko a smile and I said *koombawa* (good evening) to both of them. It was nice to know that Kiyoko, his wife, spoke a little bit of English, and better than that, she made the best curry and rice in Japan. I got on really well with Hammamula and his family and in fact a few days later when I was leaving they looked quite sad. Thank you Mr and Mrs Hammamula, for your wonderful hospitality!

When I left Katashina I returned to Afrooz. I stayed with her for a day of which I spent ten hours in bed - working in Ozè Park had drained me of all power! Early the next morning I left Tokyo for a place called Kurico, as pre-arranged, to meet the Boss and Okasawa there.

I was very much in love with Afrooz and she was very much in my thoughts on the way to Kurico. It seemed she loved me too, though soon I was to have my illusions shattered. For the last few months I had been seeing her off and on, but not all that often. Every other Saturday after I finished work I left for Tokyo and by the time I got to Afrooz it was late in the evening. I stayed overnight and was back by Sunday evening. Sooner or later, I thought, on one of these visits I would ask her to marry me. She was the type of girl I could happily spend the rest of my life with. After we were married we would stay in Japan for another year or two to save some more money, I thought, then, as she has always wanted, we would leave for India to live there for ever. I was dreaming of a fantastic future, especially since it meant I wouldn't have to spend any of it in Iran.

The Kurico ski area was situated about 2km away from the small village of Itaya. And Itaya itself was almost halfway, on the railway track, between the big city of Fukushima in the east and the medium sized city of Unezawa in the west. It took me over three hours on the train, from Tokyo, changing at Fukushima, to get to Itaya: a small station without gates or a conductor. Walking along the only street in Itaya, at the end of this small village, I came to a forest. Following a road in the forest, after walking for about a kilometre, I came to the main road; turning left here and walking for another kilometre, there it was - the Kurico ski area.

Entering the premises, I went straight for the hotel: a 5-story building, about 100 metres away from the entrance, a magnificent sight, from the outside as well as inside. At the reception a very cheerful young man of 26 by the name of Watanabè, soon to become a good friend of mine, told me that there was a room booked for me on the third floor and gave me the key. The Boss and Okasawa had bookings for the same day too, but they hadn't arrived yet.

I went to my room, which was larger than the previous ones I had occupied in Minakami or Tsumagoi, but just as clean and everything as it should be. The windows in the room opened to some beautiful scenery: on the left, about 200 metres away, was a colossal car park, almost deserted now, and beyond that a thick forest stretched as far as the eye could see. Later I realised it was the same forest I had passed through leaving the village of Itaya on my way to Kurico; then, straight ahead, much nearer, I could see part of two ski runs. One belonged to a four-passenger chairlift. Someone had left the corrugated entrance open and I could see the entire machinery from where I was standing in my room by the window. The other ski run boasted a 'Romance' lift fifty metres on the left of the first one.

It was midsummer now, the snow long since melted, the hills barren and the rest green with grass; in a few months' time Kurico would be covered with snow again, and fate, it seems, had decided my future - for who would think that I'd be among one of the staff running that same four-passenger chairlift, my job mainly punching *oikaksan'no ticketo* (guests' tickets). I left my knapsack in the room, went downstairs and left the hotel to have a look around the area. It was two in the afternoon and if the Boss arrived now there would be no more work, I guessed, until the day after, so I didn't have to worry about being back early. First I went up the mountain used as a ski run for the four-passenger chairlift. On the top, which took me more than an hour to reach, were two 'Romance' lift runs going up different hills. I chose the one on the left and climbed up. Everything was quiet: I was on my own and it looked as if the whole planet had been deserted. When I got to the top, I could see for miles around. I spent a while there looking at the scenery; then, coming down, I took a different route. I passed a single chair lift, one more romance, and at the end when I got to where I had started it was past 6 o'clock.

Entering the hotel, at the reception Mr Watanabè told me that the Boss and Okasawa had also arrived and were in their rooms - on the same floor, all three rooms next to one another. First I went for a shower, then, after a short doze in my room, I joined them both in the hotel restaurant. As usual they were drinking *saki* and when I paid them my due respects they just nodded and I sat down: a slave joining his master - with one exception: this master had no choice but to accept him at his table. I was back working with the torturers, I thought. Then dinner was served; it was perfect. Kurico was the best resort I ever stayed at in Japan. I lived like a king there. If the Boss and Okasawa would treat me with only a little more dignity it would have been a perfect life. Why did there always have to be something missing?

At Kurico we started with the four-passenger chairlift and after that worked on one of the 'Romances'. Here the boss of the area, Mr Goto, every now and then called and worked alongside us for a couple of hours. He seemed to be a nice person and one day, almost at the end of our stay in Kurico, he took me to one side and told me that when the ski season started I could come back to Kurico and work for him. Appreciating his offer, I told him I would certainly consider working for him depending on my circumstances in the near future - for until then a lot could happen.

From Kurico we went to Inawashiro, almost halfway between Tokyo and Kurico. It was a Friday and what a day! Looking back across all the years that have since passed, I still remember it (writing these notes) as a sad day - at the time a blow that nearly knocked me out. That afternoon when we got to Inawashiro I asked the Boss if he would let me have Sunday as well as Saturday off. We had been working every other Sunday for the last two months, and it was the first time I asked for leave since by now I considered myself entitled to an extra day off. Grudgingly, he said, "Daijobo." ("Okay.")

That Friday evening I left for Tokyo to see Afrooz. It would be a double surprise for her; first, she wasn't expecting me that week but the next, and then also on the Saturday, not a Friday; second, I was going to ask her to marry me! Late that evening when I got to Tokyo, coming out of the subway station with a bunch of red roses in my hand, I called for a taxi as it was a bit late, thereby making up for the thirty minutes or so that it usually took walking from the station to her place. A few minutes later after the taxi dropped me, I went round to the factory; there, going up some stairs and coming to a door usually left open, I entered the narrow corridor in front of me with three doors on the left, the last one belonging to Afrooz; the first two, until a few weeks ago, were occupied by two old Japanese women, but now by two foreign girls, one from Pakistan and the other from Sri Lanka. Looking at the glass panel on the top of Afrooz's door I saw that she was still up, the light being on. As I got closer I heard her talking to somebody in her own language, and it was a man who answered back. Perhaps a friend's boyfriend, I thought, for I wasn't going to jump to conclusions too fast: after all, I had put all my trust in her. Nevertheless I stood behind the door listening, too scared to look through the glass panel in case I saw something hurtful. Then suddenly their conversation took a different turn; she started making pleasure moans, at the same time saying, "...beautiful,...beautiful..."

There was a bucket by the door. I turned it upside-down, stood on it and slowly brought my eyes up to the level of the glass panel. I was still hoping not to see anything hurtful, but when I looked through the panel I saw Afrooz and this man both naked on the bed making love. I felt shattered! With tears in my eyes and a lump in my throat I got off the bucket and left the corridor silently. I reached the top of the stairs, tears rolling down my cheeks. In the fresh air outside it felt cool. I made my way to the nearest park and placed myself on one of the benches there. Staring at the flowers I still held in my hand, I thought what a fool I'd been. I was still thinking when dawn broke. With a lot of effort I got myself off the bench, left the flowers there and walked to the subway station. It was just opening. I bought myself a ticket back to Inawashiro. When I got to the hotel the Boss and Okasawa were getting ready to go to work, and I joined them. By working, I thought, I might get my mind off the happenings of the night before, though I knew it was almost impossible. And sure enough, I looked so downcast and depressed that neither the Boss nor Okasawa asked me anything about my swift return.

chapter twenty

THE DAY WE FINISHED WORK I didn't go for dinner. I had a shower, watched some TV and then went straight to bed. On Sunday, the day after, I slept until late in the morning. When I woke up the sun had come up; I had slept for almost 12 hours without a sound. It was an amazing habit I had since childhood: encountering bad incidents, even a fight, for the following days I slept well. In the afternoon I went to the city of Aiizuwakamatsu, about 15 miles away, walked around window shopping until late; then caught the last train back. They say time is a healer, but I say walking is a faster healer.

Days went by slowly. I wasn't thinking much of Afrooz anymore; I kept my mind off her by busying myself with work and in the evenings playing table tennis, badminton and doing some weights. Going down to the city of Inawashiro was good too; a great shopping centre and the place was supposed to be one of the best tourist attractions in the country. Inawashiro

Lake, the second largest in Japan, viewed from Bandai Mountain, was a spectacular view.

We spent over two months repairing a 'Romance' lift drawn up that mountain, overlooking the city and a vast area around. I took so many photos up there. On some weekends I met a few foreigners climbing this mountain, most being from America and Germany.

Something funny and somehow strange happened one afternoon. As Okasawa and I were working at the bottom of Bandai with no one around apart from the two of us, I saw two foreigners approaching; in a remote place like this it was more or less standard procedure for us foreigners to be drawn towards one another. After exchanging smiles and a few words, they asked me where I was from. I answered, "Iran, and you?" When they said Israel, we almost laughed our heads off. Okasawa, amazed, stood there and just watched us: two old enemies had met in the middle of nowhere and he was probably expecting a fight, but neither they nor I felt any enmity towards each other. In fact, when I realized they were looking for a beautiful place to visit I tried to be most helpful and told them about Lake Ozè National Park. In the end, shaking hands, they departed, and as soon as they were gone Okasawa asked me, "Anata wa zettai Irangin daya?" ("Are you sure you're from Iran?")

Work finished and entering the hotel one evening, Mr Sasaki, another receptionist, greeted me with his usual cheerful face. He told me that Afrooz had phoned and that she had left a message asking me to phone her back. "Next time she calls tell her I'm no longer here," I told him, and he later informed me that he had given her my message. I never heard from Afrooz again. Did she ever find out why I suddenly severed all contact with her? Who cares, I ask myself as I write these notes. Nevertheless, it's the sad as well as the good memories that remain with one for life, like trophies and scars.

We were still working in Inawashiro when the snow came in early December. The ski season had started and therefore we had to finish fast. Some local workers joined us and a couple of days later all the repairs were over.

When I said goodbye to the Boss he asked me to join him again the following year. Well, I thought privately, I would join him - but only if I couldn't find myself a better job. Frankly, I had had enough of his aloof superiority.

What I really wanted, now, was factory work, the kind of job that would keep me busy all the time so that no one would try to boss me around - for exercising their authority is something the Japanese loved to do when they came across a foreigner in the workplace. But where would I find a factory without being treated like a slave? I was miles from Tokyo. On the other hand, on reflection, I recalled that there was a readymade job waiting for me right where I was. Weighing the circumstances, I chose the latter. I went back to Kurico and found Mr Goto. He had promised me a job when the ski season started, and it was well on the way in

Kurico; indeed, hundreds of skiers now crowded the area. Approaching him, I was uncertain whether he was still of the same mind about taking me on; Japanese men changed their minds as fast as typhoons hitting their island changed direction. But I found Mr Goto true to his word and he looked very happy to see me. He took me to his office, gave me both parts of the ski uniform, top and bottom, similar to the ones worn by other workers, and told me that my job would be snow shovelling and punching skiers' tickets. In 28 years of Kurico's existence, Mr Goto informed me, I was the first foreigner working on the premises.

I started as one of the staff on the four-passenger chairlift. Only a few months ago, I remembered, in the mild sunshine weather, we were repairing this same lift and now there was snow everywhere. Mr Goto told me that sometimes the temperature at Kurico during the night-time dropped to 20 degrees below zero. But the 100,000 yens' worth of each pair of uniform (top and bottom) he had supplied us with well protected everyone against this cold.

I was working with a number of others, all farmers, who had nothing to do in the winter season so worked in the ski industry. Starting at seven in the morning, we snow shovelled for about an hour clearing the entrance and smoothing the parts where the snow machine couldn't get round to pound. I found that a good workout and often put in extra effort. Then we ran the machinery: the chairs coming down were all covered with snow and we swept them; this was followed by a few minor jobs that needed to be got out of the way in time for 8:30 a.m. when the area opened for skiing, the hard work apparently over.

Two of us punched the skiers' tickets and one of us led them to their seats, and the rest went back to the staff room, warming up around the heater waiting for their turn to replace the ones working outside half an hour later. I found punching the tickets an entertaining part of the job, especially since some girls had their tickets clipped to their jackets right over the breast. This went on for the rest of the day.

Next to the staff room was the control room, separated only by a door, always left open, which contained all the electrical equipment in connection with the lift. A middle-aged man by the name of Morohashi with short, pointed ears - quite similar in appearance to the impression I had of the devil! - was in charge of this room. He sat, or rather slept, in front of a panel covered by keys, and whenever something went wrong - a rare occurrence and usually minor - he stopped the lift and switched it back on again. His resemblance to the devil seemed appropriate for he could often be a real bastard!

Staff and control rooms, appearing as one from the outside, were next to the main machinery of the lift. From where I was sitting in the staff room, looking through the window I could see the biggest wheel of all going round and with it the main cable; hanging from it, the seats passed by at intervals of 15 metres. It was a non-stop process, the seats coming down empty, at the end of their journey going round this big wheel, each taking up to four passengers, then moving forward in a row at the head of four long queues, passing in front of my window taking the passengers up to the top of the ski run. And it was here, near my window, that most problems occurred - when the skiers had to get onto the moving seats. If a skier was too slow to come forward for the seat to pick him (or her) up, he (or she) was hit by it and fell; then everything had to be stopped. The man leading the skiers to their seats was standing next to a short pole, at his right, on which there were two buttons, one to slow the lift down, the other to stop it; for beginners he pressed the slow button so that they would have more time to ready themselves for the approaching seats. Most of the time, however, he didn't know who was a beginner and who wasn't, though by their second time round most beginners learned what to do; still, there were a few who did not move fast enough, so were hit by the seat and fell - in which case the man leading the skiers to their seats had no choice but to stop the lift so he could pick the skier up and clear the way for the others; then he would signal Morohashi to switch the lift mechanism back on again.

All lifts stopped at five in the afternoon, apart from the four-passenger lift which kept going up to ten at night - for which purpose four of us, on a rotary basis, stayed on for the extra hours. Not many liked working till that late; most were a lazy bunch, and there was always one asking me to cover for him. This happened so often that, looking back a month later, I realised I had been working seven days a week right up to ten at night, with the exception of only two days when I had been on duty until the normal closing time of 5 o'clock. I rarely claimed my right to a day's holiday per week. Trying to be compliant - the job would last for just over three months - I allowed myself to be manipulated by the person I was covering for, who made me feel he was doing me a favour by letting me have his night shift. Trapped in this situation, I worked late on many occasions. The pay wasn't appealing either, for almost 14 hours' work a day I was being paid 10,000 yens; but then again we weren't doing much, and even less in the evenings, and there was the bonus of meeting a lot of girls!

Workers were lodged at their quarters; a large two-story rectangular building, beyond the car park, with its own showers and restaurant. In here the rooms, about ten in all, were much smaller than the ones in the hotel; about 3x4m in size and with two bunk beds in each room at opposite corners, they looked like prison cells. There were four people to a room, but as most workers lived in the nearby villages hardly anyone stayed overnight. The man in charge of the rooms, Mr Jimbo, a cheerful good-looking middle-aged man who could polish off a bottle of saki in the space of two hours, stayed most nights, to my delight - since he was very good company and he gave me a bed in his own room. We joked, laughed and often drank together, sitting on his bed with the curtains separating the beds drawn back.

A few weeks later, with Mr Goto's approval, I took a day off. By now Mr Goto had proved to be very good-natured, almost unique among those I had met or am ever likely to come across. Taking the same day off himself, he took me in his car sightseeing. We went to the city of Fukushima and he showed me where the museum, library and a couple of sport centres were, and also where he usually played Pachinko. We spent about an hour together while he played the machine. I didn't try my luck on the machine since I was reluctant to gamble away the hard-earned cash earned by the sweat of my brow! By midday, both feeling hungry, we went to a Sushi shop to have lunch. Sushi was becoming one of my favourite foods in Japan: a piece of raw fish on a half handful of rice dipped into Shoyi sauce; there were two of the same on a saucer that customers picked up from a moving belt.

After our meal we enjoyed another short ride around the area, and then went to Mr Goto's house. He lived close to the ski area and being the eldest son of the family, as well as inheriting everything, he was obliged to look after his parents. The house was massive, with its own rice field at the back. His father looked after the rice field, I was informed. Entering the house, he introduced me to his wife and two sons who greeted me quite warmly. This family certainly didn't harbour any prejudice against foreigners. They sat on the floor round a low table, and I was asked to join them in a cup of ocha and some sweets. We watched some TV, which was followed by a little bit of *hanashi* (conversation) and before long it was time to leave. When they said goodnight, their leave-taking was as warm as their welcome. Once outside Mr Goto told me that if I ever found myself with nowhere to go I was welcome to stay with them. It was very apparent that in saying this he was quite sincere and spoke from the heart. I greatly appreciated his offer. From my heart, too, I thank you, Mr Goto: may you be happy and prosper wherever you are.

Back at Kurico I spent a quiet evening drinking alongside Mr Jimbo. After working seven days a week and till late at night, having a day off seemed more than just a holiday, especially spent the way I did: being driven around, "shown and explained", as my roommate put it.

I started the next day feeling refreshed, yet a bit uneasy. Recently I'd been running into some difficulty getting on with two of the workers in the rest room. One was a fat bastard by the name of Itto, the other a real pain in the neck called Kikuchi. Both were in their early thirties. Though it was their very first time having a foreigner working alongside them, they began to display the same kind of behaviour I had faced working in the Kobayashi factory. It looked as if some Japanese were naturally sadistic, probably carrying some kind of unknown endemic virus that was activated as soon as they came across a foreigner who was naturally in a weaker position as they were. It was the only way I could explain this kind of instinctive prejudice. And since it seemed an epidemic one as well, it soon spread to a few others who began to display the same symptoms. There were always a few who remained neutral, neither taking sides nor trying to calm the situation; medically speaking, I called them the immune ones, for coming across me they showed no reaction. Finally, there were those very few who, you might say, carried the antidote inside them. Out of a staff of ten permanently working on the four-passenger chair lift, only one man, a senile and diminutive man by the name of Kirisawa, displayed compassion towards me, backing me up if he felt I was the recipient of injustice. Though small but big in conscience, Mr Kirisawa tried to stop anyone using rough or uncouth language when talking to me - which was the main problem I was facing there. Pointing at me, the old man, talking to the others, reminded them, "Karè wa dorèii janayiyo!" ("He is not a slave!"). I heard him say this on a number of occasions.

But still the abuse went on, and the only way to avoid it, I came to realize, was by staying out of the room - and working was one way of doing so; but unfortunately that went in turns, or rotas, and half an hour later I had to hand over to the next worker. Then, instead of going back to the room and warming myself round the heater with those bastards in there, I chose to walk around the area till my next turn; sometimes I spent just five minutes in the room warming myself before starting work again. Even in those few minutes they found a way to get on my nerves. This caused me to become sensitive to every move they made, especially the moves of those two bastards, Itto and Kikuchi. I was safe if Mr Goto was present; he was the extreme case of the last condition the virus took - the antidote; no one dared treat me badly in front of him, for they knew he wouldn't tolerate it: "...watashi wa omotta cohi to hajimè gayijin tomodachi..." ("I intended that coffee for our foreign friend first")", I once heard him say to Deboo (fat) Itto when he was handing cups of coffee and missed me out. But Mr Goto wasn't always there; going round checking all the lifts in the area, he spent little time in our rest room.

Taking walks outside between shifts was a cold way to stay out of trouble, but it seemed the only way to keep my job. It was just a couple of months till the end of the ski season which meant it would soon be *sayonara* (goodbye) to the jobs we were holding, so I would try to be patient over this short period; on the other hand there were moments when, as in the case of Kobayashi, I felt like storming out the place. Walking on the borderline between these two kinds of feelings, but a mite closer to patience than combat, I managed to carry on working largely by staying away from the room as much as possible.

The days went by slowly, the snow melted away, and on the 31st of March all the farmers left and the lifts shut down, leaving a handful of us running only the four-passenger chairlift. And as there were no more skiers or snow, a few days later the area closed down. I thanked Mr Goto, who told me I could work for him the following year again, said *sayonara* and left to find myself another job.

chapter twenty one

MY LIFT BOSS, when I phoned him, told me that maintenance work wouldn't start for at least another month. Going that long without a job was unthinkable; it would drain me of a lot of money, and also meant spending the nights at a sauna. Finding a job was essential, therefore, if only to provide me with a roof over my head.

I went back to Fukushima since there was an industrial estate just outside that city, and I thought I would try my luck there. After spending the night in a Fukushima sauna, I left early in the morning for this industrial area. On the first few places I entered, hands were crossed and I was shown a 'no entry' sign - it all took me back to my first day in Japan, in Kawaguchi. At about 10 o'clock I entered a factory premises where workers were busy outside, standing on a platform loading lorries with drink crates. A man also standing on the platform, watching others with pen and paper in hand and now and again writing something, seemed to be in charge. I decided to approach him.

"Ohayo gozaymasu" ("Good morning"), I said to him; he barely turned his head and I carried on: "Watashi wa shigoto sagashdè, arbaito iroo?" ("I'm looking for a job, do you need a worker?")

"Do you speak English?" he enquired.

"Sure I do," I confirmed.

With his passable English and not wasting any time, he said, "Help that man at the end." The Japanese always liked to show off when they spoke English.

They were all working in pairs apart from the man I joined; he seemed busy enough on his own. Not a word exchanged, fifteen minutes later we finished loading our lorry with crates carrying drink bottles; the rest had finished a few minutes earlier. The lorries loaded, four in all, left, another four took their places. They were small ones and, fresh as I was, about thirty minutes later, loading ours, we finished first - minutes later, as did the rest. The man in charge had left, but as soon as the loading stopped he came out of an office-like room and called me in. Once inside I felt as I did the very first time I entered the Kobayashi factory office; and again, like it was there, some women and a few men were busy working, all stopping to stare at me. From that moment on I called the man in charge Boss - not to be confused with the other bosses I've had; I shall refer to him as Drink Boss, a funny name that will later serve to remind me of him. He was in his early forties, a bit fat with a small potbelly, about my height, dark thick hair, clean-shaven. He told me my job would be putting bottles and sometimes packets of drinks into crates, them on trollies; when there was enough on one trolley, it would be pushed outside to the platform and then loaded onto lorries. The work started at eight in the morning and finished at five in the afternoon; there would be an hour lunch break and my pay - something I'd been waiting to hear all along - would be 1,000 yens per hour. Did I have a visa? "Yes, I have a six months' visa," I said. Could he have a look at it? "No. I have my passport in safe keeping at the Iranian embassy, because I could lose it carrying it around." In actual fact I had it on me, in my pocket. He then told me that if I didn't have a place to stay I couldn't have the job. "Yes," I responded, undaunted, "I have a one bedroom flat in Fukushima." After telling him all these lies I left the office to start my job in Tanabè factory.

I had been lucky again, having secured a job on my first day searching for one. It felt as though a hidden hand was looking after me. Also, it turned out to be the kind of job I enjoyed. Mostly physical work, especially when loading the lorries. But how long would it last? If it were in a country with a more refined brand of people - the British, for instance (talking from experience) - I'd be thinking of years or perhaps a decade. What did I want from life, if not a steady job and somewhere quiet to live, and no one to get in my way - was that too much to ask for?

Though often working in pairs which meant working away from the main body of workers - my partner was a quiet little man, and I was yet to find out his reaction towards me - I knew that, sooner rather than later, the rest would find a way to get on my nerves; once the virus was activated, the place would become another torture chamber for me. And a few days later, when it came, I felt like getting hold of a gun, going back to work and shooting them all, one by one. (Perhaps saying before I shot them, "Sorry, you're too infected by this endemic virus, so...") I began to understand why someone suddenly loses his temper and, introducing a gun, starts shooting those around him; I dare say there's a reason for such an irrational act, and perhaps society should share some responsibility for the person's action.

Every evening, work finished, I went back to Fukushima, had something to eat, looked around till late, then went to the same sauna to spend the night. Living like that I was thinking of the same course of action I had successfully taken when I started in the Kobayashi factory: in a couple of weeks' time my Drink Boss would trust me enough to let me stay, once work was finished, at the factory. But, unfortunately, my lifeline at Tanabè didn't last that long. A few days later one of the workers, an ugly bastard, deliberately, bumped into me while passing by, then shouted abuse calling me *baka* (stupid). Feeling like turning back and killing him, I restrained myself and with a lot of effort I managed to calm myself down; showing no reaction to avoid further trouble, I kept on working. That was the first incident, but others soon followed, all adding to the tension inside me until almost a week after I had begun work at the factory it reached the point where I could put up with it no longer and I stormed out. Again, it was not through any fault on my part. This is how the trouble started: as we were working my partner dropped a crate full of bottles and broke a few. The same bastard who had deliberately bumped into me a couple of days earlier, now working some distance away, assumed I had dropped the crate and, waving his fist in the air shouting *baka*, came running to me. They say the quiet ones are the worst ones. My partner, a quiet person, looked at me in a way that suggested I was the one who had actually dropped the crate and reinforced this notion by clearing the way and moving to the side; moreover, anticipating some kind of action, he seemed quite excited and stood back to watch as the ugly bastard got close to me, still waving his fist. The man was going to put his fist into my face, he shouted, now standing a metre in front of me. I pretended I didn't want trouble and, wanting to carry on with my work, picked up a crate from the trolley, swinging it back; then, instead of forward handing it to the man inside the lorry, something snapped inside me and I threw it at that bastard's feet, hitting him on one of his shins. He gave a painful shout and when he bent over to hold the shin in pain, I punched the cunt in the face before pushing him off the platform, where he landed on his ass. At this the rest of the workers ganged up and were about to jump on me, and anticipating their action I got hold of a bottle by the neck and broke it, which seemed enough to keep them at bay. With the broken bottle firmly in my hand, they froze where they stood. I backed off slowly, but though the trouble was apparently over, they had succeeded in their goal - since I knew my time at the factory was now well and truly up. I got down from the platform. In the office everyone was staring at the scene through the window. Seeing this, I threw the broken bottle in my hand away. The Drink Boss, coming out of the office, joined me. He wasn't a bad man, as I had come to realise in the week I had worked there. We walked slowly to the entrance, not a word said until we got to the gates; there we stood for a moment and he said, "They don't seem able to get on with foreigners. I was thinking it might be different this time." Then, almost half talking to himself, he added, "No, it didn't work." All the same, he wanted to know what happened.

Feeling downcast, I wasn't in any mood to talk, and whatever happened, I thought, it wouldn't change the final result; their goal was to get me out, and I was out. In a few short sentences I said, "I dropped a crate and broke a few bottles... one of the lads on the platform didn't seem to like it..." What was the point of telling him the truth, I thought? This was how he would get to hear about it. Now at least, lying, I could leave an honest impression, and not leave him thinking of me as someone who had done wrong and then tried to shift the blame on his partner.

After a long pause during which he seemed to be in

deep thought, he looked towards the platform and then, turning to me, he said, "Come back tomorrow to get your money." Extending his hand, I shook it. We parted and he went back inside and I walked away.

So much for my notion about being lucky and the hidden hand I had imagined was looking after me; these were my thoughts as I made my way back to Fukushima.

What was I to do next? I sat on a bench in one of the parks and I cursed the people of Iran for their stupidity in getting rid of the Shah and replacing him with someone like Khomeini. Would I ever have come here to work and face all these insults if the former was still ruling Iran? The economy then was so good that we had people from all over the world working in our country, and I doubt if they were treated badly. Too late now trying to put things back the way they were, and thinking about it was a waste of brainpower.

The next day, quite cautiously, I approached the factory. A glance towards the platform told me no one was there, so I assumed they were working inside. Unnoticed, I slipped into the office. On the right, a few metres away, the Drink Boss sat behind his desk, head down sorting papers out, and I went to him. "Kanichuwa" ("Good mid-morning"), I said, standing in front of his desk. He looked up and, after returning my greeting in English, he extracted an envelope from a drawer in his desk and handed it to me. Nodding his head, he said, "Goodbye."

"Thanks Boss," I said, "but before leaving I'd like to tell you something. You know that day when you asked me about my passport…?" I got my passport out of my pocket, replaced it with the envelope he had just given me, and carried on, "Didn't I tell you I had it inside the Iranian embassy? I was mistaken, it was right here in my pocket, and when I looked at my visa" - now showing him the page where it was stamped - "I realised the visa had expired almost 15 months ago." Then I closed my passport, put it in my pocket and left.

On the way back to Fukushima I laughed non-stop, remembering Drink Boss's face. When I showed him my expired visa, his expression betrayed mixed feelings: his eyes wide open, his lower lip well inside his mouth, he leaned forward with his hands clenched on the table, feigning an angry appearance; but underneath all that I could see he was trying hard to hold back a laugh which might burst out any moment.

I phoned Hammamula from Fukushima and after telling him that I had lost my job but not the true cause behind it, he asked me to go and see him. I got on the train, later changing it for a bus and then another one, and a few hours later I knocked at his door. He seemed glad to see me and invited me in. There was no one else in the house and when I enquired about his wife and daughter, surprised, I heard him say that he had divorced her. I didn't know whether to be happy or sad, though thought it wise to display the latter feeling. It was a good turn of events for me, probably, since it meant I might be able to stay with him now. He didn't seem to want to talk about it and so I questioned him no further. He only told me that he and his wife "kangaeru chigaiy" ("thought differently"), literally meaning they were not of the same mind.

Hammamula was a really nice guy. Knowing that I had lost my job, he phoned one of his friends at work and asked him if they needed anybody there - even if only for a short time. Because soon, he knew, I would be joining my Lift Boss. Ten minutes later his friend phoned back and gave a positive answer. He would be coming round in the evening to talk it over with me.

Job opportunities in Japan for locals were fantastic. In regard to foreigners, the Japanese just didn't trust them; otherwise the opportunities would have been the same. A local looking for a job is likely to find one in ten minutes. Even the shop next door had enough workers yet wouldn't mind taking on another one. By now I had come to realize that if a Japanese said he was unemployed, it was probably because he hadn't found the right job, one with suitable hours, for instance, or one that wasn't in a particular area. The pay was good too; a local worker on average earned about 250,000 yens per months with a bonus every six months. Foreigners did not qualify for receiving bonuses.

Anyway, at that moment, Ozè National Park being closed due to the still remaining snow, Hammamula was working in the Katashina ski resort hotel as a waiter; the area there hadn't closed yet. But once the park opened about a couple of weeks later, he would go back to his job as a porter and I would probably join him too even if only for a few days.

At about 7 o'clock that evening Hammamula's friend, the one who was going to give me a job, came round. Tall and slim, he was 29 years of age but looked much younger. Though he didn't know much English, he was eager to learn how to speak the language and in fact he loved everything English, even to the point of calling himself by an English name, Tomi. I got on really well with Tomi who, like Hammamula, was modest and didn't care that I was a foreigner. He told me that I could start the day after the next and my job would be putting eggs in cases, ten eggs to a case, starting at eight in the morning and finishing at five in the afternoon. There would be a lunch break of one hour between twelve and one, which would hardly give me time to eat since Tomi wanted me to teach him English during that hour! In fact, during my three weeks working there, just about every hour, for about ten minutes, he took me to a corner asking me how they said this or that in English! I often wondered why he didn't get fired, until one day Hammamula told me that the factory belonged to his uncle.

I had no qualms about quitting my job at the egg factory in order to start working alongside Hammamula in Ozè National Park, where the public had started visiting for the last few days. Due to the lack of hikers and Shibuts Sansoii being the only place open, just five porters were required to begin with. Each carried just 30kg, an arduous task after such a long period of inactivity, but it was the most one could handle to begin with. My stay at Ozè didn't last long either; a few days later my Lift Boss came round and told me that he had taken a job repairing some lifts, and asked me to join him. When I said goodbye to Hammamula I didn't know I was seeing him for the last time.

Working on the lifts, we went through the same procedure as the previous year, but in different areas. Days, weeks and then months went by without anything exciting happening; then one day as we drew nearer to the snow season and almost the end of our working days repairing lifts, it dawned on me that I didn't have much to lose by being fired from my job - for quite soon I would be working for Mr Goto again. I therefore decided I'd had enough of my Lift Boss and Okasawa treating me like shit. Picking on Okasawa and calling him a few names, we exchanged a few punches and when Boss came to his rescue I picked up an iron bar and threatened him with it. Boss backed off and Okasawa fled. I followed him through the forest but couldn't catch the bastard. Now knowing that Boss would never have anything to do with me anymore, I went back to the hotel, had a shower and waited for him to come. It was close to finishing time, so I expected him to call soon. I would get my pay and leave, I thought. And perhaps, before that happened, some further trouble might befall Okasawa, I thought.

It was hours later when Boss appeared at the hotel and a bit drunk. As he was going into his room I came out of mine. Reaching into his pocket, he had my money ready; he gave it to me and said, "Koobi" - the same old familiar word. Putting the money in my pocket, as it was too late then to leave, I asked him if I could stay for the night and instead leave in the morning. He just shrugged his shoulders in answer and went to his room. Okasawa, coward bastard, stayed away that night.

Early next morning, with my knapsack over my shoulder, I left my Lift Boss never to see him again. What next? I could afford to be idle till it snowed, which would be in a few days' time, as it had been forecasted, but then again who could tell? Or I could go to Hammamula and work with him. My second choice was a doubtful one; being in close contact with the Lift Boss, Hammamula might refuse me, I thought; but then again, if I told him the truth about the way Boss and Okasawa had treated me, he, being a sensible bloke, surely wouldn't turn his back on me and cross his hands. However, it came to none of these.

chapter twenty two

I WAS BACK in Fukushima again, that all-too familiar place. Though I had been working on different ski areas since the year before, I had never been very far from this city. The place had become part of my comfort zone, though this time my visit proved to be disastrous. Standing in front of the railway station I noticed three people watching me. Looking up I recognized them: workers from Tanabé factory, the place where we used to load lorries with drink crates; and the man I had exchanged punches with, pushing him off the platform, was among them. They were about half a dozen metres away, and now that I had noticed them, I realised they were closing in on me, clearly looking for trouble, having seen my presence there as an opportunity to settle old scores. It seemed a bit too late now to walk away and ignore them. I thought about dropping my knapsack and running - not a wise move, since there were innumerable people around and some police standing close by. Surely with me running and them following, the crowd would react and alert the police whose involvement would mean the end of my stay in Japan. What about trying to talk my way out of this predicament? No, it was too late for that! Before I could even reach for my pocket to get the blade out, they were upon me. A fight broke out and in no time the police were putting handcuffs on us.

I don't know where those three were taken, but I was stuck into a police car and a few minutes later found myself inside Fukushima police station. There a policeman searching me found my passport and handed it to his superior sitting at a table; turning the pages over, he found the right page and, obviously looking at my visa, said, "San tsuki bisa" ("three months visa"), "daiitaii san nen iku, mada kochi" ("almost three years gone, still here"). Looking up, he asked me, "Shigoto?" ("Working?")

"So" ("Yes)", I answered, though to have admitted working, I knew, would not place me in a favourable position. But what other reply would account for such a long stay in the country?

He wrote down a few notes and, having finished with the passport, put it away. He picked up my return air ticket to Iran, which was also on the table, having also been found on me, along with my knife and the money I had received the night before from my Lift Boss. The ticket, valid for a year, had long since expired. Informing me of this, he said, "Atarashi ticketo iroo."

("New ticket needed.") Regarding the last item, I was aware that people in Japan were allowed to carry a knife.

He nodded to the policeman who took me to the next room where I was photographed and fingerprinted; after the ink was washed off my fingers I was returned to the first room. The same superior from behind his desk told me he would hang on to my passport, air ticket, money and knife, and then put these items into a side draw of his desk. With all this attended to, he seemed satisfied with his work and gave a sweeping gesture with his finger to indicate that I should be taken away.

The policeman took me down some stairs to where the cells were located and pushed me into one of them. The door was closed and bolted from the outside. It was a medium sized tidy cell, a single bed with clean sheets and blankets in one corner and a small table with a chair in the other. The bars on the window, in contrast to the rest of the cell with its white walls, for some reason were painted green; outside the window a nearby wall obstructed the view so that only a small part of the sky could be seen. A few minutes later my cell door opened and an officer politely handed me my knapsack. There was nothing of importance in the knapsack apart from my bank book and cash card which I found were still there.

Everything was quiet until noon, when I heard footsteps approaching. A metal plate in the middle of the cell door was pushed to the side, revealing a square gap through which a policeman said, "Lunch." After he passed me a tray through the opening, the metal plate slid back in place. Two hamburgers, a portion of chips and a can of Coke was what I received on that tray. I was relieved, for there was no Japanese food I didn't like; possibly they were aware that foreigners were not always partial to their cuisine! I had my fill and went to sleep.

It was dark when I woke up. The old depression crept over me as I became aware of my surroundings, for it seemed I was no stranger to prison cells! I put the light on and went back to bed, everything still very quiet. I felt certain I would be returned to Iran, the country I had always tried to get away from. But it would be different this time. I was 40,000 US dollars richer, and with the war ended, I may find the place more tolerable. Three years had elapsed since my last stay there, and the situation might have improved. Trying to solace myself with these thoughts, I resigned myself to my fate. "Do I have any other option?" I sighed.

My spirits downcast, I stayed in bed for most of the evening and only rang the bell once to use the toilet. Dinner, handed to me in the same way as before, still lay untouched on the table a couple of hours later.

I spent a restless night. In the morning, after being served breakfast, I was handcuffed to a policeman and led out of the station into the back of a police van, where the handcuffs were removed. Locking the door from the outside, the policeman took his seat next to the driver and we started moving.

After a few turns the van entered the motorway heading for Tokyo. Familiar surroundings, for I had been on that road many times before with my Lift Boss driving. Now I had a good guess where they were taking me. I tried to enjoy this journey, which was probably my last one through Japan. I had guessed correctly, for a couple of hours later I was handed over to the authorities at Narita Airport. I recalled that it was Thursday, which meant there would be a plane back to Iran that same day.

I was taken to a medium sized saloon with rows of chairs, the first few occupied, I noticed, by Iranians. Later, talking to some of them, I learnt that most of them had been picked up in the streets of Tokyo where, for the last year, unbeknown to me, a massive hunt had been going on in search of illegal immigrants. I was made to sit next to the last seat occupied; on my right all the seats were vacant, but were soon taken, including the rows of seats behind me, by other Iranians who were brought in one by one every few minutes; running out of seats, later, some sat on the floor at the back.

In the front immigration officers sat behind readymade desks with computers at hand, five in all. They all seemed busy, hastily sorting things out. Names were called, including mine after a few minutes. When I approached the right desk, the immigration officer had my passport open in front of him; my cancelled ticket was also lying on his desk. Pressing a few keys on his keyboard, he handed me my money, then pointing behind him where Iran Air had temporarily set up a few counters, he told me to collect my ticket.

What a rip off! Well aware that we had no choice, now that we were being sent back, but to use Iran Air, and also that we had been working and had been paid by the Japanese standard, they charged each of us 145,000 yens for a single flight back to Iran - *four times* what I had paid for the same flight, in the opposite direction, three years ago!

I had only 120,000 yens on me; that didn't seem to matter, for once back in Iran, my passport would be held at the airport and not returned to me till I settled the difference. But I had the money, not in Iran but "here in Japan". Only if I could get myself to a cash machine could I draw all my money out from the bank before leaving.

Turning back to the immigration officer I showed him my new ticket; nodding, he threw the cancelled one at me too. Later, back in Iran, at one of the Iran Air offices, handing it in, it might prove to be worth something. My passport, however, was not returned to me. Now was my chance to try to collect the rest of my Japanese money, so I told the immigration officer about my money in the bank. A good fellow, he called over one of the policemen and spoke to him, then told me to follow the policeman.

Leaving the saloon and following the policeman along some corridors, we came to a great hall that was half crowded with passengers, most with tickets in hand, some sitting down, a few walking around looking at the shops; obviously all were waiting to board their planes to leave.

The policeman looked at the cash card in my hand. "Fuji bank," he said.

"So" ("Yes"), I answered, nodding my head.

Following him to the other side of the hall, at one point I thought about dropping my knapsack and running away! But with all those people around, even if I got away, which seemed doubtful, would I be able to leave the airport? It seemed we were at the wrong section; all these people, now at the end of their stay, had officially checked out of the country; therefore, I thought, if a passenger for some reason tried to go back, he or she would encounter officials who would ask to see his or her papers; not like some sections where one could just walk out through doors. In spite of all that, I was still tempted to give it a try. We came to where they had the cash machines. Pointing at one of them, the policeman said, "Sorè." ("That one.") Above the machine was a sign that read, in large, clear letters, 'Fuji Bank.' Sticking my cash card in and pressing the four digits of my pin number, I withdrew all my money, just leaving some change behind to keep the account open - just in case I ever needed to use it again. At the next machine I changed them all to US dollars, the currency worshipped in Iran. It came to just over 40,000 US dollars; four bundles made up of one hundred dollar notes, all in my hand, I had a job to believe it. But I had worked hard and deserved it. I put them all in my pocket which I zipped up securely.

While being conducted back once more I thought about escaping. If caught, I would face just the same fate as I did now; but if I managed to get away it would be a different story.

I don't know what came over me, but suddenly I dropped my knapsack and started running! The policeman who was walking a step ahead of me instantly turned round and gave chase. I heard him blowing his whistle. Time seemed to stand still for all those around; all stopped dead in their places and turned back to see what was happening. Encountering another policeman running towards me from the front, I noticed some stairs to my right and made for them. I took three steps at a time. When I was halfway up I looked up and saw two policemen waiting for me; another two were at the bottom. Clearly there was no point in going further so I turned back. At the foot of the stairs the two policemen lost no time handcuffing me, with my hands behind my back. The hall now seemed crowded with policemen. One on either side of me held me by the arm, the one I had started with following from behind. On the way I saw him go to where I had dropped my knapsack, and he picked it up. I was taken back to the same saloon where, surprisingly, the handcuffs were removed, and like the rest, I was allowed to take a seat. Did they think it was my right to attempt an escape?

Long after everyone had been dealt with, the sky had turned dark outside; now more policemen joined the throng and we were told to form a single queue. Under watch from both sides, we were led out of the saloon - through a different door to the one I had taken earlier to the cash machine - then along some corridors until we reached the last one, trunk like, by means of which we entered the plane. It felt like entering my coffin, destination hell.

It wasn't long before the door was closed and the instructions were read. The 'seat belts on' sign flashed on and we started moving, faster and faster, until the plane left the surface of the planet.

In the plane there was plenty of time to think. After all, I thought, besides the Japanese, maybe I'd been infected too, by the virus of prejudice. I had been sent back, first, from England, then from Yugoslavia, and after that from Greece, and now from Japan - and still to come, twice from Cyprus and once from Malaysia. Only Turkey, it seemed, had given me a chance to serve myself with an honorary leave.

Less than two hours later we landed at Beijing airport. A few Iranians, for some reason more women than men, plus some Chinese-looking people, boarded the plane there, and not long after we left for our final destination. All the faces on the plane looked grim; no one looked happy going back against his or her will; half were being deported, the other half returning for various reasons: most not able to find jobs and, running out of money, had no other option but to return. I thought about the plight of the would-be Iranian refugee: back at home he had a roof over his head with three meals a day, paid by father and prepared by mama - then suddenly he finds himself in a foreign country in a down and out situation; yet still most preferred to go on living like that, tenuously, for as long as possible rather than face going back.

It was a long tiring flight, but it somehow ended and the plane landed safely. Now in Iran, we were herded into buses and ushered into a big hall. There, those without passports were called to one side to receive them back. Then, after a long wait in the queue with only two immigration officers to deal with all the passengers of the plane, my passport was checked, stamped, and handed back to me. Leaving this area, going up some stairs, I came to another big hall - in the front half of which passengers' luggage was coming out of openings and dumped on conveyor belts going round. At the other end of the hall the luggage items were being checked. I had nothing to pick up from the conveyor belt since I had my knapsack close with me during the flight. With every single item of baggage to be checked, it was some time before the queue moved forward and it was my turn to have my knapsack searched; all parts were unzipped and thoroughly checked, and it was well past midnight when I left the airport. It had taken more than three hours to get through the last 100 metres of my journey!

We had left Japan around seven in the evening; after a 12-hour flight, plus an hour stop at Beijing airport (13 hours in all), we had arrived at Mehrabad International Airport in Tehran, amazingly enough, on the same day and with only two hours delay.

I called a taxi and asked the driver for a good hotel, for I could afford it now. Even at this time, early in the morning, there was traffic on the road. I had always hated this city and everything it stood for; above all, the two-faced people who occupied it. Once more, finding myself back there with the full realisation of where I was, I felt dispirited. Soheila and her kids were no longer there, Sepideh was dead, and I was so far from my mother: I felt lonely, wanting to cry. However, I could still go and see my father.

chapter
twenty three

AFTER MY FIRST NIGHT in the hotel in Tehran, I found myself a two-bedroom flat to rent. Since one never gets a furnished flat or house in Iran, whether rented or bought, the place is always empty so I had to provide everything. Within the next few days I spent almost 10,000 US dollars and got the flat fully furnished. I bought almost everything one needed inside a flat. Though five-fold price increases had taken place since I had last been in Iran three years ago, food rationing and coupons had almost disappeared and one could get anything one wanted from the shops.

A few days later I went to see my father. The life of honesty hadn't paid dividends. He was in debt, living virtually in poverty and therefore contemplating going back to drug-dealing - with the same girlfriend with whom he was as much in love with as before. I didn't stay there long. I thanked him for the 2,000 dollars he had given me before I had left for Japan, gave it back to him plus another 3,000 dollars to pay off some of his debts, and left.

Then I found myself a job. Looking through a newspaper I came across an advertisement for a position to be filled by someone who spoke English, and who for some reason had to be fit. I applied for the position and the very next day started working as a taxi service receptionist at the biggest and best hotel in Tehran; my salary 50 dollars a month. Compared with what I used to get in Japan, it seemed farcical - especially since inflation was running at an alarming rate of something close to a three digit number. But I couldn't go round being idle and the job also promised to be an interesting one. I was meeting people from all over the world entering Iran to do business - added to which the drivers, about 30 in all, were quite amusing as well: I went through at least one fight a day with them! No wonder within the year preceding my debut they had 15 receptionists replaced in that period alone - six leaving with a gash on the head caused by drivers' club blows. I understood why the position called for someone who was fit!

Sitting behind the table they called the taxi service reception in one corner in the main lobby of the hotel, my job was simple: customers, mainly foreigners, in need of taxis came to me and told me where they wanted to go. I handed them over to the drivers and since they didn't use taxi metres, I told the driver how much to charge. Out of this charge the driver had to pay thirty percent commission to the table and that was where most problems originated: they would do anything to avoid paying their dues.

Mr Pak, the owner of the business who came every day, just before I was finishing for the day at 14:00, to receive the collected commissions, had left me in full charge of the table and had asked me to protect his interests in all possible ways. There was no apparent reason for me to worry about the amount of the commissions and to be at loggerheads with the drivers on that account - as I mentioned earlier, my salary was fixed regardless of the amount of commissions collected; at the end of the day, whatever the total was, I handed it over to Pak and nothing of it came my way; so there was no need for me to worry about the size of the commission package. The only reason why I had to be tough with the drivers was because I realized that if I let them have it their way, quite soon I would be left with no commissions at all, and then my job would be in the balance. This explains the frequent replacement of the receptionists that preceded me - things had got out of control. And anyway, my boss Pak, not all that bad a person, tried to be helpful to anyone in financial difficulty, especially the bastard drivers, who at the end of the day called him all the ugly names they could think of!

It was my responsibility to keep things running smoothly. I was catching up fast and the amount of commissions collected was increasing. The drivers began to realize that I was there to stay.

The drivers had a big caravan in the open, on the edge of the hotel premises, about 100 metres from the entrance to the lobby, where I had my table about a dozen metres away. I called them up using an intercom system; the next driver on the list, when needed, would drive to the entrance, park, then walk inside to the table.

I could tell the driver how much to charge if the customer asked for a one-way trip only, in which case I looked at the price sheet that listed a straightforward charge. But that wasn't always the case, some of the customers finding it cheap compared to the money they paid the drivers back in their home countries; consequently they asked to keep the car to call at other places as well, in which case, at the end of the journey, the driver, not me, was the one who told the customer how much he had to pay. In the latter instance, on returning to the hotel to be put in the queue for the next trip, most drivers didn't report the true amount they had been paid; and if I didn't get the chance to see the customer again to verify the amount paid, the driver would get away with having to pay the commission on the unreported amount. But usually I did see the customer again and, checking on the driver and finding out that he had lied, telling him and penalising him for the missing commission not surprisingly caused trouble.

One of the drivers, who I shall call 'Mr B', would try anything to pay no commission at all. This is what happened with him one typical working day:

Early in the morning, calling Mr B to the table and pointing at a customer standing by, I said to him, "Take this gentleman with you, please; he wants to call at a few places so he'll be keeping the car."

Almost five hours later Mr B, coming back from the trip, asked me to put his name down in the queue for the next trip. I asked him how much he had been paid.

"Two dollars," he said with a straight face.

"You must be joking!" I said. "You've been gone for almost five hours and that would be at least fifteen dollars."

Mr B. said, "I took him to the first address and my car broke down, so I left him and went to the mechanics."

At this point I had no choice but to accept his word. But not long after I saw the customer again: checking with him, I found out that Mr B had stayed with him (the customer) for the entire journey and had been paid twenty dollars!

Calling Mr B. to the table, I told him what his customer had said and added, "You leave me no choice but to suspend you for three days." It was the only available way to punish the drivers.

Then he started calling me names and that's how the trouble began.

"Listen Mr B," I said, "I know last year alone fifteen receptionists had worked behind this very table, one after the other, and most had left because of you. But let me tell you that I'm here to stay. Get that into your head!"

Three days later, coming back to the hotel, I ran into more trouble with him. "Mr B, you know that customer I gave you this morning, the German guy?" I said, and I let him look at the day's list in front of me to refresh his memory. "It was your second trip this morning," I added. Though I was sure he knew full well who I was talking about and what I was trying to get at, I still asked, "Remember?" I didn't expect any answer, and he just stared at me. I carried on: "He came back to the table and said that you took another customer too, with you, picked up at the door. We charge these people for the whole taxi, not half of it." I asked him if he had a logical explanation for his action. He had none, of course. I pointed out that he had tried to get away with paying commission on the money he had been paid by the second customer, and told him, "Therefore, again, you leave me no choice but to ask you to stay away for another three days." Then, threatening him with dismissal if he didn't mend his ways, I carried on, "I know you've been working here for the last 25 years and me only a few weeks, but that doesn't stop me from talking to Mr Pak and advising him to get rid of you once and for all."

For the first month I was working there, most of the passengers were taken to the airport at the end of their stay and were therefore soon out of the country, in effect leaving me with no means to check up on the drivers who would come back to the table, saying, "When I got him to the airport he told me he had lost his wallet, so had no money to pay me!" Consequently, there was no commission. After that first month I got wise to this and started charging anyone heading for the airport in advance, at the table.

What I went through with Mr B, I went through with the other drivers, though to a lesser extent. After a while, however, things began to run more smoothly: checking the drivers by getting feedback from passengers was paying off; and drivers finding out that having to stay away from work for three days, sometimes more, was a great financial loss, fewer and fewer began to lie about their fares. It was an amusing and challenging job.

When business was sluggish drivers played ball games, but most often sat drinking tea and gossiping. They usually talked about me and, though I didn't have spies among them, the news reached me almost immediately. Talking in the caravan, they would conjure up all sorts of things they would do to me: if I checked up on him one more time he would call me out and beat the fuck out of me. If I dared to check up on him again, he would give me a head butt. Some even went as far as thinking of running me over with their cars, and a few cutting my throat! But when they came to the table they were beginning to stand to attention, for I had shown some of them that I could use my fists well.

It was a job that gave me valuable experience, too. I was meeting people from all over the world of all kinds: the Chinese coming in connection with missiles, the

Japanese with cars, the Germans with electricity, the French with oil. Funny enough, coming across the Japanese, I never bore a grudge against them. Thinking of the few good people I had met in Japan, like Goto and Hammamula who were very helpful to me while there, and also because essentially I was not a revengeful person, I tried to treat them as fairly as I could. When the Japanese visitors came up to my table and I addressed them in their own language, most of them turned red and, embarrassed, avoided eye contact with me. They just ordered their taxis without saying anything and walked away. In time I stopped talking to them in their language or ever mentioning I had lived in Japan. While I received a similar reaction from the few British visitors who came to my table, I was able to reassure them that I never faced mistreatment of any kind during the years I lived in England. Had they known how discourteously we behaved towards one another in our country, none would have needed to feel embarrassed.

A German gentleman, coming to my table, wanted a taxi, and I asked him, "Wohin gehin zi?" ("Where are you going?") He went red and I hastened to inform him that I had never been to Germany and that I had merely learnt that sentence in German from a previous German client, thinking that it would come in handy.

Most foreigners asking for a taxi requested a receipt as well - probably because back home their employers would refund the amount of the taxi fare. Now, in the case of Iranians - but also in a few instances where the clients came from some western European countries, the ones we thought of as the most honest - would ask for a receipt and, finding me of a friendly disposition, would indicate that they would prefer the amount on the receipt to be left blank; they did not always come out with this request openly, but I was quick to understand their request. I presumed they wanted a blank receipt so they could put down a much higher amount later on. I had no qualms about this for the request was usually followed by a generous tip that I graciously never turned down.

Then I started making some real money by changing customers' dollars into Iranian rials. This was risky for, if caught doing this or searched by the security at the door and found with some dollars on me, my job would be gone for sure - indeed, I could even have found myself facing a prison sentence; so the transactions took place under great care.

While foreigners were obliged to change their money in the bank, most did not, since in exchange for each dollar, they received 100 rials. On the black market the same dollar could be exchanged for 14 times that amount. With the county's economy in tatters, inflation running high, the value of major hard currencies against the Iranian rial was increasing almost daily; while the banks maintained the same exchange rate they were inadvertently (and stupidly) helping to keep tourists away from the country.

On their first visit to Iran, most foreigners at the

hotel didn't know, to begin with, where those running the black market were to be found; on the other hand, they had heard it was a very risky procedure, and that, apart from the people running the black market being in dangerous places, they might end up being the recipients of forged notes. Armed with this knowledge, I would ask a visitor when he came up to my table - though not before looking around carefully to make sure no one was within earshot - if he wanted to exchange his dollars as well. (They all carried US dollars on them.) If he nodded in affirmation, I would ask him how much he wanted to change. To save time, I had money in bundles ready, of different amounts, in my pockets. Then, with utmost care, I would cautiously hand over the right amount, asking him to do the same, and in this way the exchange took place. I paid these people 20% less than they would get on the black market. Nevertheless, if they later found out they could have got a better deal from the black market, they still chose to come back to me if they required further exchanges since they did not consider it worth the hassle and danger they might face by going to an unsafe and inconvenient place.

Work finished, I went down to the black market and changed all the dollars obtained during the day back into Iranian currency. Sometimes what I made in this way in one day equalled what I earned working normally behind that desk for a month! But all good things come to an end, and a few months later the government, changing the laws, placed a small box-like counter in all big hotels with the sign EXCHANGE printed in red on a rectangular piece of glass hanging from the top, well in sight of everyone in the foyer, and started changing all currencies into Iranian rial round the clock, and at a rate of only10% lower than that offered by the black market.

chapter
twenty four

❖

NOT ALL FOREIGNERS came to do business in Iran. One day as I was reading an article in the *Washington Post*, given to me by one of the customers, a good looking young man of about thirty with light brown hair combed backwards, of medium build and wearing glasses, stood in front of my table and pointed to the item of news I was reading titled, 'Corruption in the Middle East.'

"Interesting?" he asked.

"Yes," I nodded. The news was written by the American journalist Pattrick Tailor. Mentioning his name, I carried on, "He always writes a good news story."

"You know him then?" the man asked.

I nodded again. "I've heard his name mentioned many times on the BBC and VOA (Voice of America - the English service was the one I listened to). He lives in Cairo and covers the Middle East. But I've never seen him, or know what he is like."

The man smiled. "You are looking at him now," he said.

Dismissing his remark as a joke and smiling back, I asked him where he was going.

He stuck his hand into a pocket and produced his card. He handed the card to me, biting his lower lip to suppress a laugh.

With my eyes and mouth wide open I looked at the card bearing his photo with his name below it: 'Pattrick Tailor, *The Washington Post*.'

I got on really well with this cheerful man who was in Iran to talk to the President (then Rafsangani) and a few other important people and also to write a report on Iranians trying to enter other countries illegally. He only told me about the part about illegal immigration when he decided he could trust me. "What about some Iranian who have left Turkey to enter Greece illegally, but who were sent back?" I asked. He seemed interested. Did I know anyone who has attempted to do so? Nodding my head, I added, "But I don't know if he would be willing to talk because of the risks involved." No names would be mentioned, only aliases, this journalist replied. "Then I'll see what I can do," I said.

Two days later, asking my aunt over to prepare a great meal, I invited Pattrick Tailor to my flat. He placed himself comfortably in one of my newly bought expensive armchairs and asked for a cup of coffee. Then not long after the pro journalist got his notebook out of his jacket breast pocket, a small pencil at its binding, he started writing as I told my story.

Stopping me every now and then to ask a question, he listened and took notes as I explained almost everything about my illegal entry into Greece, being sent back, then my arrest by Turkish soldiers and concluding with my release.

This chapter closed, he just listened to my encounter at the Bulgaria Yugoslavia border, which I very briefly elucidated, during which he took only a couple of short notes.

Done with the writing, he closed his notebook, replaced the pencil in its place inside the binding, and returned it to the same pocket. Dinner was ready and we sat at the table.

Now his turn to talk, he asked my aunt to pass him the salt - the American learned how to say that in Iranian!

A week later Pattrick Tailor left Iran and not long afterwards I received a letter from him in which was enclosed a page from a copy of the *Washington Post*, half of which was allocated to my story, my name having been changed to Ali. In his letter he informed me that he had arranged with the VOA Persian Service for the story to be broadcast, and gave me the date.

My uncle told me that the VOA Persian Service was on the air every night from 20:00 to 22:30 - the most popular station in the country, second only to the BBC. Listening to this station on that particular day as my story was broadcast I felt a degree of sadness, for it made me aware that a chapter in my life had closed in failure, when fate had decreed a change in the course of my destiny by a few thousand kilometres.

The days went by without much happening until one day I received a letter from my father informing me of what I had been expecting but not wanting to hear. He had been caught in possession of more than 30kg of opium and was in prison awaiting trial. How did that come about? There was nothing in his letter to explain the mystery - only his pathetic explanation that, like last time, he had been set up again; and I thought, like the last time, they wouldn't believe him. I knew this was coming and he must have expected it too.

He had been caught at the checkpoint only some 150km away from Tehran, not like the last time when at Yazd over four times further away. A day off work, I thought, would suffice to go down, pay him a visit and come back. Knowing that he wouldn't be going anywhere for a while, I decided to put this visit off for a few weeks; but if I was going to be honest with myself, I didn't care what happened to him anymore. Meanwhile, writing back, I acknowledged receipt of his letter and let him know I'd pay him a visit soon.

Five weeks later I did so. He had been caught at the checkpoint near the holy city of Qom, therefore taken to a prison there. I was seeing him after almost eight months and he appeared to have put on some weight. He had been in prison for three months by then, having been arrested after he had been back drug-dealing for over six months. In his last trip he had risked almost everything he had earned on previous occasions, calling it a 'make or lose-it-all trip' - and he had lost.

"Had I succeeded," he said, "it would have made me a rich man and the last deal in my life." Plus just 'one more' trip after that, I thought, would have almost certainly followed - and then, probably, one more, and one more, and so on.

He explained that he had been extremely unlucky. With more than 50kg of opium wrapped in plastics stashed away inside his car doors, he had passed through two of the most notorious checkpoints in the country, one outside Kerman and the other one outside Yazd (where he was caught last time) on the road to Tehran, without anyone suspecting anything; but then at Qom police block, where normally only car documents were checked for theft and hardly any cars touched for drugs, he encountered a problem. While the sentry had been in front of his car checking the number plate with the car documents, another driver, losing control of his car, crashed into my father's car's side door just behind the driver, causing the inside panel of that door to come off, exposing the drugs to full view when seen from the opposite side, though nothing could be seen from the crash side as the drugs remained inside the door. Now only concerned with the accident, the sentry walked back to my father and, handing him back his documents through the window, turned his attention to the other driver and asked for his documents. "Up to this point he was still ignorant of what I had almost right under his nose," my father said. Then the sentry ordered the offender to reverse back, and in so doing, my father's car door came off its hinges, falling onto the road, right in front of the sentry with its inner side upwards and the plastic wrappings in full view. "You should have seen the sentry's face looking down at those plastic wrappings inside the door," my father said, smiling sadly.

Other sentries were called to the car and then all the doors panels were disengaged, revealing more kilos of opium. "I was taken in, and the rest you know - and here I am," my father concluded.

He was still as brave as ever; but no matter how brave, who would have thought that a small accident like that would cause my father to face the rope five months later? When he finished speaking I shook my head, sadly, and said, "Very unlucky." Then I added, "Well, anyway, I suppose you know as well as I do that when you go up for your trial this time, in view of the amount of narcotics you have been caught with, what the verdict will be?" He nodded his head in a quiet way and I carried on, "Therefore that leaves us with no choice but to buy you out again, like the last time in Yazd" - referring to when he paid the judge presiding over his trial and got his sentence mitigated down from death to just a year's imprisonment. "And of course, with a lot more money, this time," I went on.

He had been caught with 50kg of opium, and 20kg had since vanished; how much did he think would be needed to get him off that 30kg he had been charged with?

"Maybe around 30,000 US dollars?" he suggested.

But did he have the money? He had almost lost everything in that decisive trip; but his girlfriend still had 15,000 left, and selling their belongings would fetch another 5,000, at the most.

"What about the remaining 10,000, then?" I still had 20,000 left from that 40,000 I had brought back from Japan, therefore asked him, "If someone gave you that 10,000, how would you repay him?" By 'someone' I meant myself, of course. This was my undoing - always prone to a soft touch, even to the point of helping the enemy!

"Once I'm out, the day after I'll do a 30kg job and pay the money back at once," was his answer.

If he ever got out to make that trip, I thought, in his situation he would need all the luck in the world. But never mind, I'd still be willing to give 10,000 away if it meant saving my father's life - and I told him that.

So at his trial I'd be there, equipped with 10,000 dollars and his girlfriend, Mahin, with a further 20,000, totalling 30,000 US dollars, to see if we can, once again, redeem his life - just as we had done before in Yazd. He would write to me again and let me have the date.

As we parted I said, "And meanwhile, as the Japanese say, 'Kiyots kètè - look after yourself', and the Iranians, 'Movazèbè khodèt bash!'"

chapter twenty five

BACK IN MY FLAT I was facing problems trying to get rid of small ants in my kitchen. Having nothing to do one afternoon I amused myself watching a few of the ants. I placed a drop of water on one and noticed that it spread its legs and arms, so to speak, and seemed to have died. But I couldn't have been more wrong. A couple of hours later when the drop had dried, the same ant, getting up and cleaning its antenna, started moving again. I was surprised because the drop of water seemed to have covered the ant fully, leaving it no room to breathe - yet somehow it had managed to survive. How? To get the right answer, I got hold of about twenty ants, dropped them all into a small jam-jar filled with water, fastened the lid to the jar, shook it for about half a minute, then took the lid off and left the jar in a corner to settle. About ten minutes later when everything seemed settled, most of the ants had sunk to the bottom looking dead; those few still on the surface, I took out and threw away. Leaving the jar where it was, exactly 24 hours later, with the ants still lying at the bottom of the jar, I emptied the water and then quite carefully, without causing any harm to any of them, I got the ants out with the tip of a toothpick, one by one, and spread them on a dried piece of paper. Keeping an occasional eye on them, I noticed, about five hours later, that one showed some signs of life; this was followed, a few minutes later, by the others. Soon afterwards, one by one, to my surprise, they all got up, so to speak, cleaned their antenna and moved away.

I wrote down my experience with my findings and sent a copy to the program 'Discovery' that was broadcast weekly from the BBC, asking how the ants survived in such conditions. I never received a reply.

Back at work I faced an experience of a different kind - again to do with Mr B, but almost for the last time. As I mentioned earlier, most foreign customers asked for a receipt, and if he intended to keep the car, I just put the Iranian date[2] on the receipt. Then I would hand the receipt to the driver, so that at the end of his journey, calculating the cost, he would write the amount down on the receipt, give it to the customer and receive his fare. On a one-way trip I wrote the date as well as the amount on the receipt myself; then handed it to the driver; at the end of the trip he received his fare and gave the receipt to the customer.

One afternoon a British man coming to the table told me that I had put the wrong date on his receipt. I remembered the man; he had asked for a one-way trip in the morning and was given a lift by Mr B. Looking at the receipt I could see that the date was days old and when checking the amount against the driver's list in front of me on the table, I found it to be much higher than what I had there in front of Mr B's name for that particular trip. Giving the British man a new receipt with the right date and charge, I handed him back the amount he had paid extra. When he was gone, I called Mr B to the table. Not realising how canny and perceptive the British were, he had changed the receipt I had given him in the morning for one he had had from days back bearing a higher amount. Standing in front of me I told him about it and he went red and anger flashed in his eyes. Then, like a cornered animal looking for a way out but finding none and accepting defeat, he turned back and said angrily, "So you checked up on me again, did you?"

"I'll always be checking up on you Mr B," I replied. "It's proved necessary in your case." I then suspended him for seven days.

In a threatening manner, he said, "I'll get my own back at you!" He was known among the drivers for making empty threats and I had come across a few of them myself, most resulting only in a stare or two; but then he cursed me and that, maybe because I anticipated some form of retaliation, gave me a sense of foreboding. Whatever the reason, it turned out to be a successful spell this wizard had cast on me. On the sixth day, just a day before he was supposed to be back at work, standing in front of my table, he really got his own back on me. Listening to him, on that day, it was my turn to feel like a cornered animal and, looking for a way out but finding none, I resignedly accepted defeat and left my job never to go back to it ever again, not even to ask for my pay.

Two days after I had told Mr B to stay away from work I attended my father's trial. His girlfriend, Mahin, and I, were almost the only ones in the courtroom, like the last time he appeared before the judge in Yazd. We took our seats next to each other waiting for the judge and my father to arrive. A few minutes earlier Mahin had told me that she had provided the 20,000 US dollars, and with the 10,000 US dollars already in my pocket, I was thinking, the sum of 30,000 dollars would probably be enough to get my father's sentence reduced from rope to one, or at the most, two years imprisonment. The judge, again a preacher, entered through the back door and took his seat behind his desk; he was in his forties, thin, a bit tall with a big lipless mouth, very thick bushy eyebrows almost covering his eyes, pointed chin with about fifty long strands of beard, each pointing in different directions. With his cloak about him, all he needed was two horns to complete my mental image of the devil himself. Holding my smile back, I stole a meaningful look at Mahin; our glances met and later she told me she had the same impression that I had. Outwardly this creature looked so much like a devil that I couldn't help thinking that if his external appearance was any clue to his inner state, then my father stood little chance of mercy. Minutes later my father, handcuffed to a sentry, was brought in. His handcuffs were removed and he was made to stand before that devil who sported a sarcastic grin. I shivered, thinking the Koran was right saying demons and fiends lived among us.

Asking my father his name, the judge took a file out of his briefcase, obviously my father's, put it on his desk, opened it and, still grinning, said, "So, this is your second time; 0.9kg to start with and now 30kg. I suppose it'll be a ton next time, if I ever let you out." No, I thought, it'll only be another 30kg, to start with, to let him pay his debts back, if it ever came to that. The judge carried on, "Are you pleading guilty or not?" To my surprise, my father pleaded "Guilty". He had told me that he would enter a not guilty plea, so he must have changed his mind. Then the judge asked him if he had anything to say, and my father just asked to be given another chance so that he could prove himself worthy of living with integrity in society. It was obvious that my father wasn't in a situation to be able to put in a good word on his own behalf; and then again, I thought, whatever he said wouldn't have really mattered. The devil of a judge cut my father short and, giving another grin, said, "I'm afraid you have left me with no option but to give you the death sentence…" Avoiding all preliminaries usually discoursed prior to the sentencing, this bastard came out with his verdict so casually and bluntly that, for a moment, I doubted my ears. When it sank in a second later, my mind froze with fear and I ceased to hear him anymore. My heart felt as though it was about to come out of my mouth. It was long after the judge and my father had left the room that I noticed their absence. "Quick, I have to go and see my father before he is taken back to prison," I heard myself say. Mahin, next to me, had turned pale and looked as though she was about to pass out.

Seeing the sentry in charge I managed to pay my father a short visit. He was in a huge cell down in the cellar of the court building with about thirty other prisoners mainly in for political reasons but some soon to be hanged for the crime of drug dealing. This latter piece of news I first heard from foreigners at the hotel who told me it was all over their newspapers, that Iran was treating some political prisoners as such. In fact, once one of the drivers told me that in one public hanging he himself had attended, a young man, just before being picked up by the crane, threw a rope round his neck and had shouted that he wasn't a drug dealer but a political prisoner.

"Don't waste your money," my father sighed, then pointing at some of the prisoners in the cell, he carried on, "They tell me that he is a bastard of a judge; he'll take the money but hardly ever keeps his promise." For the first and last time in my life I saw fear in my father's eyes. I dropped my own eyes so that he wouldn't notice my fear. Those were the last words I heard my father say, and that was the last time I saw him alive. But as I told him, I had to try, because if I didn't he would go to the gallows and I would be asking myself for ever, with a very guilty conscience, whether I could have saved his life.

Once outside I explained to Mahin what my father had told me about the judge, and that we had no choice but to try our luck. I asked her for the 20,000 US dollars she was carrying and told her, "I won't be seeing the judge today but tomorrow." I had an idea: if he was a bastard of a judge with the chance of not keeping his word, I had to meet him suitably equipped. Getting on one of those fast taxis travelling in between cities, a couple of hours later I was back in Tehran at the hi-fi marketplace where I got myself a mini tape recorder and a microphone in the shape of a clip-like pen end. I was planning secretly to record whatever would be said between the judge and myself when I went to see him next; then use it later in evidence if the need should arise. So if he took the money and failed to keep his word, there would be a backlash from me!

Later that day, back at my flat, I learned how to work with the equipment. Leaving the tape recorder in the inside breast pocket of my jacket, I would clip the microphone on the edge of the outside breast pocket, just like one would clip a pen there. The microphone and the recorder would be connected by means of a wire passed through a small hole made in the material. This done, I left for my friend's house. There, after talking to him for about ten minutes with the tape recorder and microphone both on, I pointed to the microphone and asked him what he thought it was. It looked like a pen end clipped to the top edge of my jacket's outside breast pocket, and he confirmed this. "It's your pen," he said. When I took it out he was surprised to notice the difference. Also, getting the tape recorder from my jacket inside breast pocket, we listened to our own conversation. The whole thing seemed amusing.

Once again back at my flat that night, before going to bed, I knew there was something else on my mind. Trivial as it seemed at the time, remembering, I gave it a quick thought: that morning in Qom, while Mahin and I were standing outside the courthouse waiting for our names to be called, for a second I thought I saw Mr B's face among all those people there. But under so much stress I had dismissed the idea as an illusion then, and thinking about it that night, dismissed it again for the same reason. Forgetting all about Mr B, the bastard, with so much else on my mind, I hardly slept that night.

The day after at 3 o'clock in the afternoon, armed with the tape recorder and microphone, both switched on and in the right places in my breast pockets, I knocked at the devil's door and entered his office. My heart was beating hard for I was so scared, afraid I might give myself away, in which case I would have to face the dire consequences - no doubt being marked as a spy, collecting information for foreign countries. But then again, even without the tape recorder and the microphone, in a situation like that, I thought, anybody would be in a fearful state, and I was hoping the judge would be thinking the same.

After introducing myself he asked me to sit down. He hadn't sent my father's file away yet, correctly anticipating it might be worth keeping for another day. Looking at the file he gave another one of his grins and said, "He is six times over the limit, to say the least, and on top of that there's the previous conviction."

"Which is why I have come to beg for clemency," I answered.

From this point forward everything went almost like the last time when I spoke with the Judge Zargar after my father's trial in Yazd: he pointed out that he was an honest judge, he wouldn't take bribes, he was a responsible person... and so on until at the end when, with another grin he came to the point: "If we take the limit at 10,000 US dollars, then six times that would be 60,000 US dollars."

In the interests of the recording everything was going according to plan, I thought, because if it ever came to providing evidence of his corruptibility, I now had the proof that he was the one who first proposed the bribe.

I feigned surprise and he knocked 10,000 off the proposed amount, but that was still too high. Then, just like one trying to haggle when buying a second-hand car - wasn't it funny that instead of a car it was a human life? - I negotiated with this greedy bastard of a judge to bring his price down a further notch or two.

I said, "Selling most of my assets, plus borrowing from friends and using more than half my earnings from hard work, I have managed to put together a substantial sum; but then again, it's not close to what you're asking for." Then, half bluffing and half pretending to find the whole thing too much to take, I rose from my chair and said, "Then you leave me no choice but to let my father meet the rope." Part of me genuinely wanted to end this swiftly though I was reluctant to leave my father to his fate.

Inviting me to sit down again with a wave of his hand, he wanted to know how much I had managed to obtain.

I took the bundle of 30,000 US dollars out of my pocket and placed it on the table, telling him how much it was; then, tapping my pockets to show that I had no more money, I said, "That's all I can afford."

He took the money and with words to the effect of "you seem to be honest and that'll do", he got his pen out and, looking at my father's file, said, "If we cross the nought out in this 30 then your father has been caught with 3kg of opium. Being his second time, that carries a sentence of four years imprisonment." When I objected to four years being too long, he stopped me by saying, "He has already done six months so I'll put him down for parole at the end of a year." Then, with a sense of finality, he said, "File closed."

Back in my flat I made a copy of the tape and listened to it again. As far as I was concerned I had done my job. I had stretched my luck to the last thread and now if the judge snapped it, no one could blame me for it. I had even put in 10,000 dollars from my own pocket without expecting ever to get it back. How much more could I have done?

As I write these notes, my mind reaches out to my sister Soheila, who has been living in America now for the last twenty years. During this time I have spoken to her many times on the phone and, not surprising, she has learnt to speak English well. If ever this book were to be published, then she will almost certainly have read it. So to her I want to say this: "Soheila, don't jump to conclusions and pick up the phone and blame me for our father's death. I know, when you've finished reading this book, what you will be thinking; but let me tell you that when he died he had sold everything in his possession to buy his freedom and all he had left was a small carpet and an old radio set. Therefore I wouldn't have inherited much by his death; on the contrary, I was even expecting to lose the 10,000 dollars I had contributed to buy his freedom; therefore his death does not only amount to a moral loss, though not much since he was our father just in name, but a financial loss as well - to me; and though things turned out differently, in the end, quite by chance I gained more than 40,000 US dollars out of the whole case; but, to start with, my only aim, I can assure you, was to get our father off the hook - or off that rope, as you can see from my recorded interview with the judge, which I have written down in detail apart from a few trivial sentences; and remember, nothing was meant to go the way things turned out.

"And I also need to tell you, after all these years, that I have been telling everyone that our father was living in Pakistan farming, whereas in fact he has been only a few miles away, buried in the same cemetery as our beloved Sepideh. To you, Soheila, what good would it have done if I had told the truth apart from causing grief and sorrow? As for mum, I never wanted her to enjoy the satisfaction of knowing that he no longer was with his girlfriend but lying dead under the ground; and regarding the other relatives, you know what kind of tongue lashings they like to indulge in - and they are still like that; so knowing the truth about father's death, that he was executed on account of being a drug dealer, imagine the heyday they would have had with such shameful news, and how intolerable they would have made life for me; not me only, living next door, but even for you, living thousands of miles away, for they would have taken great delight in making you feel perturbed."

After being absent from work for two days, early the next morning I went back to the hotel and placed myself behind my desk. With Mr B away I felt a bit easier, but still a lot on edge. I was wishing for no news from my father until I paid him another visit in four days' time: probably the only hopeful way I was going to see him alive again. And to add no more concern to my state of mind, I decided not to check on the drivers until then.

I tried to keep my mind occupied by reading a foreign magazine, but I was unable to concentrate. My mind was too occupied by my father's case. It was in the middle of the morning when I was struck by a new thought. It occurred to me that if my father was executed in spite of my having paid out the money to prevent it, and if things went the way I hoped they would, I could actually earn a lot of money. As I gave the notion some more thought and, to be honest, a few hours later I came to a point where I didn't care whether my father lived or died. Anyway, thinking about the past I asked myself, what had he really done for me? I was ten when, after constant fights with mum, he left the house to work in other cities, coming back home only every couple of months, and then only to stay as many days as he had been away. Then, at the age of 18 I left for England, never to see him until I was sent back over ten years later; and since then I had seen him once every few months, minus the three years I had spent in Japan when I never saw him. Therefore, when I came to think about it, he was almost a stranger to me - so why should I care whether he lived or died?

Back at my flat now I felt indifferent to the phone calls I was receiving, whereas the day before every ring caused my heart to tremble, expecting the call might be from the prison authorities in Qom asking me to present myself there to collect his body. Nothing exciting happened that evening and as the night drew to a close I went to bed and slept soundly until early morning when I woke up. After a hearty breakfast, I left for work.

At work that day we employed a new driver. This was his first day working and on his second trip, checking up on him, I found out he had lied to me about the amount of fare he had received. Firing him, I said, "That is why we don't deserve to be let free."

It was sometime past afternoon when, looking up from my magazine, I was surprised to see Mr B standing in front of my table. The way he was staring down at me with a sinister smile made me feel uneasy. He wouldn't dare look at me in such an overtly intimidating way, I thought, unless he had found a strong winning card up his sleeve. My first instinct was that he must have seen me changing dollars for some customer and could prove it, but I must admit I didn't have a clue as to what he was about to come up with. His half-hidden smirk gave way to a sarcastic smile as he shook his head slowly, continuing to stare down at me. For a second I wondered if he had gone mad. Coming to myself, I kept my composure and, returning his stare, I said, "I thought I told you to stay away till the day after tomorrow."

Barely relaxing his superior smile, pure hate in his eyes, he took out a folded newspaper from beneath his jacket and placed it on the table. Catching a glimpse of the front page I realised it was a copy of the *Qom Daily News*. Mr B paged through its pages, obviously looking for a specific item of news; when he found it, I saw that he had encircled the article with a red pen. Tapping the page with his finger, he almost threw the paper at me with a theatrical air. Now in the role of a tough guy, he demanded, "Read!"

My eyes and mouth went wide open as I took in the first two lines. No mistaking what was written there: '… fifteen drug dealers were hanged in the city of Qom this morning, among them the notorious drug cartel leader Iraj Kamrani who confessed, before being hanged, to have killed two sentries in the course of his dealings…' I didn't need to go any further.

I remembered then how, only six days ago, Mr B had stood in front of me and said, "I'll get my own back at you!" And now he had done so, with full force. Resignedly and with a Herculean effort, I picked up my belongings and left, never to go back there ever again, not even to ask for my pay.

Once outside tears rolled down my cheeks - and I had thought I would be indifferent in the eventuality of my father's death! I felt cold and shivered. So that bastard of a judge hadn't kept his word after all! Yet his prophet, Mohammed, had emphasized that all Muslims should keep to their promises even if it meant doing good to the enemies of Islam. I wondered why most of these clerics disobeyed their master, not only in failing to keep their promises, but in deeds as well; was it possible that they didn't believe in their master anymore? Either that, or they had found some flaw in him we ordinary people are ignorant of.

Soon afterwards, when I got home, the phone rang. I answered it and, as I had expected, it was from Qom prison. I was to go there and claim my father's body. Before leaving I phoned Mahin and told her what had happened. She became hysterical. When she calmed down, I asked her to go down to the main cemetery, buy my father a grave and make it ready so that when I returned with the body we wouldn't be wasting much time. Tears rolled down my cheeks as I said quietly, "Hopefully we can bury him today." I had work to do the day after but first I wanted to go and see that bastard of a judge, Roshan.

A few hours later at Qom prison mortuary my father's body was delivered to me. It was well wrapped in a white shroud apart from his face which was left uncovered. Aware of four pairs of eyes watching me, I didn't dare unwrap the body to look for signs of brutality and obvious lash marks every prisoner was subjected to before he met his death. I called an ambulance, since that was the only way bodies were allowed to be transported - and it cost me a fortune. Picking the body up, his head fell right back reminding me of his broken neck. My father was put in the ambulance and I sat next to the driver and we headed back for Tehran. The cemetery was situated just outside the capital, along this very road. When we got there Mahin was waiting with a grave ready. As it was getting dark I paid some cemetery workers to take my father's body out of the ambulance and place it in the grave. As they lay the body in the grave I heard them murmuring some prayers.

And so, with only Mahin and I present who had known him, my father was laid to rest - about 300m away from where his daughter lay. It was a sad moment and I realized how much Mahin, weeping uncontrollably, had loved him.

chapter twenty six

BACK AT MY FLAT that night I decided to keep my father's death a secret from all those around, even close friends and relatives. Therefore a few days later when Soheila phoned up and during our conversation inquired about our father's health and his whereabouts, I told her that he was fine and was living in Pakistan. "What is he doing there?" she wanted to know, and in fact everyone close enough to care asked me the same question. Anticipating their curiosity, I had a ready answer: "My father has bought himself a piece of land in Pakistan and is farming there." People were nosey, but I was prepared. "No, I couldn't let you have his address," was my answer to the second question I had thought might come up, "first, because of the situation his girlfriend is in, and second, they left the country illegally; there was a chance someone would cause him trouble."

At 10 o'clock the next morning I stood in front of

the Qom courthouse building, my heart full of vengeance. The sentry at the door told me that Judge Roshan was presiding somewhere else and wouldn't be coming back to Qom for a few days. I knew these judges sometimes presided in the surrounding cities and, accordingly, to catch up with him, I had come early. But where was he? The sentry didn't know and even if he did they had orders not to disclose the judges' whereabouts. Parting with a ten-dollar bill quietly slipped into the sentry's hand, I found out five minutes later where Judge Roshan at that moment was: at court in the City of Arak.

Arak was only 100km away from Qom, no great distance, so I went after him. I had all the time in the world, and on the way there I was thinking that I would be prepared to cover any distance, no matter how long it took or however far away he was. I was travelling in one of those between-city taxis which was going fast and not long over an hour later we reached the outskirts of the big city of Arak. Changing this taxi for a local one, it was some time before noon when I got to the main courthouse building in the city. The sentry at the door knew Judge Roshan well but told me he wasn't working there that day. "Wasn't he?" Could the sentry at Qom courthouse have lied to me? Parting with another ten-dollar note I found out differently: Judge Roshan was in Arak, but in the courthouse on the other side of the town.

It was past afternoon when I arrived at the other courthouse, building no. 2, and found out that the judges, among them Roshan, had gone to the mosque for midday prayers. I waited and about thirty minutes later the judges came back, though Roshan wasn't among them. Enquiring again from the sentry at the door, he told me that Roshan was working there during the morning but wasn't sure about the afternoon. Could he find out? (I slipped another ten-dollar note into his hand.) Yes, judge Roshan had finished for the day in Arak and was to preside in the City of Kashan during the afternoon. Sighing, I thought: another 100km to travel! The three locations of Qom, Arak and Kashan, if a line were to be drawn between each, would make an equilateral triangle.

At 2 o'clock that afternoon, thirsty and hungry, I stood in front of the only courthouse in the city of Kashan. At last I had caught up with him! Judge Roshan was there, but at that moment was busy at the bench; he would see me from 3 o'clock onwards.

Busy at the bench sending more people to their deaths, I thought, and from 3 o'clock onwards, "for a few insignificant thousand dollars", as some people had heard him saying, he would promise to be the saviour angel of the condemned - a promise hardly ever kept, and the people, though they knew that, were prepared to be hoodwinked as a last resort to save a loved one.

It was well past 3 o'clock when I was allowed to see Judge Roshan. After knocking at his door I entered his office. He was at his desk writing in a file, probably someone's who had just been consulted about and on behalf of whom he (Roshan) had been paid to change the figures which he was now no doubt putting back to what they were in the first place. He looked up and it took him a few seconds to recognize me, and when he did, as I had expected, standing up, he pushed his cloak back and drew his pistol from his waist shawl; it reminded me of those western movies, the jacket in this instance replaced by the cloak. Pointing his pistol at me, he said, "Leave before I shoot you!" Surprisingly at that moment I didn't feel fear; in fact, I didn't care if he shot and killed me, for then at least I would die proud in the course of trying to get back what was mine. With the mini tape recorder already in my hand, showing it to him, still standing at the door, I cut him short and said, "But before you do that, I think you'd better listen to this!" Approaching him, I said, "I have a surprise for you." My relaxed manner, most probably, made him lower his gun. I put the tape recorder on the table, with the tape already in it, and pushed the 'on' button.

As he listened his weasel face went white. Sitting down, with a motion of his hand, he asked me to do the same; it seemed he didn't want to miss a word of what was being said on the tape. The pistol went quietly back in his waist shawl, his cloak pulled over his shoulder covering it. Sitting there looking at him, I didn't know what to make of this monster in human shape. Incongruously at that moment I recalled something from the past, when I was a boy: I had thrown away an apple because there was a small area of the skin that had gone bad, and my father, who this creature had sent to his death, picked up the apple, cut the bad piece away and handed the rest back to me. "This is still eatable," he said, and I had asked, "What if half had gone bad?" - and he had answered, "You'd have the other half to eat." And then, thinking deep, talking as if to himself, my father had carried on, "But there'll be a time when the whole thing would go bad, and in that case nothing of it could be saved."

Now, looking at this corrupt individual sitting in front of me, I felt I would fight the whole world, all those democratic countries included, if I was told there was still a small chance that this creature might be saved. Even if he died, his body should be cremated and the ashes thrown into a volcano, I thought, because if buried, a few years later a tree might grow on his grave, and anyone eating from that tree would surely be poisoned.

He listened to our taped conversation right to the last word, which took almost ten minutes; at the end, after I had said goodbye to him on the tape, he turned it off. He looked at me, but before he could say anything, I said, "Don't get any ideas about destroying this tape: that is only a copy you listened to." Then, lying, I carried on, "My mate has the original one, and if I don't get to him in time, tomorrow morning at the latest, he will be down to see Yazdi..." Nodding my head, I concluded, "...with the tape in his hand." Yazdi, the head of judiciary for the last half year, even in such short period had made a name for himself. He was considered honest and also to have said, "Any judge proven to have been bribed to change the course of justice will be dealt with harshly." Indeed, even in the short period of his position, he had sent many judges to prison and also a few to their deaths for miscarriage of justice. And now six months since his appointment not only judges but other people in positions of authority were beginning to feel the weight of his power. Yazdi was feared, and as some had said, also cruel like a devil, but in the right way.

At the sound of Yazdi's name, Roshan's eyes flashed. He knew he had done wrong. Accepting a bribe of 30,000 US dollars would call for a severe punishment. To start with he would be lashed 36 times, lose a hand from the wrist and after that heaven knows how many years imprisonment he would be given; and while inside, if someone recognized him, never mind his hand, he would lose his head too. There was no protection law in Iranian jails like the one (Rule 43) that existed in British prisons. So why didn't he just put a bullet through my head and then leave the country? Surely with the money he had saved up he could live more than comfortably for the rest of his life anywhere on the planet.

There was one problem he couldn't overcome, and that was his greed; this virus was hard to shake off.

Looking at me, he said, "Okay, what do you want?"

"I just want my money back, plus the 100 dollars I spent today to reach you."

It was all too clear on the tape how much I had paid

him, or rather been deprived of as a result of his demands. Realizing I meant business, he wasted no time and made a phone call, asking the person at the other end to get him the right amount. Putting the phone down, he told me, "Your money will be here soon."

While we were waiting, showing him the microphone, I explained how I had done the taping. And since he was giving me my money back, I promised once I got home to destroy the original tape, and only if, I said, "you destroy this one now, because if anyone got his hand on this tape we'll both be in trouble." He broke the tape open, took his lighter out and burned the strip inside to ashes; by doing so he got my plan a step closer to succeeding.

Not long afterwards, knocking at the door, a man entered, put the money on the table and left. I counted it - 30,000 US dollars, plus the 100 dollars he had already given me. I put them in my pocket and went to the door; but before leaving, he reminded me: "You promised to destroy the tape." And I answered, "Sure."

Once outside I said to myself: "Sure. Sure I will keep my promise in the same way you kept yours."

On the way back to Tehran I was trying to decide whether I should in fact put my plan into action. Why not forget about the whole thing and carry on with my life as usual? I had my money back and my father wasn't all that innocent either. But, if I went ahead with my plan, there was a chance that I might earn myself a further 30,000 US dollars, and if not that, at least it would mean the end of Roshan.

Back at my flat that night I was still in two minds about what to do before going to sleep: forget all about that bastard or take the tape to the authorities and make him pay for it? Though, by then, all thoughts of money had left my mind. Then I decided to sleep on the matter and would make up my mind in the morning.

My sleep was restless that night in which my father appeared to me, first, asking me to take Mahin's money back to her - in answer to that I told him he was better dead - and, second, to take vengeance on Roshan.

Getting up, first thing in the morning I picked up the phone and made an appointment to see Yazdi. There were many people like Roshan, and one less probably didn't mean more lives would be saved; but, when news of his fall from grace got around, others holding similar positions would tread much more cautiously when handing out death sentences and accepting bribes - *and* making empty promises. Yazdi was a very busy man and his secretary told me that I had to wait for another week before I could see him.

Now that this case seemed almost settled, my mind went back on Mr B. How had he found out about my father? I kept asking myself this question. How had he come by that paper, the *Qom Daily News*, which was hardly ever sold anywhere apart from in Qom. He was 80% illiterate and barely able to read papers; in fact, none of the drivers ever read anything. Therefore, how had he come across this piece of news? Whichever way I thought about it, no suitable answer presented itself.

In the end I came up with one possible solution, and even that failed to explain properly some of the conclusions reached. My thoughts went like this: whenever I was off work at the hotel, I left a driver in my place to do the job. Now the drivers I had asked to stay off work, in my absence, got the chance to go back and carry on as usual; I was not in charge so they worked. On the day I attended my father's trial, finding out that a driver was in charge of the table, Mr B goes back to work and, being his lucky day, is given a customer going to Qom. Being the holiest city and boasting the biggest mosque in the country, many customers asked to go there every week. Qom was the city where the Iranian revolution got its impetus from; I remember the Shah was always having trouble with the clergy there. On his return from exile in France, Khomeini visited this city the day after he entered the country; Qom was the only place in the country capable of giving the rank of Ayatollah to the clergy; and finally, one of Mohammad's daughters was buried in Qom.

Entering this city one passed by the main courthouse building which, being built so magnificently, it could hardly be missed. That day, passing by this building, Mr B sees me standing in front of it; dropping his passenger, he comes back to find out why. He must have thought, what was I doing there? Was I in some kind of trouble, out on bail, now waiting to appear before the court? Seeing the sentry at the door he finds out. Then, asking a friend in the city to keep an eye on the local paper for my father's name, or to let him know if anyone got hanged in the city by that name, he duly received news of my father's execution a few days later.

Therefore, that day, in front of Qom courthouse building, I had actually seen Mr B's face among those people standing there, not a vision of him, as I had imagined at the time. Later thinking about the incident, I reminded myself never to doubt my eyes again.

Almost a year later I was walking in the area where I was living when I spotted Mr B's car parked outside a big house. I looked at it, wondering what he was doing there, when the door of the house opened and he came out. Suddenly a funny situation arose: our glances met and I turned round, thinking of running away, and at the same time he nearly went back inside, half closing the door behind him. But for some reason our thoughts ran in parallel lines, for at the same time we both turned round to face each other; we crossed the space between us, shook hands and kissed each other on the cheek; no hostilities were felt - all that suddenly seemed to belong to old times. What was he doing now? (And he asked me the same question!) It was his friend's house, as it turned out, and he was just leaving. He offered to give me a lift and we both got into his car. As he drove we were quite reluctant to talk about the past to begin with, feeling a bit embarrassed to do so, but that seemed inevitable. As if reading my mind, he turned towards me and said, "I suppose you want to know how I found out?" Though a long time had passed since my father's death, we both had our thoughts on the same subject.

"Yes, I'm interested," I answered, though to be honest the incident no longer occupied my mind to any significant extent.

In his own words: "...I have a son working in Qom. A couple of days after you asked me to stay off work I went down to see him. He has been living there for years now and I pay him a visit every now and then. Entering the city it surprised me to see you standing in front of the courthouse there. Were you in trouble, out on bail, and now, I thought, waiting to appear before the court? I was curious and decided to find out. Parking my car somewhere I sneaked among the people standing there." He gave me a glance while driving, and smiled. "I was quite careful not to be noticed and for a moment I thought that you saw me there among all those people, but then you kept on talking to this woman standing next to you..." Cutting in, I said, "My stepmother." He nodded and went on, "Then I heard your name called on the speakers and you entered the building. After you'd gone in I approached the sentry at the door. Giving him a five-dollar note, I found out that not you, but your father was on trial. Thirty kilos of opium." He gave me another glance while driving. "Surely you knew what the verdict would be?" I nodded and he carried on: "Then I went back to my car and drove off. Now you could have bribed the judge and got your father off, I was thinking while driving, otherwise he would hang; and I never understood why you didn't get him off."

I didn't want to tell him that I had tried but failed,

so I just shrugged and he went on: "That evening I told my son about your father and he thought that if he was not bought off that rope he would be hanged in the middle of the city in the next couple of days, with his name printed in the local paper the same day. 'That was how it usually happened,' my son said to me; and that was exactly how it happened. My son informed me a few days later."

As if talking to myself, deep in thought, I said, "And that's how you got to know about it." It was all fresh in my memory once more, as though all that had happened just the day before.

"My son was there when they hanged your father and the rest of them. It took place at five in the morning. Your father was among the first four to die and the bravest also, my son said."

At 9 o'clock in the morning on my appointment day, with the tape and the mini-recorder in my hand, I entered the justice ministry building where Yazdi had his office. I had come so far, but still doubtful whether if I really wanted to go ahead with this. On the second floor I was led by a guard to his secretary and introduced myself. Consulting a list in front of him, he asked me to knock at his door. I opened it and then I just walked into Mr Yazdi's office. People knew him for his honesty and as someone responsible, so I was expecting justice from him and hoping that he wouldn't jump to the conclusion that I was trying to tar all judges with the same brush in the belief that they were all corrupt - which in fact was not far from the truth with the exception of very few indeed.

I closed the door behind me. He looked relaxed and quite cheerful, sitting comfortably at his desk - quite different from what I had expected. He pointed to a chair in front of his desk and asked me to sit down. Though I had seen him a few times on TV, I hadn't noticed he had such bright eyes and so clear a complexion. He had a short white beard, as white as his turban, and was wearing a light brown cloak. Though not standing, I knew he was a short person, about 5'3" tall.

Very briefly, he asked me to tell him why I was there.

"My father was caught with 30kg of opium, went in front of judge Roshan, was found guilty, so obviously sentenced to death. Then I paid 30,000 US dollars to judge Roshan to reduce my father's sentence, and he promised me he would do so; nevertheless, he hanged him, and also kept the money." I omitted to tell him of my later visit to Roshan in accordance with what I had planned. Yazdi asked me if I had any proof to this.

I turned the recorder on and after listening to the tape for a minute he stopped it. What was the problem? I thought, perhaps tapes were not accepted as proof. Leaning forward on his desk, he spoke into an intercom and asked a Mr Karimi, obviously somewhere within reach, to come in. In no time the man presented himself; also a cleric, tall, sporting a dark brown beard. Pointing at me, Yazdi put him in charge of my case, and said, "Let me have the final result." After that he dismissed Karimi and the subordinate, showing due respect, withdrew.

I followed Karimi into his office which was next door. There he listened to the full ten minutes of my conversation with Roshan on the tape, turned it off, then said, "Leave this tape with me and come back…" He paused to look at the calendar and then a sheet of paper on his desk, "…in four days' time." Meanwhile, he said, he would follow it up. I informed him that all I wanted was to see justice done concerning Roshan: "…being paid and still hanging my father." Also to my next question, he reassured me that I would not face any punishment for bribing the judge since I went to them of my own volition. But I was made to repent and swore, with my right hand on the Koran, not to repeat the breaking of such a sacred Islamic law again.

Later I enjoyed a walk in the park thinking of Roshan: he was only a drop in the ocean of corruption that was engulfing the country; and funny enough, all supported by outside interference from unsuspected quarters.

About five years ago an earthquake measuring 6.9 on the Richter scale shook the north-eastern part of Iran, destroying at least 20 villages plus one big city, and killing, according to reports, 2,500 people which, I believe, was actually twice that number.

Referring to the earthquake in Iran, the next day the BBC announced: "France was the first to respond followed by America." I understand that quite well: *of course* they'd be the first ones to offer aid - so long as

Rafsanjani, the ex-president and now the head of the expediency council, Karoobi, the ex-head of the organization taking people to Mecca in Saudi Arabia every year and now the speaker of Parliament, Rafighdoost, the man who drove Ayatollah Khomeini from the airport to his stronghold in the north of Tehran after entering the country from France and at present the head of martyred foundation, Khameneii, the current leader, and Khomeini's grandson - all kept their more than 50 billion dollars in American banks and almost half as much in France; so *of course* they'd be the first ones to respond. There'll be even a faster positive action and on the same day next time, with America probably apologizing behind the scenes for being second, determined to try to beat France in the future.

The BBC went on: "It's been the most generous donation the UN has ever handed out on one single relief operation; 8 million dollars." If this book ever sees the light of print and Mr Secretary General of the UN ever gets the time to read it, could he tell me why he didn't, before handing out that amount of money, ask one of those people I named above, with so much money in banks all over the world, to bring a fraction of that money back to where it belonged and help those stricken areas? I lost faith in the UN long ago.

And then, when Zaire's dictator, Mobutu Sese Seko, was no longer in power and therefore of no use to them, they revealed his wealth at 4 billion dollars in Swiss banks, and also drew attention to his ownership of a mansion there and one also in France; whereas until then they all had kept quiet, calling him a man in need of help. I'm beginning to think that maybe the BBC is under some sort of control as well.

At this point it seems appropriate to refer to another eminent figure, the respectable monk called the Dalai Lama, though I am more than willing to concede that in doing so I may be pointing my finger at the wrong person; the question is, is he in effect the head of Tibet or just the exiled spiritual leader of that large nation? If the latter is the case, were the former residents of the White House fully justified in supporting him? Doesn't it sound ironic to say that Khomeini, in exactly the same situation in exile in France preceding his entry into Iran, found more support from leaders of state, among them Jimmy Carter, then the President of America?

The Dalai Lama in an interview on the BBC said that once back in Tibet he would choose a suitable place of worship and dedicate the rest of his life to prayers and the teaching of Buddhism. Didn't we hear the same promises made by Khomeini, that other so-called religious leader who, when enthusiastically interviewed by CNN in France, said he would be in retreat in one of the mosques, his main agenda being merely to promote Islam? "Politics is best left to politicians," was his catchphrase. I ask with tears in my eyes, was that what he really did?

I'm not trying to draw a parallel here, but are we to see this pattern repeated if the Dalai Lama is reinstated?

Whatever his intentions now, we will judge him when he is placed on the throne of Tibet and his hand kissed a few times. Will he be Dalai Lama, The Emperor?

But now, back to my story! Four days later, at 10 o'clock in the morning, as prearranged, I knocked at Karimi's office door, and entered. Inside were two sentries armed with pistols in the holsters at their waists. Standing on either side of the door, they looked intimidating and made me want to turn around and run! But, from behind his desk, Karimi assured me that the sentries were there to take care of Roshan who had just phoned saying he would be present after a few minutes delay.

Karimi asked me to sit down, gave me a book to busy myself with and turned his attention to writing. I tried to read but I couldn't concentrate on the words. It wasn't long before there was a knock on the door. Karimi stopped writing and looked alert. I was scared, anticipating an unpleasant outcome. Would it all go against me, when over? With the people I was dealing with, anything seemed possible. The door opened and Roshan walked in. Karimi nodded to the sentries and in no time they got hold of Roshan's hands, who started struggling, twisting in resistance. Searching him, the sentries found his pistol and took it away. During the struggle Roshan's turban came off his head and fell on the floor. He shouted, "How dare you! I'm the brother of a martyr and have been to the war zone myself..." So that was how a person with inadequate learning, I concluded, had got himself a professional job like the one he held as a judge! I also remembered when talking to him in the city of Kashan, looking at the open file on his desk, that he had misspelt a few words, which gave me reason to think of him ever since as semi-literate! But that didn't matter, since another one of the same ilk was ruling the country!

When the struggle was over, Roshan, almost subdued, put his cloak in order and picked up his turban from the floor. He brushed it off as through brushing off the dust and replaced it on his head. Karimi gave a nod to the sentries and they left. Surely, I thought, he was thinking he could handle this thin nonentity of a bastard himself, now that he was disarmed! Pointing at a chair in front of his desk on my left, Karimi asked Roshan to sit down. Doing so, this brute in human form tried to ignore me, obviously pretending to show unfamiliarity.

Nodding towards me, Karimi asked him, "Do you know this man?"

Turning his head, he gave me a quick look, then turned back to Karimi. "Never seen him in my life," was Roshan's answer.

Karimi gave way to a sarcastic smile and said, "Now I want you to listen to this." And he turned the recorder on.

The tape hadn't gone for a minute when Roshan said, "This is not my voice. It's faked."

Karimi turned the tape off. "That's what we thought to begin with," he said, "but two days ago I sent someone to Qom to tape your voice; you were there. Comparing the two tapes at the laboratory..." He pointed at the recorder on his table, "...we found this is unquestionably your voice."

Changing tactics, Roshan said, "Tapes are not accepted as proof of someone's crime in court."

Karimi answered, "Unless it's proved to be authentic; and this is authentic." Then, clearly convinced of Roshan's culpability and not waiting for him to blab any further, he carried on: "First, I want you to hand over this money" - pointing his finger at the recorder.

Rather belatedly, Roshan, at this point, decided to tell the truth. "I gave him his money back a couple of weeks ago, when he came to see me and I realised he had taped me..."

Karimi cut him short and almost shouted, "First you didn't know him and now you have given his money back!"

Roshan repeated, "I gave it back to him when he came to see me..."

At this point I couldn't help butting in and in a sarcastic amateurish way, trying to show that he was lying, half telling and half asking him, I said, "You gave me the money back but never asked for the tape, is that right?"

His devilish eyes sparked with hate: "You had a copy of it with you..."

Karimi, stopping him again, asked, "Where is that copy?"

"I suppose you destroyed it," I said almost in a whisper as I looked at Roshan sideways out of the corner of my eye. I asked the question quickly, before he could say anything.

"You bastard, you told me to do so!" he hissed, his weasel face distorted.

At this point Karimi, getting impatient with the lies he obviously thought Roshan was telling, got up from behind his desk and with some anger told him, "Listen, if you give this man his money back he is willing to withdraw his complaint."

That was new to me! Karimi walked up to Roshan's briefcase where it lay after falling to the floor during Roshan's struggle with the sentries. Putting it on the table, he opened it and found Roshan's cheque book. He selected one of the cheques and made it out for 30,000 dollars, and put it in front of Roshan and made him sign it. Was that meant to be handed to me? I withdrew my complaint and received the cheque from Karimi who said to me, "So far as the matter concerns you, you are free to go." I heard these words in a near numb state, for a second doubting my ears.

With my heart almost coming out of my mouth, somehow I walked on wobbly legs to the door - aware of Roshan's eyes following me furiously. I opened the door, went out and closed it behind me. Leaning my back and head against the door, my eyes closed, I let out a very deep breath. I left the building and once outside, got myself a taxi, and went straight to the bank. The taxi waited for me while I went inside and cashed the cheque. Back in the taxi, I asked the driver to take me to my flat.

chapter twenty seven

WHAT WOULD I DO NEXT? I had almost 70,000 US dollars in my possession now but still lived in a rented flat. It wasn't right - I should have a place of my own. Seeing the owner of the flat every month coming round to collect his rent was making me sick. A few days later I bought myself a two-bedroom flat on the top floor of a six-storey brand new building for 40,000 dollars in a middle-class area and a week later moved into it. Meanwhile I went to see Mahin and gave her 7,000 dollars. "That was all I managed to get back from that bastard judge," I lied.

To get away from all the tension of the last few weeks I decided to have a holiday. I bought myself a ticket to Cyprus - another place where Iranians didn't need a visa to enter. They were issued visas at the airport there where more than 50% were sent back by the same plane, I was told by some friends. One shouldn't trust rumours, of course, but the only way to test the waters was to go!

Cyprus was another place Iranians were entering by the planeload to find jobs with better pay. Ever since a few years ago Japan made it nearly impossible for Iranians to enter that country by setting up very strict visa regulations - asking them to obtain permission from the Japanese embassy[4] in Tehran before getting on the plane - people were looking for an alternative destination and most decided on Cyprus. (The influx slowed down considerably a short while later due to the tougher rules introduced at the airport in Cyprus, stopping youngsters entering the country. Also, the high cost of air tickets, increased by half every six months, made many think twice before heading for that small island.)

It was a Wednesday when my plane touched down at Larnaca Airport in Cyprus after a flight of under three hours from Tehran Mehrabad International Airport. When the passengers got out of the plane, a bus waiting at the foot of the steps conveyed them to a big hall where visas were being issued. Everyone looked tense as they entered this hall and I heard a few youngsters murmuring prayers, probably nervous, thinking they might face deportation. While I was standing in one of the queues, an immigration officer asked for someone who spoke English - obviously in need of a translator. Realising this would virtually guarantee the issue of a visa, I went forward and said,

"I speak English." The immigration officer, who looked very young, probably not more than 25, asked me to stand aside and translate for the people in the queue, all Iranians.

He first asked each person that came forward for his passport. I didn't have to translate that! Then, how much money did he have? Anyone with less than 1,000 US dollars on him wasn't questioned any further and handed over to one of the uniformed officers standing at the back, then taken to a room at one corner of the hall - a very large room, I supposed, able to hold half the passengers of a very big plane; from where I was standing I could see the room had a light blue colour wooden door with armed policemen on either side guarding it. When all these passengers had been dealt with, they were taken out of the room and put back on the same plane that had brought them in - in other words, they were deported.

Why had he come to Cyprus? That was the next question asked. Most youngsters in reality could give one answer: to work. But if they said so, the deportation order followed swiftly. And though the immigration officers knew that almost all had flown in with this purpose in mind, turning a blind eye, they still permitted half to enter the country. About eight months later when I got caught overstaying my visa, an immigration officer at the police station told me that the number of people they let in was equal to those caught who were in the county illegally *plus* the ones who were leaving of their own accord; in other words, you might say, the flow of those entering and those going out was always in some kind of balance.

Other questions followed: What was his job back in his country? Did he have a card to support this? Most people over the age of 50, only a handful of them seen around anyhow, passed through; but it was the other way round regarding the youngsters. The visas, a square seal 5cm each side, printed in red in the middle of a page, costing 5 Cypriot pounds (almost equal to 10 US dollars), when issued, were for the duration of a week or at the most two weeks.

All that questioning, to my mind, was part of a bullshit procedure and in the end I didn't understand what standard the immigration officer was working by to allow some people in and to deport the rest. Also, when he asked for one's passport, turning the pages, he started pressing buttons on his computer keyboard - which to my mind was a lot of bullshit too; for, a few days later when I shared a flat with seven other Iranians, I looked at a passport belonging to one of them and noticed that he had been deported from Cyprus only two weeks before, yet had managed to enter the country, through the same channel, again. How could that be? He had covered the prints (visa and exit) with Iranian postage stamps and the immigration officer, not noticing this or realising what he had done, had issued him another visa to enter the country. Yet passports had numbers and bore the holders' names, I was thinking; didn't immigration officers store them in their computers?

In fact, during my eight months stay in Cyprus I met many Iranians who had used the same trick, and for most their present stay was the result of their second attempt to enter Cyprus. The ruse was not unknown to the immigration authorities, for one of the entry questions was, "Did you use the postage stamps trick to enter again?" What that meant didn't need explaining to us, for we were all familiar with it. One had been asked by the immigration officer, pointing at the stamps, what they were for, and he had answered, "Exit tax paid in the form of stamps." Why, then, did not everyone have these exit stamps? The canny answer: "Only those who have not served in the army paid to receive them."

Others, instead of sticking postage stamps over the old deportation stamp, had just torn out the page bearing the record of the previous attempted visit - using a razor with great care so as not to leave a trace at the binding; in some cases leaving out the matching page too. The passport would then be handed to the immigration officer, and though all pages had numbers both in Iranian and English quite clearly printed at the bottom of each one, the immigration officer, not noticing a page or two was missing, had issued the visa. So you can understand why I thought all those questions and tapping of computer keyboards was just part of some sort of elaborate bullshit!

Many Iranians had come to Cyprus, been deported, had tried again a week later and been successful. Some had finally succeeded to enter on their third attempt, a few on their fourth; since no stamps whatsoever were printed in the passport when deported straight from the airport, the deportee had a chance to repeat the journey without the hassle of using postage stamps or tearing the page out of the passport, apart from the cost of a return air ticket. There were a few who had tried more than four times. Later I met a couple in Cyprus who had attempted entry many times, but in the end had got through. Fools, some might call them, but people will try anything in search of a better life elsewhere.

Some entered Cyprus illegally: Iranians through the Turkish part of the island, Syrians and Egyptians by boat straight from home, landing anywhere on the beach. These people, if caught, spent 45 days in prison and were then deported by air. They had to provide their own air ticket as well. Most had worked and therefore could afford it. But with some nationalities, the ones with no money were kept in prison till somehow they managed to make the arrangements to cover the cost. With Iranians who were short of money, the embassy paid for their air tickets, but when home, at the airport, their passports were kept and released only when the deportees came up with the money.

I am reminded of another one of our flatmates, a good looking 24-year-old fellow by the name of Hojat who was losing his hair badly and, concerned about this, was ridiculed by the rest of us every night when we gathered to talk shit; after being deported three times at

Larnaca Airport, he had gone to Turkey and from there by boat to the Turkish part of Cyprus where, meeting a few other Iranians, had sneaked into the Greek part of Cyprus during the night.

Iranians travelling to Turkey were allowed a one-week visa, if asked, to visit the Turkish part of Cyprus - but as the number of Iranians entering this part for the purpose of slipping into the Greek side increased, they stopped issuing such visas. Not long ago Japan, and now this - so where next? Doors were closing for Iranians.

A year later Hojat got caught, spent 45 days in prison and was then deported. He tried, flying, twice more, to enter Cyprus, but was sent back both times at the airport. So far as I know he has resigned himself not only to the baldness of his head, but to the futility of trying to enter Cyprus. Shortly after his last deportation, stuck in Iran, he got married, and now has a son and is working for himself.

Syrians and Egyptians were treated worse when trying to enter Cyprus legally. Almost 70 to 80 per cent of them were deported at the airport, I was told; how much of it was true I couldn't really tell, but the ones who had managed to pass through and with whom I later got the chance to work with had paid up to 2,000 US dollars to a go-between who had some influence in immigration at the airport to get them through - or a trafficker, again the same amount of money, to assist in a night landing on a lonely part of the beach. There were more Syrians than Egyptians and more of the latter than Iranians in Cyprus.

Going back, again, to the time I was translating for Iranians at the immigration desk of the airport, I recall that as they were coming forward, one by one, half were being refused a visa and sent to the so-called deportation room. One youngster, ignoring me, tried to show off that he knew a couple of words in English when asked why he had come to Cyprus. Reluctantly translating the question for him, he ignored me again, answering back using the two words, *country* and *look*, the only ones he probably knew, and the rest in Iranian, obviously trying to say that he had come to the country of Cyprus to look around sightseeing. I translated it to the officer as, "He has come to this country to look for a job." He was deported and as he was being taken away, I told him in Iranian how I had really translated his last sentence. He was furious and shouted, "No, no. Stop. Job."

When they were all dealt with, the immigration officer thanked me for being helpful but apologised for not being able to issue me more than a two-week visa.

Coming out of the airport I joined three other Iranians going to the city of Limassol where everyone looking for a job was heading. I had come to spend my holiday, but the thought "Why not work and earn some money?" passed through my head. If the pay was good, I would consider a job. A few days later, changing my mind altogether, I decided to stay on. Sharing a taxi, four of us, an hour later, reached Limassol where we went our various ways. Two went one way with me following little Eskandar to his friends' place, where he promised we could spent a few nights - a one-bedroom flat shared by six Iranians. Eskandar and I brought the group to eight. Somehow we managed; one cooked and the rest took turns to wash up. It was a first-time experience for me in that I had never shared a place with so many others before, and in as small a place as a one-bedroom flat! Also, most of the party were of the type who had left their hometown for the first time and were therefore hard to get on with. However, as I mentioned, somehow it worked out and instead of staying for just a few days, I remained there for a while: the others, finding me useful with my knowledge of English, asked me to stay longer. Furthermore staying there suited me because it was so cheap: just two days' work paid for a month's food and rent. I also decided to stay until I got to know my way around. Then I would try to rent a place of my own, or at the worst, have a flat-share with one more person.

That first night, finding an empty space, I spread the sleeping bag I had with me on the floor and before long I was dead to the world. Early in the morning at five everyone was up. Those with permanent jobs waited for their *mastros* (bosses) to pick them up, and the rest, after having breakfast, left for a place they called Labour Square, where, as Hojat explained on the way, workers waited till picked up by people in need of them. But why didn't Hojat have a permanent job after six months in Cyprus? And, in fact, why did only two stay at home and the remaining six, including Eskandar and I, set off for Labour Square?

I was soon to find out: most foreigners, especially the ones who had recently arrived, worked on privately owned construction sites where work abruptly ended with the completion of a building - unlike company employees who, when a building was completed, would start work on a different building. The foreign worker might find himself cooling his heels for some time before he found his next employment. A second reason was that in some places you would find your co-workers to be Egyptians, and Iranians didn't get on with them. Egyptians who landed in Cyprus a few years earlier than Iranians felt they could lord it over the Iranians. Therefore after a day's work, facing that problem, most Iranians got paid and left - and quite often not before a bloody fight broke out between the two nationalities. I suppose two cultures with bloodlines stretching a few thousands of glorious years behind them wouldn't give up easily. The third reason was that some of our group didn't get on with their *mastros* (bosses), though I found them not at all bad, ten times better than their Japanese counterparts.

We got to Labour Square, which wasn't a square but a crossroad, and everyone looked alert. "Be ready to run if the police show up," I was told. People in the area, shopkeepers, office workers, motorists, pedestrians and even the minister at the nearby church, had filed a complaint to the police against us gathering in the area, which in days when jobs were scarce, around mid-morning, our numbers reached close to a hundred and sometimes more.

The police also knew we were in the area waiting to be picked up by people in need of labourers, and were aware that most of us had entered the country as tourists with a week or at the most a two-week visa that had probably expired. Indeed, at the end of the visa's period of stay hardly anyone was willing to leave. Therefore we were liable to be picked up for committing two offences: being illegally in the country and sustaining the same status while looking for a job. But then again the country was in need of foreign workers; therefore the police, perhaps by order of the authorities at the top, turned a blind eye to our presence, or went through the motions of following up people's complaints - thereby in effect playing a kind of cat and mouse game with us, for the sake of appearances snatching a few illegal foreign workers each day.

It was early in the morning, not many people around, and with us joining the group, maybe about fifteen in all. Suddenly someone spotted a police car approaching and gave a shout, and everyone started running in different directions. Though it was just my second day in Cyprus and I had a valid visa with most of my two weeks' allowance still intact, I was aware nevertheless that, if caught in the area, I could still face deportation. I followed a small pack, mainly my flatmates, and going round the bend we came up against two other policemen who had got out of their car ready to give us chase. If I wasn't mistaken, one of the policemen touched my elbow. I managed to get away but the guy behind me, who was a bit slow due to him being overweight, got caught. The rest of us kept on running until a suitable hiding place presented itself, where we took refuge. After about ten minutes, when the police were gone and those who had been around longest felt it was safe to return, we went back to the area. "They won't be back for another couple of hours," was the general opinion. The word got around that three people had been caught in the chase, and when confirmed, one of them, as it turned out, was our flatmate, a quiet young man by the name of Ali.

Back at Labour Square we were soon picked up by someone wanting us all for the day to work in his vineyard. "How much is he willing to pay?" was the first question everyone asked. The man had a station wagon and we climbed in and he drove off. No one spoke about those caught anymore.

Apart from Eskandar and me, they all had worked in a vineyard and I was told that in the right season it was one of the most common jobs around. The name of the man in charge was Marios and everyone started calling him Mastros Marios.

Limassol was not a very sizable city, and in a few minutes, entering the countryside, we had left it behind. I had always thought that Cyprus, being an island surrounded by water, like England and Japan, would be green with grass and trees everywhere - but it was nothing of the sort, for there was no green to be seen anywhere; all looked like wasteland apart from a few trees here and there. I had observed the same kind of aridity the day before, from Larnaca to Limassol. The country was covered by hills rather than mountains, and being small, an hour later, getting to the vineyard, I had the impression that this was the general view of the whole land. Later, as I found out, this was exactly so.

At the vineyard we were met by more than ten local women and Mastros Marios told everyone to start. Unfortunately these women were all old, otherwise it would have been an ideal place among those grapevines to have a quiet game with someone a bit younger.

The women cut the grapes from the vines, put them in big baskets, plenty of them around, and when they were filled we carried them over our shoulders to a lorry parked close by. They were quite heavy. Climbing a ladder at the back of this lorry, we emptied the baskets, climbed down, and took the baskets back to the women and waited while they were being filled again. As the work went on, we moved further away from the lorry and therefore with each journey a longer distance had to be covered; and by the time we brought the empty baskets back the next ones were almost ready to carry.

Cyprus was hot, hotter than anywhere I had ever experienced, and this was only the beginning of summer! What would it be like in the middle of it? "On fire," I once heard somebody say. As the day wore on, the job got harder and it felt hotter. At 10 o'clock Mastros Marios left and half an hour later came back with a few cool watermelons, bread, cheese, butter, sausages, tomatoes and quite a few drink cans, my favourite, cola, among them. The Cypriot cheese was delicious. We had our fill and started working again.

They were good golden grapes and Mastros Marios told me that at the end of the day he would be heading for the wine factory in Limassol. "Wine is the main export of the country and the liquor people drank most," he said. "There are wine factories in every city and major town." But in general Cypriots didn't drink much - just a can of beer and a few glasses of wine every now and then.

At 1 o'clock Mastros Marios left and half an hour later came back with his hands full once again: roast beef, chicken, potatoes, carrots and cans of drink - enough to go round three times over! After such work we needed a repast like that! We had another bellyful and a few saved some to eat after work on the way back. It must have cost Mastros Marios a lot of money, all that food plus the drink cans - or did he knock it off our pay? To make sure I asked Hojat and he answered "No", shaking his head. "At most places one works at in Cyprus, one is given breakfast and lunch." I was beginning to like Cyprus! It wasn't like Japan where a foreign worker is pushed around physically and verbally, and I began to entertain thoughts of staying longer than the two weeks my visa allowed me - in spite of the chase every morning! In fact, within the next few days, working here and there, though I found the work much harder in Cyprus, I never had to suffer the indignity of those shouts and calls of *hayacoos* (hurry up!) and the rough treatment I used to be subjected to in Japan. We did our jobs and no one bothered us.

At 4 o'clock, with no more grapes to cut, having gone through the entire vineyard, we finished. Mastros Marios paid us 15 pounds each, as we had agreed at the outset, plus a plastic bag full of grapes and a lift back home.

That evening, back at the flat, after everyone had his shower, we got together in the medium-sized sitting room and talked about Ali who had been caught in the morning and how his arrest posed a threat to us all in the flat. Lucky enough, one of our flatmates, Hamid, was due to start work late in the morning and therefore, was still in bed until quite late, Ali has had his passport with him at the time he was caught and we knew that soon after one was caught the police would take him to his place to get his passport as well as his belongings, and anyone unlucky enough to be in the place at that time the police would take along with them. Hamid hadn't noticed anything out of the ordinary so slept in. Fortunately, however, the old residents at the flat knew the score and warned us newcomers that Ali would be brought back home by the police to get his stuff. When? Most probably early Wednesday morning, they conjectured, just hours before he would be taken to Larnaca Airport and flown back to Iran. That gave us a few days grace, and everyone made plans to stay with a friend on Tuesday night right through to Wednesday afternoon, when it would probably be safe to return.

Early the next morning we made for Labour Square again, which would be the start of my second working day in Cyprus. On the way there, about a 2km walk, I thought how lucky I was that there was a place I could go to and by just hanging around find a job, though with a little bit of hassle; but then again, Iranians weren't the only ones who had managed to establish a job seeking area; about 500 metres away from Labour Square there was a café in front of which Egyptians in need of work would gather, and not far from the café, farther away, Syrians had their base. None of these nationalities dared to stray across the boundaries of their own territory when seeking jobs, not daring to enter enemy territory, as we called it.

After the encounter with the police, and when everything seemed quiet, back at Labour Square, I was picked up and spent the day working for the local brewery unloading sugar bags, each bag weighing 50 kilos, from a 6-metre long truck trailer, of which there were 400. Two people were allocated to each trailer, and when all 400 were unloaded, they were paid 20 pounds - in other words, 10 pounds each. It was a much harder job than working on the vineyard. All my flatmates had worked emptying sugar bags in the same place, and though the pay was good, apart from one - a very strong and likeable young man called Koorosh who had a very good physique and who later shared a flat with me - all stayed away and asked me to do the same. "It's a very tiring job," everyone agreed, "emptying that long trailer of those sugar bags;" it was early yet and everyone else was reluctant to go because they all thought that people with easier types of work would call around later. But when I realized that the brewery job would be like having a good workout, I decided to go. The man who called wanted eight people, but no one already there was willing to come forward. They were all after easy pickings and since the job opportunities in Cyprus, at the time, were relatively good, one could afford to be choosy and miss a few opportunities.

We got to the brewery and saw a few trailers parked outside on the road and when we entered the factory, there were a few more inside: "Twelve trailers in all," Mastros Andros explained. "You empty one and it'll be replaced by a full one outside." Two Egyptians were emptying the first trailer, two Syrians the second one, and, Mastros Andros said, "You can start with the third one." He later explained that we had to cover for the extra people he hadn't managed to get. He had planned for twelve people, and with twelve trailers, that meant two trailers to each two; but now that he had only six people, each two had to get through four trailers. "A very hard job and hope you manage," he said.

Opening the trailer door we found it was full of sugar bags, right up to the sides and up to the roof. And so we started: holding the end of a bag by its two corners with both hands, and Koorosh the opposite side of the sugar bag, we put the first one on a wooden pallet placed just outside the trailer door, on a platform level with the trailer bottom, and then the next one. Four to a row, in the shape of a square, somehow left a small square gap in the middle; there were seven rows in all, one on top of the other, stable enough not to be toppled; that done, the forklift truck picked up the pallet and carried the whole thing away. We placed the next wooden pallet at the same place and repeated the pattern, and before long another 28 sugar bags were taken away. Two forklifts were available, carrying the piles of sugar bags away from the trailers. When enough sugar bags had been unloaded and there was room inside the trailer, we put the pallet there and the forklift took it from there. As we worked our way into the trailer we were given rollers to place the pallet on them; once seven rows were loaded, we pushed the pallet to the trailer door and so to the forklift.

It took us more than an hour to unload the first trailer, almost a few minutes behind the Egyptians and Syrians. Then an engine truck going to-and-fro a few times would stop at the right place, its tail under the front of the trailer; the driver, getting out and pushing a few handles, would connect the two together; back inside his truck, he would drive away taking the trailer with it. A few minutes later he will have changed the trailer for one packed with sugar bags outside, and the big truck would come back rolling in through the gates.

In less than half an hour he replaced the three empty trailers and meanwhile, having had a good rest, we started again emptying the second one.

Koorosh was strong, sometimes picking up the sugar bags by his own as if they had no weight at all. By his accent I could tell he was from the north of Iran, a city alongside the Caspian Sea and probably close to where I used to live, staying in my father's villa. We emptied the second trailer in one and a half hour, had something to eat, then while having a rest waiting for the trailers to be replaced, he told me where he was from and I thought, what a small world! He was from a city where, while living in the north of Iran, I used to shop; and being a small city, I may well have passed him in the street without taking notice. Later, sharing the flat with him, I brought up the subject and told him about my stay by the Caspian Sea.

With a lot of effort we started on the third trailer and, when finished, with hardly any energy left, we began to unload the fourth and last one. Somehow we got through, and when it was over we could barely stand on our legs. It had taken us over eight hours to empty the four trailers of sugar bags and all we wanted now was, after being paid, to go home and rest. We were paid 45 pounds each, 5 pounds extra, which, like a battery, recharged us a bit!

As we were leaving the Egyptians were in the middle of the fourth trailer and Syrians a few bags behind them in theirs. We got a lift back home and, once there, crashed out.

In the evening our flatmates got back and, despite the noise they were making, Koorosh and I kept on sleeping. At night when we got together to have dinner I heard Hojat talking to Koorosh, asking him how we had got on at the brewery; he told Koorosh that once, with some of the flatmates, he had done the same job but after emptying one trailer, they realized they had had enough, got paid and left. "That was all we could do, one trailer," Hojat said, "we had no more energy left!" When Koorosh told him we went through four trailers, he sat back in surprise.

Living with the others I was becoming more streetwise about working in Cyprus. A few days later one of our flatmates, after a hard day's work, came back late one evening, looking sad and dead beat, and said, "Donkey's day!" That was a phrase commonly used by Iranians in Cyprus when one worked for the day but never got paid. This didn't happen often but still, it happened. You worked for a day (sometimes more), and when finished, the mastros took you somewhere, anywhere, often to your doorstep, dropped you there, then without paying you, took off! This is what had happened to our friend; he had been dropped somewhere far from home and been told to wait for a few minutes. He had waited for three hours and when it was clear the mastros was not coming back as promised, he had called for a taxi to take him home - a cost of 5 pounds on top of the loss of his day's work.

Once Hojat had fallen prey to a donkey's week, or

so he said. After working for a week his mastros, knowing that he had no visa and therefore couldn't go to the police, had decided not to pay him. Some of the flatmates who had seen his mastros a few times coming round to fetch him for work every morning readily agreed that he looked like a bit of a bastard - yet they all had some reservations about whether Hojat had told them the whole story. Though he denied it, Hojat, they felt, must have done something wrong to cause his mastros to behave in such a dastardly way. A few months later, not to lose face, Hojat was still telling everyone that he would soon be going round to his mastros' house with a blade to get his money back, and everyone, knowing that he didn't have the guts to do anything like that, took the piss out of him.

Listening to these stories and a few others, I thought, when would my turn come? Was I safe enough as long as I kept my eyes open? There was no easy way one could tell a good mastros from a bad one, and with most of us having no permanent jobs and having to change one's mastros almost every day, one was bound to come across a bad one in due course.

Days went by. With a number of my flatmates I was still regularly visiting Labour Square to find myself a job. Police gave us an awakening chase every morning and as Wednesday approached this chase picked up momentum, peaking on Tuesday. "You will be on the plane the next day (Wednesday), reducing the costs of keeping you in the station," I was told by a policeman when I was caught months later, when my stay in Cyprus was brought to an end.

Approaching Labour Square on Tuesday everyone took extreme caution. On this day the police appeared every half an hour and took the biggest toll. *Any* kind of job offered on Tuesdays was welcomed. That day, after being chased twice by the police, we took the first job offered to us - which was working in a vineyard again and doing the same thing as before, carrying baskets. Sometime late in the afternoon, when the last of the vines were all cut clear of grapes, as usual, we were paid and given a lift back.

At the flat, after we had something to eat, we packed Ali's stuff and left it by the entrance door, so that when brought to the flat by the police he wouldn't have to look around for his belongings; in the short time the police allowed people to fetch their belongings, Ali wouldn't be bothered trying to decide which item he wanted to save: he could easily pick it all up now in a single bundle. That done, everyone left to spend the night away from the place.

Eskandar and I, that night, decided on 'Hotel Bench'! Going to the seaside, we each found a bench and, spreading some cardboard on each bench, we spent the night under the stars with our knapsacks under our heads. The next day, after a hard day's work, we returned to the flat and noticed that Ali's stuff had gone with his flat key left on the table.

For the first few weeks I worked doing odd jobs, the

longest being for five days on one building site making concrete with a machine they called Mihani; when ready, turning a handle, the concrete was poured into a wheelbarrow I had positioned in the right place; once the wheelbarrow was filled I turned the handle back to stop the concrete running down and took the wheelbarrow to wherever it was needed on the site.

Then I met Mastros Glitos and all things changed, to begin with for the better. He was two years older than me, about my height, very strong, with a thick moustache, bright eyes - one of the nicest guys I ever met in my life.

He picked me up from Labour Square one morning, looking for someone to take his AC's (Air Conditioners), ten of them, each weighing more than 50 kg, to the roof of a seven-storey building. About an hour's job, I estimated, and he was willing to pay 10 pounds.

I got into his double cabin Mitsubishi van with the AC's, all Mitsubishis, each packed neatly in its own cardboard box piled up in the back and tied down with a rope round them; about 20 minutes later he stopped in front of a big building block that looked newly built and still unoccupied. "Offices," he said, "soon to be taken over by firms from all over the world." Changing Cyprus into a free trade country like Singapore and Dubai, I supposed.

Taking the rope off, I got the boxes down and started carrying them, one by one, over my shoulder to the roof. The lift wasn't running yet; two people were working on it, obviously finishing the last touches, so I used the stairs. It was hard legwork and by the time, just over an hour later when I took the last one up, the stairs were slippery with my sweat! Did I want to stay a bit longer and earn some more money? "Sure," I replied. Mastros Glitos looked very honest and I was soon to find out he was the same inside.

Those were the outdoor units I had just taken to the roof, he explained to me, and now, getting in his van again, he started for the Mitsubishi AC's office to collect the indoor ones.

The office was close by, only a few minutes' drive away, and something funny happened on the way there. While driving Mastros Glitos turned back and asked me, "Esi (you) Pepsi?" Thinking that after an hour's hard work and the weather being hot he was offering me a cool drink, I answered, "I'd rather have Coca Cola than Pepsi…" He cut me short with his loud laugh, then, reading my mind since I was looking puzzled, wondering what the joke was, he explained slowly: "You Persi? This is the Greek word meaning Persian, Iranian." Now it was my turn to laugh out loud!

We got to the office and I realized that it was also the shop where AC's were sold. They had a small warehouse in the back full of Mitsubishi AC's of all kinds.

I followed Mastros Glitos inside and met Manos, the man in charge of this office in Limassol; tall, well built, good looking, friendly, smiling, he was a graduate of London University. Then I met Sophoglis, the sales manager; also tall, friendlier, smiling more often, and a sterling human being. Sophoglis canvased for customers, then by means of some simple arrangement, handed over the addresses to Mastros Glitos who took the units in his van to the clients' houses and installed them; a job of sorts, a bit hard, and in need of some skill. Mastros Glitos was paid 50 pounds for each AC he installed; usually about eight a day, less costs, he was pocketing almost 300 pounds (600 US dollars) daily - very good money if all the days brought in the same business, though that wasn't the case. One or two days a week there were only half that number of AC's to install - not such a good enterprise considering, too, that Sundays were off and the demand for AC's ceased for six months of the year, since when the weather got a bit cooler there was no further use for AC's.

Though my first meeting with Manos and Sophoglis was very short, we had a great laugh and really hit it off. Perhaps that was why Mastros Glitos treated me so well.

I put the indoor units in the van, roped them down securely and we started back for the building. There, again taking the rope off, I carried three indoors at a time; these were 15kg each, less than one third the weight of the outdoor units. I took them to different rooms. Then I helped Mastros Glitos thread wires through some plastic pipes already placed inside the walls, connecting the indoor units to the outdoor ones on the roof. That over, handing him the tools when up on the ladder, I stayed on till the afternoon when he appeared and said, "Lunch time!"

We climbed into his car and he started off. I had no idea where he was heading for until a few minutes later we drew up in front of an old looking single-story private lodge, when he said, "My house." Then, getting out of the car, he invited me in.

What was going on? Was he trusting me in his house on the first day of our acquaintance? Did I look that honest? I followed him through the back door which led to the kitchen. There his wife, I suppose hearing us, was arranging the table. It was a nice place inside, almost newly decorated. He had a quick wash and asked me to do the same. There were new tiles in the washroom as well. (Clearly he had been renovating the house and, keeping up with the interior décor, a few days later he started on the exterior of the house; when finished it looked quite unique in the row of houses in the street.) Coming out of the toilet I was asked to join the family at the kitchen table: Mastros Glitos, his wife and their two daughters, Viyoletta (18) and Sofi (15) already there. It was a round table and I sat on the only empty chair between Viyoletta and Mastros Glitos. When the food was placed on the table everyone stood up, as did I, and Sofi started to give thanks for the food in prayer. She went on and on to a point where I thought she wouldn't stop! In time I learned that anywhere in Cyprus before people started eating, prayers were said. I also learned that most people attended church on Sundays. They were religious but not fanatic.

Within the next few days I found out that Mastros

Glitos' daughters were pious and chaste, though I never tried to make a pass at them. Viyoletta, about my height, had a beautiful figure; with her black hair, she was very pretty and very quiet; she had just taken her 'A' Level exam in pure mathematics and had failed. She was planning to take the same exam again soon, hoping to pass it this time. Looking at her pure maths books brought back some memories; they were the same two books I was given at Basingstoke Technical College when preparing for the same exam. Not able to contain my surprise, I told her about it and that I had passed my 'A' Level in pure mathematics with grade 'A'. "And if you encounter any problems, I might be able to help you!" I told her. I'm pleased to say that a couple of months later, though not without my help, Viyoletta passed her 'A' Level exam in pure maths.

Back at work that day, I stayed with Mastros Glitos till late evening; by the time he finished he had all the AC's running. Then, giving me 25 pounds and a lift back home, he asked me to join him again the next day, provided I had my visa. I lied to him about having a year's working visa, and the next day was the first of a number of days I spent working for Mastros Glitos. Now that he meant me to stay with him, there were no more daily payments; like all other workplaces in Cyprus, when one was asked to work for more than a few days under the same mastros, one received one's pay weekly.

I didn't have to call at Labour Square anymore. Mastros Glitos came round to our place every morning at about seven and I was always waiting downstairs - cautiously, on the lookout for the police as well.

After I was picked up we always went to the office before any work began. Being too early, no one was there, but Mastros Glitos had the keys. We got the AC's, according to the list Sophoglis had prepared, noting how many were required and of what BTU's (British thermal units); then we called at the first customer - usually a private house. Starting at 7:30, I got through some hard work with the biggest drill one can work with, making a hole in the wall to pass the wires and pipes through, sweat dropping from all points of my body. Around 9 o'clock the household we were working in asked us for breakfast. Everything one wanted was laid on the table. My choice of job, it seemed, couldn't have been better! We had our breakfast and went back to work again. Most houses had three bedrooms, therefore there were three AC's to install in each house. When the work was completed we left, around 11 o'clock.

We went back to the office, had a short laugh with Manos and Sophoglis, got a few more AC's, then left to call at the next house. We would either have lunch there, if the members of the household were in, or otherwise at Mastros Glitos' house.

Most places we called at suggested affluent owners who were able to afford AC's, and had a Philippino maidservant helping with the housework. Some of these maids I talked to told me they were being treated like a member of the family by their employers. The situation was quite different to that in Kuwait, I thought, where 400 of them, as I once heard on the BBC, had run away from the houses they were working for, most bearing cigarette burns and bruises all over their bodies and a few with broken noses. They had taken refuge in their embassy, asking to be sent back home. No wonder Saddam attacked them!

chapter twenty eight

IN GENERAL I found Cypriots okay, though most of my mates disagreed with me. Maybe I came across only the good ones! But without any doubt Mastros Glitos treated me the way one would treat a brother. To start with, working for him, he might have kept an eye on me when entering different houses, for his job was the only source of his income and could have been at stake, but he did it in a way that never made me feel uneasy. Also, the money he paid me was generous, an amount that even most Cypriots longed to earn. No, I have to say I have no bad memories from the time I worked with this very kind man. My sincere thanks to you, Mastros Glitos, and also to your family.

A few months later when I got to know my way around I rented a flat which I ended up sharing with Koorosh. This was in a different part of the building and though it turned out to be much more expensive, I was tired of living with so many in such a small place, and felt I needed more privacy.

As for the building - it was the most notorious and ill reputed one I had come to know in Limassol, something everyone recognized. It was called Rialas Building consisting of a complex of three blocks, A, B and C, each eight stories tall, four flats to each floor, mostly occupied by foreigners, thieves and smugglers.

If a crime took place anywhere in Limassol, the most common one being a burglary, and if someone had managed to see the culprit and was able to describe him, the next day, first thing in the morning, there was a police car parked about 50 metres away from Rialas Building entrance checking all the people against the description they had been given. And that is what made Rialas Building, in my opinion, a safe place to live in Limassol; one was always on the lookout for the police, but for this safeguard to work, leaving the flat, one had to remember, going down, to use not the lift but the stairs. In every block the lift door, on the ground floor, opened opposite the entrance door of that block, and if a policeman were to be standing there, a person coming out of the lift had no choice but to be subjected to an identity check - imperative if a foreigner. Then, on being found out that he had no visa, he would be arrested on the spot and later deported; whereas, using the stairs, there were windows through which a person could check out the area all around him and, if noticing anything out of the ordinary, could open the window on the second floor, jump into the adjacent car park next door and make good his escape. At the other end of the car park there were ropes left by some foreigners to expedite an escape; by means of one of the ropes tied to a handrail one could lower oneself down to the level of the pavement, jump over a fence, and melt into the side streets and private houses. On a couple of Tuesdays a year when the police raided the building for the purpose of rounding up illegal foreigners, there would be five or six people climbing down these ropes at the same time.

The flats themselves were raided too, every now and then, but not for the reason of arresting illegal foreigners; the police always had other good reasons for doing so, and what a mess the place was left in after they had gone! One of these flats was occupied by six Iranians I had recently come to know, all addicts, drug dealers and smugglers, who had come to Cyprus, some carrying hashish and opium in plastic bags inside their stomachs; they were all thieves to boot, who would come back home from the Saturday market - held every week in an open area close to Rialas Building - and the one who had stolen the most would be the boss for that week and be exempt from washing the dishes. When I entered the flat on one occasion just after it had been raided by the police, my mouth fell open and my eyes widened in shock. It was like a scene one would see in some movies, everything on the floor and nothing in one piece: the TV and stereo smashed, mattresses torn apart, furniture overturned, some even smashed, and the belongings of all six occupants thrown about.

One of these six, Rasool, a tall dark young man of 24 with a beardless face and thick black curly hair, had managed to get away while the police were carrying out their search. Using a rope, one end tied to the handrail of the flat balcony - all flats were equipped with such a rope - he had climbed down to the balcony of the flat below where, finding the flat door to the balcony open, he had walked in and out through the front door, picking up a briefcase on his way. (The briefcase looked costly, but opening it later he found nothing but documents inside.)

Rasool, coming to us, begged to stay for a few days till he found himself a new place; going back to his old flat was out of the question; police would call again and worse than that, the landlord calling at the flat at the end of the month to collect his rent, which was only a couple of days away (and it was odd he hadn't been round yet), would ask him to pay for all the damages; but now finding no one there, and the place in such a state, the landlord would probably go to the police; they would explain everything to him (the landlord), and that would be the end of any hope of staying on there and, indeed, in Cyprus.

Everyone in the flat was reluctant to have Rasool with us, since he was known as the worst among those six: an addict, smuggler, thief and anything one could think of calling him. But in times of trouble people helped one another, so we asked him in; and what a mistake that turned out to be!

Two days later Rasool got his chance to pay us back for our hospitality. Finding one of the flatmates, a quiet little fellow not yet 20, called Babak, alone at the flat, he thrashed him, took his money and fled.

Coming back from work that day, going to the bedroom, I saw Babak, head and one shoulder covered in blood, though not badly hurt, lying on the bed and the rest of the flatmates standing round, all looking grave, staring down at him. Hojat was the one who found Babak in that state. "He was tied up in ropes," he explained; then, picking up a metal pipe lying on the floor by the bedside, he flourished it above his head, imitating the action of someone bent on striking an imaginary person. He said: "He hit him with this on the head…" Then, pointing with his eyes at the knife Hamid was holding, he continued: "…and stabbed him in the shoulder, taking his 2,000 dollars from his pocket and running off." He had left a note thanking us for everything and even had the audacity to sign his name, Rasool, at the bottom.

His first chance, I thought, to take advantage of us, and he had used it; and he had probably come to us, in the first place, with the same intention, taking us for a bunch of simple people.

First we decided Babak needed some treatment. Someone called a taxi and we put Babak in it and went to the hospital, situated just outside Limassol. There they gave Babak a tetanus shot, and shortly after he received three stitches to his head and two to his shoulder. Luckily Babak had escaped serious injury. All this cost him 100 dollars and since he had no money, for Rasool had taken it all, Koorosh and I paid half each, but a few days later when Babak went back to work, first thing, he paid us back that money.

Back at the flat that evening we considered what we could do about this incident and talked about it into the small hours of the morning; but in the end everyone realized that there was not much we could do.

Like Hojat, Rasool had entered the Greek part of Cyprus through the Turkish part; and now, probably anticipating that Babak would go to the police, though he didn't have a visa, there was a chance, however slim, that he would, on account of his condition, but he must have considered 2,000 dollars worth the risk. Nevertheless, the police would still listen to Babak due to the seriousness of the crime, and try to track down the lawbreaker. Thinking all that, Rasool most probably would try to leave the country, and surely by the same way he had entered it. Hojat suggested that he knew the area where the crossing between the two parts, the Turkish and the Greek, usually took place, and that we could ambush him there. But it was too late by then, we thought, to go there and wait for Rasool; he would surely have crossed the border by now if he had put his mind to it.

In the end, whatever Rasool's intentions, he would surely want to leave the country; or if he stayed, he would go to another city to look for a job, and so we decided there was only one option open to us. To some extent persuaded by the rest of us, Babak didn't risk going to the police; therefore everyone agreed on the following course of action.

The day after Babak was feeling a bit better and, giving him some money, we sent him to the Iranian embassy in Nicosia. There he spoke to the ambassador and told him his story, and, as expected, the ambassador, looking at his fresh wounds, asked him for witnesses, four in all. According to some Islamic laws, though not present at the scene of the crime, after going through some Islamic procedures, people can bear testimony in some cases expressing ideas as to what they thought had really happened. When Babak returned and told us about this, we all agreed to testify; no one doubted Babak's story which also had more credence since Rasool had run away.

Therefore early the next morning, five of us plus Babak headed for the Iranian embassy in Nicosia. We wanted to get this thing over with early and spend the rest of the day hanging around Nicosia. At the embassy security was tight. On entering the building we were asked to stand in a queue; then, one by one, the first one being Hojat, we emptied our pockets, leaving the contents on a side desk; we were then told to walk through a wired door frame. When Hojat did so, it beeped and the sentry standing on the other side asked him to check his pockets again. Doing so, he found a coin in one of them. Leaving that, too, on the desk, he passed through the frame once more, this time without any beeps! But his entrance was not over yet; he was body searched by the sentry on his side. Didn't he trust the electronic frame? Finally the green uniformed brown bearded sentry, looking satisfied with his task, asked Hojat to take his belongings from the desk. One by one we went through the same procedure, which took a good twenty minutes.

We were met by the same ambassador who had seen Babak the day before. He took us to a small neatly carpeted room, got five chairs, put them in a row along the wall opposite his desk and asked us to sit down. The room was quiet and I was feeling uneasy.

The ambassador looked very smart in an expensive suit, his beard neatly trimmed. He got behind his desk and mentioned that in cases where the witnesses had not been present at the time when the incident had taken place, there were sermons, to start with, which had to be preached to the witnesses. For the first ten boring minutes he read us verses from the Koran, then for another forty boring minutes he started telling us about how God dealt with people bearing false testimony. "...these people had no place in Heaven... they would definitely end up in hell with fire all around... people bearing false witness would be burning in the fires of hell right up to eternity... Have you ever burned your fingertip with a match? That's painful! Now imagine your whole body burned like that…"

If I was honest with myself, when the ambassador finished, he had so brainwashed me that I would have got out of my chair and run for the door, had I doubted Babak for a second!

We were given pen and paper each and were asked to write the incident down in brief; in the course of this we weren't allowed to talk.

I finished first and also wrote the longest. When everyone had finished the ambassador collected the pens and papers; it really looked like being at school. Then, dismissing us, but before leaving, he faced Babak at the door, telling him that he would let him know if there was news.

We left the embassy around mid-morning; putting the incident behind us, we decided, if it could be helped, not to talk about it anymore. Then, going down to the city centre, we spent a great time in Nicosia, and it was well past nightfall when, all quite drunk, we got back to Limassol.

Life started running smoothly soon again; Babak found himself a permanent job, I carried on with Glitos and the rest got on with whatever they were doing.

As days went by Iranians committed more crimes, not only against themselves but also against any easy target and sometimes crossing the hard line when they found the chance. Not a night passed, watching news on TV, that we didn't hear about some Iranians arrested, most on charges of burglary; two Iranians broke into a sports shop, stole some expensive equipment and later, trying to sell the wares, got caught; four Iranians were arrested in connection with the Panasonic warehouse robbery. Every Wednesday night we watched the news eagerly to see who had been caught at the airport amongst new Iranians entering the country, carrying hashish or opium. The previous Wednesday four Iranian women were caught carrying half a kilo of hashish each inside their cunts. X-rayed, an excerpt was shown on TV.

And why not, I thought? For a kilo of best hashish one would pay 500 US dollars in Iran; smuggled into Cyprus, it would fetch sixteen times that. And talking to the people involved in it, all were of the same opinion: "Money earned this way was pleasant" - something, I remembered, my father used to say.

Thinking about it now, writing these notes, what was it that made us Iranians ready to commit crimes? Egyptians and Syrians in larger numbers than us came to Cyprus, but hardly any of them got involved in criminal activities; they just worked and left, but we Iranians, given a chance, were all too ready to commit crimes; these were the remarks I heard made by the Cypriot police, when I was caught overstaying my visa. Remarkably, I remembered, years ago, the same comments were made by the Japanese police; when arrested at the end of my stay there, I heard them talking about Iranians as criminals. In Japan we were compared with Pakistanis, Bangladeshis and Indians.

We even robbed the hospital in Limassol off 800 dollars. And this is how it happened: one of our flatmates, a tall and strong young fellow of 24, called Habib, lying on his back one day was complaining about a pain on the right side of his lower abdomen. The pain must have been excruciating for, in spite of being a brave young man, he was moaning pathetically, doubled over in agony. Speculating, some came up with the idea that the pain, being in the right place, could be due to chronic appendicitis. And if so, we all knew, he had to be operated upon without delay and the appendix removed before it ruptured, if it hadn't already. Remembering what I had heard on the BBC about how to diagnose an inflamed appendix, I put my hand on the place where Habib was feeling pain, pushed it down a bit, and on releasing the pressure he felt a sharp pain, almost screaming; now I was sure that it was to do with his appendix. About thirty minutes later the doctor at the Limassol Hospital confirmed my findings and informed us that the patient had to have an operation without delay. God be praised, it could have been more serious, and everyone was relieved that the crisis had been averted. There being no need for us to remain in the hospital any longer, we went back home once Habib had been taken to the operating theatre.

The next day, work finished, we all went up the hospital to pay Habib a visit. He was doing fine and the doctor told us that he would be allowed to leave hospital in a few days' time; the patient would be required to pay 800 dollars towards the cost of the operation.

But Habib had no intention of parting with such large amount of money! Talking it over, the day before his release, on a pre-planned decision but pretending to pay him a visit, we entered the hospital. Habib and three other patients were being looked after in a big ward on the ground floor. In this room, just opposite the door, there was a window about a metre above the floor level, going all the way up to a point just below the ceiling. This window was quite wide and opened on to a big garden where the patients were allowed to refresh themselves walking about; but now it was dark outside with no one in the garden. Habib's bed was on the right of this window close to the corner, and on the left a young English fellow who had been involved in a bike accident; the other two corners were occupied by a very old man, bedridden probably for the same reason, and by a man all in bandages apart from his eyes, mouth, left arm and right leg.

When we entered the room, Koorosh stood watch by the door and Hojat went out to find a wheelchair and place it outside the window; the rest of us started changing Habib's hospital pyjamas for the ones we had brought with us; we didn't know where the clothes were that he had worn when he had entered the hospital so we would simply abandon them - a small payment towards that 800 dollars he owed. But his belongings that were in his pockets, though not much, were in a draw at his bedside, and someone took them. Now Hojat was knocking on the window from the outside. I opened it; he had a wheelchair ready and said that he had a taxi waiting too. The young English patient, looking puzzled and then realizing what we were about to do, asked us if we really intended to leave through the window. I was the only one to understand him and answered this golden young man with the words, "Yes, it's much cheaper this way." The old man lying on his bed from the other corner looked quite amused; I went to him, put some pillows behind his back and sat him up; now he could see better and be more amused!

Four of us picked Habib up very carefully and took him to the window. The man in bandages, with his eyes wide open - the only distinctive feature in his face - was not able to move his head but follow our movements with the corners of his eyes. Resting Habib's upper body lightly on the window sill, but still holding him, two of us moved outside and held him from there; then the same procedure followed to lift his lower body, and so we got him out and onto the wheelchair. Koorosh joined us and we went round to where the taxi was waiting, got in and left. This, then, was how we robbed Limassol hospital of 800 dollars.

"No wonder the money has to be paid in advance in hospitals in Iran!" one of our party laughed on the way home.

Habib soon recovered and went back to work. But a few months later, renting a motorbike, he got involved in an accident. The police were called and, being the party at fault, he had to pay 800 dollars towards damages caused to the car he had crashed into; in addition, the incident led to the discovery that he had overstayed his visa, and so he was deported. I heard someone calling it nature's fair play.

About two months after our visit to the Iranian Embassy the ambassador wrote asking Babak to pay him another visit - there was news.

After going up to the embassy and talking to the ambassador, Babak came back home and indeed there *was* news. Rasool had been caught trying to enter Iran. The story was that late at night, on the same day he had injured Babak, Rasool had crossed the border into the Turkish part of Cyprus. There, early the next morning trying to embark on one of the boats bound for mainland Turkey, his passport was checked and he had been stopped for overstaying his visa. After spending a week in prison he had been released and allowed to continue his journey to Iran. In Turkey he had travelled to Istanbul, staying there a few weeks enjoying himself spending Babak's money; then realizing the loot was becoming scarce and Turkey was no place to find himself a job, and that soon he would go hungry with no shelter over his head, and also thinking of the crime he had committed in Cyprus, he determined to move on to Iran, where the legal consequences of his crime in Cyprus would not reach him. Clearly he was badly mistaken, for upon his entry to Iran he was arrested at the border.

Rasool was now in prison awaiting trial. "He will be convicted," the ambassador had told Babak, "though his legal aid has argued backing the same idea that the crime had happened outside Iranian soil and therefore not subject to legal procedure there; but," the ambassador, shaking his head, had carried on, "in cases where the plaintiff and the defendant were both Iranians, no matter where the crime had been committed, the trial would go ahead." About three months later, as his court case date was approaching, Babak left Cyprus for Iran to attend the hearing and secure the return of his money.

I stayed with Mastros Glitos till mid-October; then, due to the lack of need for AC's, with the onset of cooler weather and very little work to do, it was no longer cost effective for him to keep me on the payroll. By now, however, I had learned to do the job thoroughly on my own.

After he paid me generously for the last week's work, we reluctantly took leave of each other - but not before he asked me to join him again the following year. After working for over five months, enjoying every day of it with no rough treatment, for one of the most honest and kindest employers, it was time to say goodbye. By now we had become great friends and I thanked him from the bottom of my heart before we finally parted.

I was a bit richer now than the time when I had first started working for Mastros Glitos. He had paid me really well. No dissatisfaction there, but banks wouldn't open an account for people like us with such limited visa duration; though the main reason, I gathered, was the fact that the passport belonged to a person from a developing country. The money bulged in my pockets, and fortunately there were a couple of shops in Limassol that would change Cypriot pounds for dollars, thereby reducing the bulk. But there was always the danger that one could lose the money, either through negligence or through the light fingers of one of one's flatmates. Therefore, every now and then, when someone returned to Iran, those trusting him would give their savings to him, taking the risk that he would be honest and would deliver the money on the other side to a family member; one often phoned the family member to await the arrival of the trusted courier at the airport in Iran. That way one felt more secure about the money reaching its target.

chapter twenty nine

❖

BACK AT THE NEW FLAT where Koorosh and I had recently moved, sitting in front of me, telling Koorosh that my job had ended, I asked him casually about the situation at Labour Square. I hadn't been there for the last few months. At the old flat, where I had been staying until a few weeks ago, I had been more in the know about the situation at Labour Square for some of my old flatmates were still going there some mornings and coming back in the evenings; but since moving to this new place I hadn't had much news, and Koorosh, working on one building site for the last month, and before that, for a slightly longer period, on another one, didn't know much either, apart from some bits and pieces of information that occasionally came his way.

Our new flat was on the 6th floor of C block, the previous one being on the 4th floor of A block. Using the stairs, going two floors up to the roof, feeling safer that way, I walked over to block A. All tall buildings and even some one-storey private houses in Cyprus had asphalted flat roofs, and in Rialas all three blocks were connected and had exit doors at the top. Entering block A, then using the stairs again, I went down to the 4th floor, stood in front of the old flat door and knocked. Suddenly I had a funny feeling, for a second thinking that I was still living there; that irritated me since I had become used to the quietness of our new place. Babak opened the door and asked me in. He had fully recovered from his injuries that were inflicted on him nearly three months ago and the news of Rasool's arrest at the border in Iran within the last month had uplifted his spirits.

I entered the flat and as I did not intend to stay for long, I got straight to the point. I told them about my job having ended, as I had already explained to Koorosh, and said I was now looking for another. "What are the job prospects like back at Labour Square nowadays?" I asked.

Eskandar was the only one going there for the last two weeks. He had been working on a building site for three months until recently, having left after an argument with his mastros. He said the outlook wasn't brilliant, though perhaps not hopeless. It seemed more people were seeking jobs of late and the numbers were increasing daily. With the tourist season having come to an end, that wasn't surprising, I thought. Recently

Eskandar had returned empty handed a couple of times due to the lack of jobs. "I'll find out for myself tomorrow," I said and left. I didn't volunteer to join him on the way there in the morning, since it was a good half hour walk and I preferred to keep to my own company. I went back to my flat the same way I had come.

It would have been a nice break from the AC job if I did not seek any new form of employment in the meantime, but it would be six months before I could start back with Mastros Glitos and I didn't want my money to drain away. At Labour Square the next morning there were indeed more people than usual waiting to get picked up by those in need of them; and beyond the point where the last Iranian was standing stretched mixed lines of Russians, Bulgarians, Romanians and Yugoslavs. The small country, Cyprus, was being invaded by workers from Eastern Bloc countries too, financial pressure being at the root of all these migrations. Some spoke of facing rough treatment at work and the kind of demeaning jobs they had been assigned to. Furthermore, there was the recurring chase by the police through the streets; it was disgraceful, at least for us Iranians, some said, coming from a country full of natural resources, one of the largest oil producing countries in the world and with all those gas reserves. Better than that they had diamond resources, others were saying, in Africa, which nevertheless did not amount to much.

Eskandar was there already when I reached Labour

CHAPTER TWENTY NINE

Square. "Have you been here long?" I inquired, just to have something to say.

"For about half an hour," he answered.

"What's the job situation been like so far?" I asked, though I'd find out for myself soon.

"Quite a few have been picked up since I came," he said.

Within the next hour, though still early in the morning, in spite of there being so many people and the numbers steadily growing, jobs were being offered at a steady rate. Then came the shout "POLICE!" and everyone started running. I and a few others were running down a narrow street when we came across four tourists who looked British, walking in the opposite direction with full knapsacks over their shoulders. "What's the problem?" one of them shouted and I shouted back, "There's a lion loose up the road!" With that all four turned round and started running like mad behind us.

It wasn't long before we were all back at Labour Square again, emerging from all directions, some even coming down from trees.

More of us labourers got picked up by those in need of us. Then a man arrived asking in English for someone who knew how to weld. I am sure no one among those standing by understood the meaning of the word *weld*. I translated it and one came forward. Ten minutes later a van pulled up at the kerb and the driver asked for a carpenter, again in English. Again I translated the word *carpenter* and after some discussion someone came forward and was taken away.

After that a brand-new BMW stopped at the roadside close by and the driver, getting out, shouted for someone who could speak English.

Quite a few people gathered round his car. I held back watching with some premonition; as typical with most Iranians, they tried to show off the few English words their limited vocabulary allowed them; at last the man, looking dissatisfied with all those who had stepped forward, was about to return to his car and I shouted, "What do you want him for?"

Turning round, his eyes searching for the person who had asked the question, he said, "To work in my restaurant serving customers."

Before our eyes met I asked, "And how much are you willing to pay?"

Now aware to whom he was speaking, he said, looking directly at me, "I'll give him a room, breakfast, lunch, dinner, plus 15 pounds a day."

Even at only half of what he was offering, anyone there meeting his requirements would have stepped forward! I volunteered and he asked me also to choose someone among those standing by, not necessarily someone able to speak English, who would be working in the kitchen washing dishes. I pointed at Eskandar who was standing next to me and the man asked us to get in his car.

He took us back to where we were living to get our

belongings. Mastros Lefteris, as he was called, wanted us for three months; on top of his offer he would also give us lodgings next to the restaurant - a big room just for the two of us. What a lucky first day, I thought, for I was all set up now for at least half of the quieter season.

The car stopped in front of Rialas and both Eskandar and I got out. I went up to my flat, got my knapsack, but before leaving wrote Koorosh a note: "I found myself a job in the village, won't be back for another week or two." Though Lefteris promised us a job for three months, I was thinking that if I didn't get on with him I'd know that within the first week or two - then get back before Koorosh, to keep the rent down, tried to find another flatmate or give the flat up altogether prior to joining the others in the cheaper flat. On the other hand if Lefteris proved to be a nice person I'd still go back in two weeks' time to explain things to Koorosh; then it'd be up to him whatever he wanted to do with the place afterwards. I left the note on the table, banged the door shut and, using the stairs, went down.

The state of the art BMW that Mastros Lefteris was driving had now turned round, parked on the other side of the road. I crossed the road and got in, and Eskandar joined us a minute later.

We left Limassol behind on the road heading west. Going in that direction for about half an hour, Lefteris, talking non-stop, took a side road going north. Driving for another hour turning to the right and then to the left, with him still talking non-stop, the car eventually drew to a halt somewhere in the county in front of a restaurant. Getting out and getting some relief from his incessant talking right into my ear, I became aware of the cold; indeed, it was much colder here than in Limassol. Taking in the scenery I noticed there were not many trees apart from at the back of the restaurant. To the left of the restaurant and attached to it was a medium-sized house; otherwise, the terrain consisted largely of heaths and hills; in one direction I could see the rooftops of houses belonging to a small village almost 1km away.

Lefteris led us into a very big room attached to the end at the right side of the restaurant. The room was sparsely furnished; a double bed at one side, an old large wardrobe filled with bags and other personal belongings at the opposite side, a table and couple of chairs placed somewhere in the middle. We left our belongings in one corner. At the other corner a fire was burning, a little ineffectually in such a large room. If anything, the room felt cold but there were enough blankets on the bed. It was an old room and the walls seemed at one time to have been white. Never mind, I thought, we'll try to make the best of it for the next three months - no doubt just like the previous occupants, two Egyptians who, until a week ago, lived there for the last two years - as Lefteris told me, still talking non-stop; all the time I was trying to explain some of this to Eskandar who kept poking me to know what was being said. The Egyptians had decided they needed a holiday, had left for their country, but had promised to be back in three months' time - hence the need for us to cover that period. They had left a lot of their stuff behind, all in the wardrobe, so it seemed pretty certain they'd be back.

As for Lefteris himself: he spoke good English, had been educated in London, having gone to university there; he had spent most Friday and Saturday nights in discos round that city, gone out with a few girls, all pretty, then, at the right time, had married an English girl of Cypriot descent.

Life seemed to have taken the right course for him; he had his own house in Kensington, London, where he spent a few months every year, with his wife and two children; the rest of the year he was back in Cyprus running the restaurant with his parents who lived in the medium-sized house next door. While in Cyprus he lived with his family in his house in the village.

After putting my belongings in the room Lefteris said, "Have a shave and put a white shirt on; have you got one?" I had a white shirt in my knapsack so I nodded. He continued, "You'll be serving the customers." Then, pointing at Eskandar and giving him a long look, he said, "His appearance will do. He'll be working in the kitchen so it doesn't matter much what he looks like." I translated that to Eskandar and Lefteris, leaving the room, paused at the door and said, "I'll see you both in a few minutes in the restaurant."

I got my shaving equipment and went outside. A few metres away and to the left, there were two toilets and a small shower room, all built separately adjacent to the back door of the restaurant. I had a quick shave, went back to the room, put my white shirt on, then both of us left for the restaurant.

In the kitchen I met Lefteris' parents and his wife who was deficient in beauty and, as I found out later, in manners too. But his parents were nice, his father full of joviality, and they never tried to bother us. Before anything we were offered a full breakfast; so far so good, I thought. Then Lefteris showed us how to make salad dishes, cutting tomatoes, cucumbers, a head of lettuce and on top of that grating a couple of small carrots. They had a coachload of German tourists coming to the restaurant that day. Things were rushed. But on the whole the job was easy, certainly the easiest I came across while in Cyprus; it was nothing like using shovels and pickaxes or carrying bags of cement. We were kept busy till noon when the restaurant was invaded by the Germans, Cypriot wine flowing generously and soon everyone started singing.

In the kitchen the two women (Lefteris' mother and wife) prepared the dishes, Lefteris, his father and me serving the customers while Eskandar was kept busy washing up. We started by giving them salad, then the main meal was served. There was another coach, also full of Germans, on the way, so as soon as a dish was emptied we took it back to the kitchen to be washed; the women, next, started helping Eskandar at the sink. Working efficiently we got rid of the first group, the dishes returned to the kitchen, the tables cleaned. The second group that had been rambling outside for the last few minutes, entered. The same procedure was repeated and by the time they, too, were gone, all the dishes were washed, the tables cleaned, the floor swept and mopped, and everything put back in order; it was around 3:30 and Lefteris told us that till 6:00, routinely, we were off duty. Given some of the food that was left in the kitchen, Eskandar and I took to our room to have lunch.

In the room I took from my pockets the tips that had been left behind on the tables, which Lefteris had told me I could collect. It came to more than five pounds. I gave half to Eskandar.

After a short nap in the room, I took a shower. Eskandar, feeling tired, slept through the whole of the rest period; then, just before 6:00 we were back in the restaurant. There wasn't much to do in the evening; the restaurant opened at 6:30 and, with no coachload of customers expected, we spent a relatively quiet evening until the restaurant closed at 10:30. Again, everything in order by 11, Eskandar and I took to our room, had dinner there and, feeling tired, went to bed.

We started at 8:00 the next morning. The same kind of overloaded breakfast was laid out on the table from which we helped ourselves; then the day began, outside in the back garden, by peeling potatoes. This went on till 10, then back in the kitchen we followed the same procedure as the day before, everyone back at the same job, only this time serving different groups of Germans. In the evening it was quiet again.

This working pattern was repeated for the next four days, and on the fifth Lefteris told us that there'd be no more Germans. I thought, if not that, what then? Throughout the day it was very quiet. On the sixth day, as Eskandar and I were about to leave the room in the morning to start the day at the restaurant, two Arab looking youngsters, followed by Lefteris, walked in. In their mid-twenties, I had a good guess who these two strangers might be. Had they decided to cut their holiday short? If so, I had made the right decision to wait before giving up my flat. It didn't take long before I was proved right on both counts. Lefteris, looking at me, confirmed they were the two Egyptians he had referred to who worked for him. And now that they had come back there was no further need for Eskandar and me.

What about the three months' work he had promised us? Resignedly, we packed our bags. One of the Egyptians, looking smug, gave a sly smile, and no longer able to contain my frustration, I hit him hard on his jaw. Taking a few steps back, he landed on his ass. The fight wouldn't have ended there if it wasn't for Lefteris and Eskandar who jumped between us to hold me back.

Bags over our shoulders, following Lefteris, Eskandar and I went to the restaurant and had something to eat in the kitchen; then Lefteris paid us, plus a day extra. He wasn't the type that would try to get away with his workers' earnings; on the contrary, as we had realised from the start, he was generous, also handing us a small bottle of whisky each. We were sorry to leave and knew we would miss him.

Getting into his car, we left the restaurant, not a word said on the way. A couple of hours later we were back in Limassol. Closing the car door, nevertheless, I thanked Lefteris and showed him a happy face. Though I had lost a good job, somehow I was glad to be back in that familiar place. I entered Rialas Building and went up to the flat. No one was there, so obviously Koorosh was at work; thankfully there was no trace of anyone else having moved in. I had a cup of coffee, then left to spend the day walking on the beach. Around early evening, back at the flat, I was watching TV when the door opened and Koorosh walked in. He looked more than pleased to see me! The thought 'No more lonely evenings!' was expressed in his happy smile. Like two friends who hadn't seen each other for months, we exchanged warm greetings, feeling close, like brothers; we talked; curious to know what either of us had been up to. I told him, briefly, where Eskandar and I had been working and what had happened. He had good news for me; on the building site where he was working his mastros had asked him to take a friend along to work with him till the following week. So I was back at work the following day!

It was the same old kind of job I had done anywhere working on a building site - hard but glad to be employed and earning good money. What I had in mind now was to save enough money so that when sent back home one day, I didn't have to work anymore.

Depositing all my savings in the bank, I would live on the interest drawn from it. Truth to tell, I didn't get on working alongside my own people. Not only me, but many others were experiencing the same thing. At workplaces there was always trouble; arguments flared up over minor things; people called one another spies working for the government, sent there to catch them!

Working on the building site, Koorosh was very helpful to me. When the going got tough he gave me a hand; his mastros liked him too, since he was a hard worker. But the week passed swiftly and once again I found myself back at Labour Square.

For the next couple of weeks work turned up sporadically, with a few days, now and again, with nothing to do. I was perhaps useful to others, occasionally translating the requests of those who drove up looking for workers with specific skills. I was becoming famous as a translator there. There was a Cypriot farmer in search of someone to look after his flock of sheep, and he understandably wanted a person with some knowledge of sheep. I shouted for a *choopan* (meaning shepherd in Iranian) and some young fellow stepped up. He used to look after his father's flock, pasturing them in the mountains of central Iran, often staying out for days on end - and I thought I was the only Iranian who liked a solitary life! When I translated what he had told me, the farmer asked him to get in the car without further ado. But how had the young shepherd ever come to know of Cyprus in the mountains of central Iran, I wondered? As the car pulled away, I murmured to myself: "Once a shepherd, always a shepherd."

Then came that fatal Monday.

chapter thirty

A MIDDLE AGE MAN, looking quite smart, got out of his car, wanting four people to work in his warehouse. I asked him what kind of a job it was and how much he was offering; impressed that I could speak English and probably thinking it would make it easier for him, through me, to communicate with the other three, asked me to join him and to choose the other three workers from those standing around us. I pointed at Eskandar next to me, for one, but was reluctant to choose the other two. Pretending I didn't know the others around me, I placed the ball back in his court and asked him to make the choice. In truth, they were all looking at me expectantly and I had no desire to disappoint the ones who would not be selected. In normal circumstances to have joined that many Iranians to work at the same place would have been unthinkable for me - it was like asking for trouble. But the situation wasn't normal, too many people still waiting to be picked up and jobs were scarce; reluctantly, therefore, I took the chance and accepted the offer.

I sat next to the driver and the other three, Eskandar, Mohsen and Javad, got in the back and the car moved away. The warehouse, Mastros Kostas explained, was situated in Limassol and they kept tiles there. There were tiles of all sizes from different countries, mainly Italy and Spain, shipped to Cyprus. Fifteen minutes later we got to the warehouse. There were two wooden pallets just outside the entrance, on the top boxes filled with tiles waist high. According to their sizes or whatever, Mastros Kostas told us to take them to different parts of the warehouse. Though the boxes were small, they were heavy. For this reason we carried them one at a time, but also because the tiles were costly and breakable.

It was a sizable warehouse inside with a low ceiling, dimly lit, rectangular in area. There was a small brightly lit office at one corner, its windows covered with frosted glass that obscured the view inside from the outside - presumably, the other way round too. Boxes filled the warehouse, in some parts up to shoulder height, forming corridors between the stacked boxes along which we could walk. An hour later all the boxes from the two pallets were unloaded and stacked, and we had a short rest, Mastros Kostas going to the office.

Customers and representatives from the shops in the area, Mastros Kostas told us, came to the warehouse to obtain tiles. I saw a van arrive outside. After parking it, the driver got out with a sheet of paper in his hand and walked into the office. A minute later the man came out following Mastros Kostas, still carrying the sheet. A glance from Mastros Kostas indicated that we should join them. A few minutes before this Mohsen had disappeared and now a shout from me brought him back. Joining us, it was apparent from his black looks that he didn't like me calling after him and also that I should stop my boss-like behaviour towards him - an attitude not shared by Eskandar and Javad. In truth, this was the kind of attitude he liked to display towards us. It all came down to the fact that he did not want to work half as hard as the rest of us - an intention he didn't avoid conveying from the start. While emptying the two pallets, he paused to light a cigarette, even though I had translated Mastros Kostas' earlier injunction prohibiting smoking inside the warehouse. He took his time for over five minutes standing idle outside to finish his smoke while we were working; even then, quite reluctantly, he joined us afterwards. "Eskandar and Javad smoked too," I later said to him in a friendly way, "but they waited till work finished and only then went outside to smoke."

If he disregarded the no-smoking injunction, it'd be a bad influence on the others. Quite soon, I could predict, Eskandar and Javad would be thinking: "Why should we do the extra work Mohsen is avoiding and at the end getting paid the same?" I'd give it another couple of days, I decided, then if he didn't mend his ways, I would have a word with Mastros Kostas to get rid of him. Whether that meant a boss-like behaviour or not, I was willing to resort to it.

When Mohsen joined us and conveyed his resentment by means of his dark looks, it took a lot of restraint on my part not to land one on his face; in any case, the present was not the time for such a course of action since we had work to do. Consulting the sheet of paper, Mastros Kostas pointed at some boxes and we took a number of them to the van. Moving to another part of the warehouse, looking at the sheet again, he ordered more boxes to be removed to the van; room for no more, the driver got behind the wheel and drove away. Under pressure due to the weight of the tiles, the vehicle moved considerably slower and was much lower on the road as, a few seconds later, it disappeared round the bend. Pointing once more at the sheet of paper in his hand, Mastros Kostas told us that the customer would be back. "He has gone to unload the boxes at his shop first," he said. That said, he went back to his office. Meanwhile we would rest.

Eskandar and Javad went outside to have another smoke and Mohsen disappeared again. To pass the time I decided to explore my surrounding. There were beautiful marble slates in one corner, the type one could see the reflection of one's face in, like looking into a mirror. Then I smelt hashish and panicked. So *that* was the reason behind Mohsen's disappearance, I realised! What should I do now? There was a fan on the wall right in front of me and, pulling the cord, I put it on. If I went and found Mohsen, who I had no doubt was responsible for this hashish smoke, there would be trouble; and being our first day, it would mean the end of our jobs in the warehouse. Later I regretted the course of action I took - or didn't take - for it cost me not only my job but the country I was living in.

I was thinking what to do, as I often did when facing trouble and not being able to come to a quick decision; what I should have done at this juncture was leave the warehouse altogether while I had time, though that is based on wisdom after the event. My thoughts were interrupted by a tap on my shoulder. Turning round, I found myself staring into the barrel of a pistol held by a well-built big policeman. Coming up to my face, sniffing me, he realised I wasn't the one smoking. Now another policeman appeared, talking to his colleague, and nodded his head towards me, apparently thinking I was the one responsible for the smoke, his fist clenched. The first policeman shook his head, but turning me round, handcuffed me. Holding my right arm, both pistols drawn, the policeman gave me no option but to accompany him as he and the other policeman walked towards the place where the smoke seemed to be coming from. We turned a corner and, right in front of us, were a pile of small boxes stacked waist high, and from behind it, in the dim light, smoke could be seen coming up thick and clear in a single shaft; about a foot higher than the boxes, it scattered. Very quietly, we moved round the pile. Mohsen was sitting on his ass and the soles of his feet, knees bent, his back against the boxes, hands crossed over the knees, his head bent forward resting on one forearm. He had his smoke between the fingers in his right hand. Releasing my arm the policeman took a couple of steps forward, brought his hand up, then let it go down hard, slapping Mohsen on the back of the neck where it was well exposed and positioned for the purpose. The impact was loud, as if someone had just set off a firecracker. Not able to restrain myself, seeing the way Mohsen jumped into the air, I gave way to a burst of laughter. The policeman standing next to me had a job stopping himself from laughing too. I had never seen anyone who was stoned sober-up so fast. The pistol back in its holster, the policeman could take Mohsen away, one hand held behind his back, without fear of resistance.

The joint was now on the floor where it had flown from Mohsen's hand; with the edge of his shoe, the policeman put the glowing tip out, picked the rest up and handed it to his colleague. Mohsen was just beginning to come to terms with what was happening when the big policeman grabbed his shirt just above the shoulder and pulled him up as though he had no weight. Still held by the same place, Mohsen was turned round, controlled like a puppet with no balance of his own, then pushed roughly over a pile of boxes where he was involuntarily stretched out. The policeman, searching him, found a small plastic bag in his trouser pocket with a few pieces of hashish in it. He handed that, too, to his colleague, who added the joint he still held in his hand to it; folding the plastic bag to secure the contents inside, he put it in his trouser pocket.

Satisfied with his search, the giant of a policeman put handcuffs on Mohsen while he was in that same recumbent position. What a way for my Cyprus adventure to end, I thought! Would any of this have happened had I landed my fist on that no good hashish smoking bastard when the chance was there earlier? I regretted my inaction for days to come. Then the lawman brought both hands down hard on Mohsen's shoulders and in one swift movement pulled him back onto his feet. We were both pushed roughly towards the entrance.

Outside there were three more policemen with three police cars, and I wasn't surprised to see Eskandar and Javad, also arrested, occupying the back seat of the front car. Mohsen and I were taken to another car and thrown onto the back seat before the doors were slammed shut.

There were two policemen to each car, occupying the front seats. For some reason one car stayed behind while the other two pulled away. A few minutes later we entered Limassol's main police station. There our handcuffs were removed and we were all searched down to our underpants; a few bits and pieces plus a lot of money was found on us. Mohsen, held by the arm, was pulled away by one policeman; a door opened and he was pushed in. Eskandar, Javad and I were taken to another part of the station where cells lined both sides of a long narrow, dirty corridor. There were two prisoners to a cell, but some were empty. Eskandar and Javad were placed in one while I occupied the next one on my own. The first resolution we made was that if Mohsen was brought in we would beat him half dead! Unfortunately - or fortunately - that opportunity did not present itself.

The cells were small and dirty. There was a bunk bed at one corner with no pillow cases and sheets, just a mattress and dirty blankets on each bed. In contrast to the cells I had occupied in other countries, these cells were smaller, but once the doors were opened in the morning, they remained that way till late in the evening when it was time to go to bed, when the doors were closed. There was an open toilet at the end of the corridor that hardly anyone used; with those inmates watching one didn't feel relaxed enough! There was a sink next to the toilet on the left with one cold water tap over it. I found the sink so dirty that, during my ablutions the next morning and the day after, I let the water run into my cupped hands which I then splashed over my face instead of filling the sink for the same purpose. It would only be for two days, I reminded myself, that I would have to put up with those filthy surroundings. After that I would be home - which sounded even worse! I took my shoes off and lay down on the lower bunk. Once more I was going to be sent back, I thought, through no fault of mine. How was it that my body was born in Iran but my mind was set on belonging to a different place? Why couldn't we choose where to open our eyes? I was beginning to think that there was some kind of magnetic pull between my body and the country where it first came into existence. Wherever I went on the planet, I was always forced back to that land in due course. Destiny, it seemed, could not prevail over natural selection - or was it a case of destiny prevailing over random selection? Up Charles Darwin! I'm still waiting for a chimp to turn human. Within a couple of minutes I planned my moves for the next few months.

Cyprus was a good place. I wouldn't have minded staying there a bit longer, though there was no guarantee when one's time would come to depart. No matter what, the end result was always the same; depending on one's luck, no one had managed, staying in Limassol, to elude capture for more than three years; and from what I had heard it was worse in other cities, Paphos being the worst.

A policeman came round to the cells and called Eskandar and me out. Now we would be taken back to where we lived to get our passports. While being searched at the warehouse, Mohsen's passport was found on him in a neat leather case worn round his neck by a long strap; the policeman had pulled it off roughly and thrown it to his colleague who caught it in the air. Javad also had his passport with him, found when searched at the station; plus all the keys to our flats which were also taken away.

Eskandar and I were handcuffed together, and

outside the station building we were pushed into the back of a small police van. A policeman closed the doors and took his seat next to the driver, who was also in uniform, and the van pulled away.

We stopped in front of Rialas Building. We were taken out of the van, the driver holding my right free arm and the policeman Eskandar's left arm, and in this way all four of us walked in a row towards the entrance. There, turning sideways, but our arms still being held, one by one we entered block A, then in the same way into the lift that took us up to the fourth floor. We went to Eskandar's flat first, and he was hoping no one would be in. It was mid-morning now and earlier he had told me that his flatmates should all have left by this time, two attending permanent jobs and two going to Labour Square. On the fourth floor, the policeman was first to leave the lift, Eskandar and I next and the driver behind us. Key in hand, the policeman went to the right flat, easily identifying it since the numbers of the flats were stuck on the keys by means of sticking tape; he opened the door and entered, followed by the rest of us, in the same way we had left the lift. Someone was lying on the settee placed along the right wall in the sitting room, I noticed, once through the door. It was Hamid. He woke up and, turning round, he saw the policeman and he went white as chalk, all the blood draining from his face. It was too late to do anything and in no time the policeman had him handcuffed to me.

Hamid resisted, struggling, begging to be let off,

saying he had a wife and children in Iran and if sent back he would be out of a job there and his family would go hungry, but was subdued when the policeman gave him a slap across his face. He and Eskandar were pulling me from one side to the other as they got their passports and handed them to the policeman, who gave both passports a quick look before putting them in his pocket. Hamid had overstayed his visa by more than fourteen months. Next, they were allowed five minutes to collect their belongings. I was stretched to the limit; Hamid wanted to get his trousers from the top of the wardrobe and Eskandar his spare shoes from under the bed. At one time we stumbled over one another, then trying to sort out which way to stand. Bound together, it took twice as long before each managed to pack a small bag, at which point the policeman told us we had to move on. Throwing the key on the table, he left the flat first, followed by us and the driver who slammed the door shut.

When we entered my flat on the sixth floor of C block, as I had expected, Koorosh wasn't there. Asking Eskandar and Hamid to move forward, then backwards, now to the right and then a bit left ("Leave your hands free when I say so and bend down with me," I said), I somehow managed to get my passport from the side compartment and hand it to the policeman. Since I always had my knapsack ready packed with my belongings in case I had to move quickly at a moment's notice, all I needed to do after grabbing it was to unzip it and insert my small radio and alarm clock. It all took less than five minutes before we were ready to leave. Once more, as in the previous flat, just before leaving, finding no more use for it, the policeman threw the key on the table. By doing so he didn't realise, I thought, that he was relaying a message to Koorosh, who would know that I had been arrested.

Outside, I felt helpless and vulnerable. If anything went wrong, with both my hands incapacitated, one handcuffed to Eskandar and the other to Hamid, I could not defend myself. If both my hands had been handcuffed behind me, I would at least have been able, if trouble arose, to turn round and present my back to any onslaught.

Back at the station, handcuffs removed, we were searched once more, plus our belongings which were taken away; then we were sent back to the cells, now all full, which suggested there had been a concerted drive to roundup illegal workers and immigrants. Some cells were even occupied by three people. There were many nationalities now - Russians, Bulgarians, Romanians, Egyptians, Syrians, one from Nigeria and two Cypriots. But on the whole there were more Iranian inmates than all the rest added together. One of the policemen later told me that this was because, out of all those nationalities, we Iranians were more prepared to get involved in criminal activities; so they tried to get rid of us first.

I shared my cell with another Iranian. When he told me his name I almost jumped out of my bed and ran for the door. He was called Ahmad, which reminded me of the man by the same name I had shared a cell with in the north of Iran by the Caspian Sea. It brought back the terror of that time when I almost met my death at the end of a rope! For a moment I felt myself back in that condemned cell, sweat covering my forehead. I must have displayed some kind of odd reaction, since Ahmad, taking a step back, looked concerned and asked me if I was okay. Short and in his late twenties, this Ahmad was in line for a different fate than the former one. Like the rest of us, he had been brought in for overstaying his visa, in his case by 18 months, having been caught at work. Ahmad would be sent back to Iran, a different fate from that other Ahmad who, presumably, had ended up in hell.

About an hour later we newcomers were handed, each, two boiled eggs, one large round Cypriot loaf of bread, a banana and a packet of milk. I assumed this was our lunch, but was informed by those who had been confined a day or two longer that it was a "prisoner's ration that had to last through the day" - usually received in the mornings apart from those coming in late. Thanks heaven I wouldn't be staying there long - only two days, I reminded myself again. I had been worse off in Turkey, but that was expected from most backward countries. In Cyprus my expectations were much higher - not dirty cells without pillow cases and bed sheets. But then again, in conjunction with all that, the behaviour of those running the station towards the prisoners was tolerable (with a bias towards good) and that made a lot of difference. I had the eggs with half the bread and put aside the rest for later, sticking the banana inside what was left of the bread. I would have that with my milk just before bedtime.

It went past noon and no more prisoners were brought in - certainly not from Labour Square since all workers left the area well before noon most days, knowing from experience that no one would call in need of them anymore. In early evening just two Cypriots were brought in. With no more empty cells available, they joined their countrymen, four of them in one cell.

As in all prisons, time passed quickly. Around five o'clock two policemen came round to the cells and called, "Time for exercises!" The smaller of the two, twice my size, opened the door at the end of the corridor next to the toilet, and the other one, much bigger, checked the cells making sure all joined in. Would anyone dare defy his orders? One by one, passing through the door, we entered a small yard, 10x10m square, surrounded by tall walls surmounted by barbed wire all round. Four policemen stood watch over us at the corners, all armed with pistols at the waist. There were a few toilets positioned at one side of the yard, all walled round; some of the inmates started using these while the rest walked round in circles. The air was fresh and I enjoyed the walk. Only an hour of open air - how I longed to be free!

After an hour of exercise, the light fading, we were

led back indoors. Passing the cells I noticed a few books inside one of them on the floor, placed upright against the wall. I entered the cell, followed by two Russians; it was their cell and by the looks they gave me they didn't want intruders. Pointing at the books, nodding my head and smiling since they spoke no English, I made them understand what I was after; I picked up one in English (most were in Greek), and left. I took the book back to my cell, lay down on the lower bed and tried to read it. My thoughts were scattered and to pull myself together, and also to get through those boring hours, reading seemed a good strategy; otherwise I would drive myself demented thinking about revenge on Mohsen. Ahmad, lying on his bed above me, was, fortunately, like me, not talkative. Anyway, I was in no state for any kind of conversation. I soon became absorbed in the book, so much so that when the policeman closed the door at ten o'clock I didn't take any notice; I grabbed my banana cake and milk and, while eating, read on. The cells were windowless and the lights were left on during the day. I was expecting the lights to go out when I heard the last cell door being closed with a loud clang - but they stayed on and there were no switches inside the cells to turn them off. That suited me for it meant that I could carry on reading. Ahmad above me, not stirring, was probably asleep. In the early hours of the morning I stopped reading, overcome by sleep.

I woke up to the sound of cell doors being opened. It had gone seven in the morning. No need to hurry, I reminded myself, for the cell doors remained open; I'd wash when everyone else had done so. About an hour later we were handed our rations, the same items as before: two boiled eggs, one round loaf, a packet of milk and one banana, all in one plastic bag. Not feeling hungry, I hung the bag by my bedside. In the meantime more inmates joined us, mainly Iranians, all picked up at Labour Square. And more were expected. It was Tuesday, the day earmarked for the arrest of those who had overstayed their visas. The next day, Wednesday, there would be flights to various destinations, reducing the cost of keeping us there for longer than necessary - as I heard the policeman telling the Cypriot inmates who had asked about the overcrowding.

From two o'clock onwards no more prisoners were brought in - the police station cells all full, more than twice the normal capacity, and the number of Iranian inmates making up half the total. Eskandar and Javad in the cell next door and Hamid a few doors away, left their cells to join Ahmad and me. Now, with five to our cell and with less than a day to go, we thought it best to trust each other and share the cell among us, thinking that it would be better to share with people we knew than with strangers. Better the devil you know, as the saying goes!

I took a blanket, folded it a couple of times and stepped just outside the cell into the corridor. A couple of steps to the left I put the folded blanket on the floor and, like so many there, sat on it leaning my back against our cell wall. But unlike the others, most with heads hanging down, smoking, drained of any optimism, I continued reading my book. Again at five o'clock, two policemen, different from the ones on duty the day before, came round to the cells and called, "Time for exercises!" But this time due to the large number of inmates they divided us into two groups - beginning with those occupying the cells on the left. They would walk round the yard till 6, then, for an hour following that, the ones opposite. Included in the first group, but always enjoying my walks, I managed to sneak into the second group of inmates, too, as they were getting ready to leave for the yard. Exercises over, close to two hours in total, back inside, I felt refreshed.

I retrieved my folded blanket from my cell and, sitting on it in the corridor again, I returned to my reading. (Had I left my blanket in the corridor while going for exercises it would have disappeared.) Now feeling hungry, eating my banana cake while sipping from the milk packet, I kept on reading my book. It was an epic of Henry VIII, about the way he had dealt with the clergy; even in those days, it seems, religious dignitaries were draining the country of its wealth. Good on you, King Henry! We need you back in Iran to deal with our mullahs (the men with turbans) in the same way.

Reading, time certainly flew. It didn't seem long before two policemen entered the corridor and ordered everyone back to his cell; it was 10 o'clock, time to close the doors.

Now, with five of us in such a tiny cell, everyone felt surrounded. It was a consoling thought that only just over half a day remained before we would be on the plane to Iran and, if you could call it that, freedom. Nevertheless, we were still in Cyprus and already everyone was talking about what they would do once back in Iran. I joined Eskandar and Ahmad sitting on the lower bunk while Hamid and Javad sat on a neatly folded blanket on the floor opposite us; in such limited space, their knees were almost touching ours. They were talking, putting forward various ideas, as they had been doing for the last few hours - as I knew since I was able to hear them while I was sitting in the corridor. Their session had long been in progress by the time I joined them in the cell, the talk mainly being about which countries were best to enter on leaving Iran. Inescapably I became part of the assembly, unavoidably listening to everything that was said and occasionally nodding my head.

"...Australia... ask for asylum there... and you are provided with a nice place, a good job, money..."

Let him carry on, I thought, and he'll probably come up with more things provided: a brand new car and a shapely whore in it, too.

"...but it is hard to get there... otherwise you need a lot of money... paying some human trafficker..."

"...these people often take your money and you'll never see them again..."

"...and there is no need for them either... you could do the job yourself if you are clever enough..."

"How?"

"....I was coming to that... not long ago... a friend of mine went to Indonesia (charged 25 dollars at the embassy in Tehran, he was issued a three-month visa)... for 100 dollars, paying some local there, he was taken to the neighbouring country... Papua New Guinea... parting with another 100 dollars at the border... he was driven, along with a few others all from different countries, at the back of a van, down to Port Moresby... that's Papua's capital... In his letter I received from Australia he wrote saying that the port was crowded with people from Iran, Iraq, Turkey, Bangladesh, Pakistan and also many from Africa... Some locals there, in Moresby, owning speed boats, in agreement with the police, traded openly: approaching these foreigners asking them, just saying, 'Australia?'... They charged 1,200 dollars per head... then on your way first thing after dark... After spending all night on the sea, just before dawn, they had reached land... a short walk from there to a waiting car... for 300 dollars each, being driven to civilization..."

And so on and so on! Similar stories followed.

There was no chance of any sleep that night, it seemed. For the next few hours I heard of Iranians who had travelled, by means of illegal channels, taking such routes that would leave one's mouth and eyes wide open; landing in half the countries round the world. And oddly enough, all somehow in contact with these four I was sitting next to - my cell mates: they had received letters from most of them. The ones who had failed the journey, myself included, were also in some sort of contact with them back in Iran - furtively, no doubt.

To my surprise, Ahmad was quite talkative too. The next story he began drew my attention, since it told of the same route I had taken a few years back.

Commanding attention with a sweep of his hand, as though it was his turn to talk next, he told us of a very risky undertaking. "I know of a friend," he began, "who went to Turkey, and from there sneaked into Greece…" My head half turned involuntarily towards Ahmad sitting on the other side of Eskandar. He went on, "Before I come to Cyprus he left for Turkey to repeat his daring trek to Greece again; in fact, he asked me to go with him…" Second-hand reports and letters (received from supposed travellers) no longer attracted much notice; first-hand accounts were more arresting, and so journeys told in person were the ones that began to be discussed: "…. but when he told me how he proposed to carry out his daring escape, I found the game somewhat out of my league…" In response to a question put by one of the guys, Ahmad explained that he was shown everything on a map, tracing his friend's route, leaving no doubt about the friend's capability and trustworthiness. "…you go to this border town in the west part of Turkey close to Greece… though, offhandedly, now, I can't remember the name of the town my friend had gone to…" But I did! Keeping quiet and just listening, I thought, either Edernè or, from where Osman (our Turkish guide), Ali (my Iranian friend) and me started, Ipsala. Ahmad carried on: "...there is a road stretching along the western part of Turkey, that's on the map too, a few miles away from the border..." So far so good. "...wait till dark..." Exactly! "...then get a car or a taxi to take you along this road..." That's what we did, using a taxi! "...you pass a tall bridge..." So your friend must have started from Ipsala village, I thought. "...a couple of miles after the bridge you stop the car..." Good enough, though a bit short of a ten minutes' drive, for I recalled that we went beyond the bridge. "...from there start walking towards Greece... going through mainly rice fields... a few hours later you come to a forest..." Yes! The forest which, I remembered, was not so dense with trees but covered by thorny bushes up to shoulder height; and no matter how hard I tried, I found it impossible to get through, thorns sticking to my jacket stopping me. In the end, resignedly, I had slept at the threshold of the forest, hoping I would find a way to cross at first light. "...passing the forest, my mate told me he came to the most challenging part of his journey..." The river, Maritza! Certainly it *was* challenging. My mind back in time, I felt rather than imagined myself standing by it; though a few years had passed, the experience was still vivid, up to my ankles in water, staring at the river thinking how I would cross the bastard. "...my mate told me he came to a very wide river... a natural border between Turkey and Greece..." It was like someone telling me my own story! "...very calm river... but when he tried to swim it, he was taken along with the current... he had to swim back..." This is what happened to me on the second day, in the morning after I was sent back by the Greeks. "...he found himself a log... hanging onto it while paddling with his feet... got himself to the other side... Greece..." As for the rest, with only minor differences, it was the same way it had happened to me: caught and sent back.

So it seemed not all reports, contrary to my expectation, were false or just rumours - some, as I now realised, were authentic. And so, I now knew, I wasn't the only one who had made that abortive journey. In fact, as I write these notes listening to the BBC, it is being reported that more than 400 people have been caught trying to cross the Maritza River to enter Greece in the month prior to the broadcast alone.

With no more adventurous journeys to relate, and it being well into the morning, everyone felt exhausted and agreed it was time to sleep. Eskandar and I shared the lower bunk while Ahmad and Javad took the one above. Hamid, adding one more blanket to the one already on the floor, made himself comfortable there though I offered him my own place; he declined and happily lay down on the blankets and went to sleep.

The next day, as usual, the cell doors opened at seven in the morning. Would it be our last day? Everyone had a quick wash at the only sink available; and again I took my time, one of the last to wash.

Around 8 o'clock rations were handed out. Then, past eleven, all nationalities were separated; first, we Iranians were led outside into the yard, a number of policemen standing watch. We were divided into two groups before being bundled into as many large police vans. Doors swung shut, the vehicles started moving. Destination: Larnaca Airport. Not one of us uttered any words. I could hear some long bitter sighs as some exhaled. Others, looking downcast, might have said "woe unto me" - now that at last their hopes of a future in Cyprus were finally dashed. There were close to 40 people in that not so large space, half of them sitting on the benches fixed to the sides of the vehicle, the rest on the floor. There were wire-meshed windows, one on each side and two on the doors, so dark that it was difficult to see outside. It didn't matter, I thought, for in less than six months I'd be seeing all this again, travelling in the opposite direction if all went according to my plan.

Less than 50 miles to cover, I thought. It didn't take long before we could hear the sounds of planes taking off. Some, I noticed, were actually crying now. If one didn't know better, one might have thought the tears were tears of joy, in anticipation of seeing their homeland again. One could say that thought was correct if only one could change the word *joy* for *sorrow*. We had a purposeful stop, the second van drawing to a halt right behind us. Those at the windows looked back at us and, as if reporting bad news, shouted, "Airport, airport!" The two vans rolled through some gate and entered the airport area. A minute later they came to another stop, this time the last one as far as we were concerned.

The back doors swung open and a shout ordered us out. There were more policemen than deportees, half commando types with their dark beret caps pulled to one side on their heads; they looked ready for action. Rumour had it that a few weeks back a fight had broken out between the two sides.

Following the others, leaving the van, that mighty plane, the 747 Iran Air Bus towering above us, took my breath away. Led to the stairs, I once again felt as though climbing into my coffin. At the entrance, carrying no boarding cards, we were asked to occupy the seats at the rear of the plane - all left vacant for us. The rest of passengers, in the seats already occupied in the front part of the aircraft, I presumed, were those deported at the airport. The doors were shut and the sign 'Seat belts on and no smoking' appeared on a small elongated screen. The plane started moving and a minute later we were in the air, smoothly on our way back to Iran.

In the middle of flight each deportee was handed a medium size envelope. A steward, his hands full, called out the name written on each envelope before handing it over. Inside the envelopes were the personal belongings taken away from the inmates after they went through a body search at the police station in Limassol. Passport, money and a few minor things I usually carried with me, like penknife and pocket watch, I took out of my envelope. The money I found intact, as I had expected. I was already aware of this procedure having been told about it by one of my flatmates who had been through this course of action. He had entered Cyprus for the second time using the postage stamp trick to cover the visa and exit prints, having been deported only two weeks prior to his re-entry. Those who had stayed in Cyprus for more than a year, like Hamid who was sitting on my left, found their money 300 dollars short. This is because their original return air ticket, valid for only a year, had expired, and so the cost of the airfare had been deducted from their money. That they had expected too, as I knew having been informed of this by the same flatmate.

As for me, going back I was 5,000 US dollars richer, though most of it I had sent back a few months earlier by Habib's father who had come to see his son when he had his appendix removed. Needless to say, no one told him how we had released his son from the hospital. A man of high esteem and fully trustworthy, Habib's father, going back, was the chosen courier for more than a dozen people, carrying more than 50,000 US dollars on him. The day after I arrived back in Iran I checked my balance at the bank and had it confirmed that the dollars I had handed to him had all been deposited and changed into Iranian currency.

chapter thirty one

THE PLANE TOUCHED DOWN at Tehran Mehrabad Airport less than three hours later. Standing at the end of a very long queue, passengers from another plane already there, it took almost an hour for my turn to have my passport checked and stamped. And so, back where I had started, I entered the country officially. Going up some stairs, then after a short walk, I came to the conveyor belt carrying our flight passengers' luggage around. Quite uncertain, I watched; it didn't take long before I spotted my dark blue knapsack coming out; from what I had heard, a number of deportees, for some reason, were deprived of this right, their belongings having been held back. I picked up my knapsack, which had been my companion in my travels round half the world, and joined another long queue, at the end of which everything was searched inside out. All done, leaving that behind too, then passing through the throng of people waiting to meet and pick up other passengers,

I stepped out of the airport. It had taken longer to get through the last hundred metres of my journey, I noticed, than the flight itself from Cyprus to Iran, a distance of a few thousand miles. I was reminded of the saying "Time is no factor in our country", common among people in Iran. And funny enough, they were always in a hurry.

I called a taxi and gave the driver the address of my flat. The driver took a route along main streets and I watched through the window as we covered the distance, over 20km, from the airport on the west edge of the city to my place right on the opposite side. Only eight months had passed and things seemed to have gone from bad to worse; the cars looked older, the city more polluted, and the people looked more arrogant than ever. Would you dare tell a motorist why he ignored the traffic lights, or a pedestrian to use the zebra crossing? I got home and found things the same way I had left them eight months previously.

Around late evening, when everything was quiet, I went out for a walk. As always, returning from a long time away, memories years dead, bitter and sweet, resurfaced, all giving rise to a strange sense of novelty. It seemed a bit late to enter the park I frequently used to visit, spending hours there prior to my departure for Cyprus; too dangerous even for a short excursion. I would do that the following day in the morning light, and no doubt more memories would be refreshed.

Returning to the flat, late as it was, I phoned Babak.

He had left Cyprus only one week previously, gracefully of his own volition. And how surprised he was when he heard my voice, thinking I was phoning from Cyprus! When he found out that I was only a few miles away, he wanted to know the whole story. I would let Eskandar and Hamid, Babak's flatmates back in Cyprus, do the explaining, for he would contact them as soon as I put the phone down; I just told him that I was caught along with them and sent back. Then I asked Babak - my main reason, in fact, for getting in touch with him - about his supposed court case in regard to Rasool. It was Thursday, and he had received instructions to attend a hearing on the following Saturday. "I'll be there," I informed him; then after some small talk I ended the call.

The day after, Friday, I spent almost the whole day in the park. Though it was a public holiday, there was hardly anyone there, probably because the weather had turned very cold.

Meeting my old flatmates back home had a different feeling; probably because in Cyprus emulating the kind of job a friend held, if any, and the amount of money he earned, played a key role. Both were lacking here. As prearranged, on Saturday at 10 o'clock in the morning I met Babak in front of the courthouse. He was with Eskandar and Hamid joined us a few minutes later. It didn't take long before Babak's name was called on the speakers and we entered the building and then the appointed courtroom. Three people were already there, a well-dressed middle-aged couple and a young man of

15, occupying the spectators' seats. If they were connected with whom I was thinking, it would look strange. We took our seats on the remaining chairs; there was one short but Eskandar made up for it by collecting a chair from the next room.

The only woman present extracted a tissue paper from her handbag and put it to her eyes. I realised, then, that she was quietly sobbing. The man sitting on her right, closer to us, also seemed to be in a sorrowful state. He turned to his right, facing us, and apologetically asked, "Which one of you is Babak?" His question was not unexpected and I wasn't the only one among us who had a notion of who these people might be. Babak nodded and the man, almost head down and in a quiet manner, introduced himself: "I'm Rasool's father, Razavi." It must have taken him a lot of courage, I thought, to have dishonoured himself like that. "This is my wife," he said, pointing to her, and then to the young man sitting on her left, "Rasool's only brother," he said. Razavi ruefully carried on, "We are very sorry for our Rasool's behaviour - please accept our apologies, Babak. Whatever had come over him to react like that, I assure you it is in the past now; he has learned his lesson in these few months of captivity and deeply regrets what he has done. Of course, we are all of the same heart and would do anything in our power to compensate for our son's action."

Babak, looking a bit on edge like the rest of us and anticipating Rassol's arrival any second, said, "I just want my money back, my 2,000 US dollars." Though hardly expecting to recover even half that amount, a view shared by the rest of us, he was nevertheless of a mind, as he had told us, to go further and push for the injuries he had received, whether he was awarded the 2,000 dollars or not.

Suddenly the back door opened and the judge entered the room. We all stood up while he took his seat at his desk, then sat back. A few seconds later he was followed by Rasool who was brought in handcuffed and accompanied by two sentries, one on each side. A tense atmosphere prevailed. All four of us kept looking at him maliciously, in a way that suggested only a spark might be needed to inflame us to the point of jumping out of our seats to have a go at that bastard. However, our anger and indignation was somewhat mollified as a result of Razavi's softening talk a moment before, quite a subtle manoeuvre, if that was what it was. If he meant it as a disarming tactic, however, it failed to calm us, as the next development will indicate.

My first impression of Rasool, when he entered, was that he had started on hard drugs. He was avoiding eye contact with us, but everything about his appearance suggested he was on drugs. They say narcotics of all sorts are readily available inside Iranian jails. Addicted inmates obtain them from sentries, who, as well as running the jail, charge high prices to supply the inmates with drugs - or so I've heard.

The judge put his briefcase on the desk and opened

it. Of medium build, wearing a dark grey suit, he looked to be in his forties. His short beard, like mine, seemed to have gone prematurely grey. He got a file out of his briefcase and placed it on his desk. There was no other sound apart from the slight noise made by the judge's handling of the briefcase and file. The woman's sobs had stopped. Rasool, standing to the side, presented his profile, still avoiding looking at us on his right less than five metres away. Both sentries stood a step back behind him. The judge closed his briefcase, removed it from the desk and placed it on the floor on his left. He took a moment to adjust his chair and, after a moment, opened the file. Obviously familiar with its content, he turned to Rasool at his right, then looked back to the file. Glancing from one to the other, he said, "You have been charged with injuring Babak Tavana on the head and shoulder, binding him with ropes and, following that, taking his money before leaving the place. Have you got anything to say?"

Rasool gave the same defence he had learned from his solicitor at the time of his arrest. The Iranian ambassador in Cyprus, familiar with the exact words of his statement, had relayed it to Babak not long after Rasool's arrest, and endorsed the prevailing opinion that it didn't stand a chance. Apart from all that, Rasool was clearly in the wrong, in my judgment, but I had to admit Rasool's tactic deserved some admiration, since he was expressing an opinion against the power of the judiciary system of the country. It was a remark not many dared to state at the time of such political unrest. One needed courage to voice a critical comment. The so-called Damned Cemetery embraced an unknown number of those defying this system, the rest waiting in Evin prison to join them. Then again, it all depended on the presiding judge, and this one didn't seem political. Cutting Rasool short, he reminded him that "since the case has reached the court your course of reasoning has already been rejected, and, on the other hand, your argument gives rise to the fact that you are guilty of the charges laid down against you." Firmly stated, the judge's words sounded like a concluding summation. Complacently looking as if the matter was settled and, giving his notes another glance, the judge looked back at Rasool and continued: "Now, have you got anything to say towards the mitigation of your punishment before I impose it on you?"

All seemed lost. How could a semi-literate person defend himself in a case like that, I asked myself? Even those with an educational background seemed incapable of doing so. Rasool murmured a few words and at the end just managed one sentence: "I'm sorry."

In order to sentence Rasool Razavi, the judge asked Babak Tavana to go and stand on his left - the accuser facing the accused on opposite sides of the table. The situation created was embarrassing: Rasool kept staring at the edge of the desk in front of him and Babak gave the rascal the most sarcastic smile he deserved. Looking at them, I felt as though I was appraising one and then the other: Babak looked young and innocent to have suffered such evildoing, and then Rasool with his beardless face had cruelty written all over him; outwardly Rasool seemed to have aged more than ten years since I saw him last, just a few months ago. The judge asked the plaintiff if he had anything to say. Babak tried to explain how we had accepted Rasool into our flat back in Cyprus after his had been raided by the police.

The Judge interrupted Babak, pointing at the file in front of him, saying that the details of his explanation were all in the reports we had left behind at the Iranian embassy in Cyprus. No wonder the file looked unusually thick. Shuffling through the file and pulling a couple of pages out, holding them in his hand, the judge said, "The whole drama is well explained in this one… " He paused, while looking for something at the bottom of the page, and carried on, "…made by one of the witnesses, Cyrus Kamrani."

The heads of Eskandar, Hamid, Babak and even of Rasool involuntarily turned towards me. So all my efforts hadn't been in vain, I thought.

Next, the judge got his pen out, wrote a few lines in the file, then sentenced Rasool Razavi. He turned to him, called him by his full name, and said, "You will pay back the 2,000 dollars you took from Babak Tavana; for the injuries you sustained him, three stitches to his head and two to his shoulder, you will provide him with an additional 400 dollars." He stopped and gave Rasool a long look from top to bottom, then back up again, as if appraising him to see whether the rascal scamp could stand what he was about to pass on him next; then he carried on, "You will be lashed 74 times, plus put back in jail to serve a further nine months."

With the prisons all full to three times their capacity, no wonder a crime of that nature received such a light sentence. A few years ago the same offence would have carried nothing less than five years imprisonment.

Now it was up to Babak, in accordance with religious canons, to come to a decision; would he let the punishments thrown at Rasool, all four of them, stand the way they had been announced? Or would he be lenient and try to lessen or relinquish altogether some of the charges?

Before Babak could say anything, Rasool's father took to his feet and, introducing himself (mentioning his first name, Behrooze), suggested amended terms. If Babak would agree to forego the 400 dollars he was to receive for his injuries, and also grant a pardon with respect to the 74 lashes and the 9 months imprisonment Rasool was to undergo, then he, Behrooz Razavi, would pay Babak 1,500 dollars in cash immediately, and ensure that he received the remaining 500 dollars by means of five post-dated cheques, signed by his son Rasool, valued at 100 dollars each. Babak could then cash them one at a time within the next five months, at the end of each month.

It was a good offer, I thought, more than any of us had expected, but Babak seemed reluctant to go along with it. There was one punishment - the 74 lashes - that he insisted should be carried out, because he wanted to see Rasool suffer. This charge was vehemently contested by the opposing side - Behrooz Razavi in the lead - that protested against the severity of the lashes and the designated place where they were to be carried out, which was in front of Razavi's house. Razavi was a respectable member of his community and would be humiliated by the lashes being carried out in front of his house. Babak insisted, however, on the designated place of punishment, and for the next few minutes negotiations seemed to come to a standstill and at one point looked as if everything would all slip back to the sentence as it was first announced. Then suddenly, Behrooz gave in to Babak's demands, with some modification: Rasool was to be lashed 40 times and in front of his father's house where he would supposedly return to. Papers were signed, five cheques were handed over to Babak, and we all left to watch the show which was to take place before noon prayers.

It would be interesting to see how Rasool would play his part. About an hour later through the speakers from the nearest mosque (to Razavis' house) the news of the punishment was brought to public notice. Being the first ones to know, we took our positions in an inner circle which formed round the action; rows of people, held back by sentries, were pushing from behind to get a better glimpse of what was happening. In the middle of the road, closed to traffic, Rasool, face down, was made to lie on a narrow wooden bed, but not before his jacket was removed, leaving him wearing only a shirt on that not so cold November day. The lashman, in his early twenties and a bit short, looked strong as he swept the lash in the air expertly as though warming himself up; now he was waiting for the person standing on the other side of the bed to give the signal so he could start.

It was the first time I was to see someone being lashed right in front of my eyes. Reflecting on my past it wasn't surprising, perhaps, that I felt very little disquiet witnessing this form of punishment: having been through some very testing experiences, I felt like steel which, following each time it had been melted in the furnace of life, solidified and with each solidification got harder; it was as though I had become immune to the pain of others and had lost my appetite for witnessing spectacles of human suffering. Had I become less man and more machine?

The signal was about to be given by the weak looking man with narrow shoulders, who stood apart from the rest. He would be shouting, counting the number of strikes too, and was carrying a copy of the Koran instead of handing it over to the other side, according to what was written in that same book. Now used to these wrongdoings, a few spoke of it afterwards, when the ordeal was over. In reality, since Islam was against all sorts of bodily harm, it was considered a sin to do otherwise, and lashing was introduced only to embarrass the person receiving them; the book was meant to be held under the armpit of the hand carrying the lash, thereby considerably diminishing the power behind it, so that only soft strikes were received and no bodily harm experienced. But then again, as all things worked out for the best, since there was no such word as shame in the vocabulary of the people of Iran, with every mistake they held their heads higher, and nature balanced the scale. But hundreds had died at the hands of inexperienced lashmen, some of them innocent, too; was it nature's fair play? It only took one lash at the wrong place to burst the kidney and kill the person.

Two months later after his second cheque was not honoured by the bank due to lack of funds, just like the first one, Rasool was caught at Yazd checkpoint carrying opium from Kerman to Tehran and suffered the same fate as my father. Babak, a few days afterwards, was feeling guilty for what had happened and had even sent condolences to Razavis. In the light of what happened he did not care anymore about the cheques, now worthless pieces of paper.

But for now, Rasool's arms hung from the sides of the bed exposing his back where he would receive the lashes between his shoulder blades. The sign was given, the man nodding his head, and the long leather strap at the end of a short wooden handle went round in the air before coming down, striking its target with the utmost intensity. The sound from the impact was shattering. Soon it was followed by another. The first five lashes, maintaining the same rhythm and intensity, almost ripped Rasool's shirt open. With each one he gave an involuntary shout of pain. Then the lashes started coming down softly. The man counted up to eight in sequential numbers, then jumped to 20, missing out 11 lashes; and the lashman, for the next five strikes, missed his target, lashing the edge of the bed instead. Jumping again from 24 to 37, the last 3 lashes matched the first ones Rasool had received. "He will have a job sleeping on his back for days to come," Eskandar whispered into my ear. The show over, Rasool, helped by some friends, was almost carried to his father's house, only a few steps away. The bed was removed and the crowd disappeared in the same leisurely way they had appeared.

Days went by. I either spent them in the park, at home or travelling inside the country staying at some of the best hotels. Around the middle of March I went to see the greatest historical sight in Iran, Persepolis, which is close to the large city of Shiraz, 900km away, in the mid-South. I spent a week there admiring this wonderful pinnacle of civilisation in the past, and wondered how we had managed to bring about the decline of such a mighty and magnificent empire to the shameful and disgraceful one that Iran had become today. History has it that more than 23 centuries ago Alexander the Great put fire to it in retaliation for the burning of Acropolis by Xerxes 150 years earlier. Apart from all that, thinking of it, standing where Darius used to address his army of 200,000 men, how did he relay his messages to so many people without the aid of speakers, walkie talkies and the electronic equipment without which commanders today wouldn't dream of moving their forces? Maybe not technologically, but politically they must have been more advanced than us. Mr President, would you consider changing places with Alexander the Great? And in that case, whose job would be harder? He'll probably last about five minutes, but I doubt if you would in as many seconds!

From Persepolis, only a short drive away, I went to see the tomb of King Cyrus the Great in Pasargadae, the mightiest king who ever ruled Persia. There was a great story behind his birth. When Cyrus' mother, herself the daughter of a king, was pregnant and soon to bear him, she dreamt one night that a tree grew out of her belly and its foliage spread over the land. Calling his soothsayers, the king came to know of it and was informed that the child inside his daughter's body would be a boy and one day would conquer his kingdom. Therefore, when Cyrus was born he was given to one of the generals to be discarded, by taking the new-born to the forest and leaving it there to be preyed upon by wild animals. Such cruelty was beyond the general's comprehension and unthinkable to be carried out by himself; so he took the child to the king's shepherd, ordering him to do what his sovereign had demanded. Back at his hut the shepherd's wife the same day had given birth to a dead boy. Replacing the stillborn child with the living one, he took the former to the forest and left it there. A few years later the truth came to light.

Back in Tehran I changed my passport, as its validity had expired, and got myself a new one - clean as a baby's ass! Then, in keeping with the decision I had taken that day lying on my bunk in the Limassol police station cell, I sold all my belongings, including the flat which had increased in value by 20% within the last six months alone. Adding to that the money I withdrew from the bank, leaving 3,000 dollars to cover my expenses soon to come, I had a total close to 80,000 dollars. I sent all that plus a copy of my new passport to my sister, Soheila, in America; then, a couple of weeks later, according to my instructions, I received a statement from the Bank of America bearing my name and passport number, giving my balance which was 70,000 dollars, the amount she had deposited in my account. The 10,000 dollars shortfall I had asked my sister to divide between her two sons. Would they now refuse me a visa to enter America when, as I planned, I called at their embassy, soon, in Cyprus? The answer to that question would decide my fate, or destiny.

Withdrawing the remaining 3,000 dollars from my account the next day I bought myself an air ticket to Cyprus, costing me 250 dollars, a rise of almost 80% from the previous year. Each passenger was allowed 1,000 dollars in his possession leaving the country. The same old knapsack over my shoulder, passing through the airport on the following Wednesday, I was well searched. I had my remaining dollars rolled inside a durex, buttered, up my ass. Cleared, I got on the plane bound for Cyprus.

Nothing had changed at Larnaka Airport since a year ago, not that I expected any changes; the same tense atmosphere prevailed amongst Iranians queuing up in front of half a dozen desks, immigration officers seated at them, only their heads to be seen. I took my stand in a queue on the far left. No translator was called for this time, and by the time I reached the desk, six had been sent to the so-called deportation-room - the same one as the year before. Was it possible that they had improved their computer records so that the names of those who had overstayed their visa in Cyprus within the last few months could be identified? My new passport had a different number from the old one, so hardly any question there; if other information pertaining to me was stored on their computers and now checked against my current passport, then I'll most likely be on the same plane back to Iran.

I handed over my passport and air ticket when the immigration officer asked for them. He was casually dressed. Picking them both up from the top counter I heard keys pressed on his computer keyboard. My heart was beating fast - I so much wanted to enter Cyprus again.

Whatever he came up with, most probably nothing, didn't seem a problem; he looked up at me after he had finished tapping the keyboard and asked, "Why have you come to Cyprus?"

"To spend my holiday, sir."

Realising I could speak English well, something I had in mind to emphasize, since it meant a great deal to these immigration officers, he didn't bother to ask me the many questions others were usually required to answer. He was certainly not concerned with my money which, during the flight in the plane's toilet, I had pushed out of my ass, now all ready at hand in my pocket. Just one last question he asked me: "Have you been in Cyprus before?"

Did he know the answer already and now wanted to catch me out? Trying hard to keep a straight face, I lied, "My first time coming to Cyprus, sir."

He charged me five Cypriot pounds (equivalent to ten dollars) and issued me a visa for two weeks.

Outside I wanted to jump in the air. Knapsack over my shoulder, I called a taxi, the latest model Mercedes, and headed for Limassol. Sitting at the back, looking through the window, wasn't it funny, I was thinking, that only a few months ago, travelling the other way, captive, I had promised myself this same journey I was enjoying now. It all seemed to have happened yesterday. We got to Limassol and I felt back at home, like seeing an old friend. The taxi stopped in front of Rialas Building. I paid the driver and walked to the C block entrance. Koorosh was still in Cyprus; just before coming over I had spoken to his parents on the phone and they had told me so. But where was he living - still at the same flat we had rented together a year previously? That was a question soon to be answered. Using the lift, I went up to the sixth floor. Memories flooded back! The last time I was there I was handcuffed to Eskandar and Hamid following a policeman.

I stood in front of the old flat and knocked. I heard footsteps approaching, then someone from the inside asked who it was. I answered and the door opened to reveal an old acquaintance, Majid. We had worked together once moving someone's furniture. He asked me in and over a cup of coffee told me that soon after I was arrested, finding the rent too much to cover just by himself, Koorosh had asked him to share the flat with him. This suited Majid: in search of somewhere quiet, tired of living with five others in a small one-bedroomed flat for over ten months, he felt the need for some privacy and accepted the offer. And now he wouldn't mind, he said, if I joined them - and he was quite sure that Koorosh would love it if I joined them. That was very nice of him, I said, for only a fool in my situation would reject such an offer.

It was late afternoon and Koorosh was expected any minute. Suddenly the door opened and he walked in. For a full ten seconds, his hand on the key inside the door, his mouth and eyes wide open, he stood there, as if frozen, staring at me! His smile broadened and I was happy to see him too. We shook hands and hugged - a very joyful moment. He insisted that I stayed with them.

That same day in the evening I phoned Mastros Glitos. I had decided to wait for a week before presenting myself at the American embassy in Nicosia to ask for a visa to avoid giving the impression that I had come to Cyprus with just one purpose in mind - and until then I didn't want to go round doing nothing in a place where I could earn good money. Last October, parting with Mastros Glitos, he had asked me to join him again when the working season started next; it seemed well on the way for, entering Cyprus, I had taken notice of the weather, the kind that cried out for air conditioners - it was hot!

The phone kept ringing, and eventually it was answered by his wife who passed the receiver to her husband. Mastros Glitos was a nice person - honest, just and generous. It was good to hear him after such long time. I'd had no contact with the man for over five months. He wanted to know where I had been. I couldn't tell him the whole truth. I had lied through my teeth when I told him that I had a working visa for a year in order to secure the job of working under him last year. The same visa needed to be renewed, I expected, if that help was to continue, since he would probably ask if I had such a visa, though I doubted that he would expect me to show him the actual document.

"I've been around doing some odd jobs here and there, then renewed my working visa to legalize my stay in Cyprus for another year," I said. The old bullshit came out naturally, unavoidable if I was to serve him again, and it seemed to serve the purpose.

He asked me to join him the next day. Though I had meant to stay with Mastros Glitos working only for a week, things didn't turn out the way I had planned. I went to the American embassy, armed with my bank statement showing 70,000 dollars in my account, plus an invitation letter I had received from Sohrab, my brother in law, undertaking to cover the cost of my stay there, providing me with a room in his house and three meals a day for the duration of one month. All I needed was a one-month visa, since, once in the country, I had no intention of leaving. It took the embassy worker less than two minutes to reject my application for which I had paid 45 dollars!

My fate was now in the balance! Certainly my destiny had been changed by that rejection. What would have happened had I been able to follow that course in life? But as it turned out, I stayed on in Cyprus, working with Matros Glitos doing the same thing as before, installing ACs, till early October - throughout each day, just like the year before: waiting somewhere close to the block entrance at seven every morning, and remembering, once my two-week visa had expired, to use the stairs instead of the lift going down.

I was forced to leave the country, flying to Istanbul in a few days' time, while writing these notes; otherwise I would face arrest for distributing leaflets among the people calling for a popular uprising against those who had committed the serial murders of writers and translators in Iran - a familiar piece of news that travelled all round the world. To cut the story short: two months after leaving Mastros Glitos I was caught and sent back to Iran. I stayed there only long enough to arrange my air ticket to Malaysia. Upon my arrival at Kuala Lumpur Airport, I was issued a 12-day visa.

Overstaying it by eleven months, working in one restaurant throughout that time, I was eventually caught, spent three months in jail, fined 2,000 Ringgit, and then - the same old story: back to Iran.

Ah, Sue, if you were satisfied with just one man, your husband, I wouldn't have had to go through all that trouble.

Perhaps one day when settled and with more time on my hands, I'll write about my experiences back in England and the way I was deported from there.

[1] Referring to a Muslim.

[2] The year 2000 AD corresponded with 1379 in the Iranian calendar. When Mohammed left Mecca for the City of Medina, both in Saudi Arabia, this trip, called Hijrat, marks the dawn of history in our country.

[3] A notice on the door of the embassy for the last few years had read: 'No visas will be issued until further notice.'

ND - #0055 - 270225 - C0 - 203/127/26 - PB - 9781909544161 - Matt Lamination